CONVERSATIONS
ON THE NATURE *OF*
POLITICAL ECONOMY

CONVERSATIONS
ON *THE* NATURE *OF*
POLITICAL ECONOMY

JANE MARCET

WITH A NEW INTRODUCTION BY *EVELYN L. FORGET*

Routledge
Taylor & Francis Group

LONDON AND NEW YORK

First published 2009 by Transaction Publishers

Published 2017 by Routledge
2 Park Square, Milton Park, Abingdon, Oxon OX14 4RN
711 Third Avenue, New York, NY 10017, USA

Routledge is an imprint of the Taylor & Francis Group, an informa business

Library of Congress Catalog Number: 2009006466

Library of Congress Cataloging-in-Publication Data

Marcet, Mrs. (Jane Haldimand), 1769-1858.
  Conversations on the nature of political economy / Jane Marcet.
    p. cm.
  Reprint. Originally published as: Conversations on political economy :
  in which the elements of that science are familiarly explained. 7th ed.,
  rev. and enl. London : Printed for Longman, Orme, Brown, and Green, &
  Longmans,1839.
  Includes bibliographical references and index.
  ISBN 978-1-4128-1010-4 (alk. paper)
    1. Economics. I. Marcet, Mrs. (Jane Haldimand), 1769-1858. Con-
  versations on political economy. II. Title.
HB161.M3 2009
330--dc22
                                                           2009006466

ISBN 13: 978-1-4128-1010-4 (pbk)

Table of Contents

Introduction to the Transaction Edition

Evelyn L. Forget

JANE MARCET AND THE GENEVA HERITAGE

Jane Haldimand (1769-1858)[1] was born in London to an English mother, Jane Pickersgill, and a Swiss father[2] named Antoine Haldimand. The prosperous banking family had ten children, of whom she was the eldest. Following the tradition of the Genevan bourgeoisie, Jane was educated at home by tutors and studied mathematics, astronomy and philosophy alongside her brothers. Her family ensured that she was also trained for her anticipated role as society hostess by hiring a governess to teach her dancing, music and painting. She attended a formal school only once, for two months, and very much disliked the experience. The Haldimand home was a social focus for the expatriate Geneva community in London; her father entertained a large circle that included bankers, writers, scientists and politicians, and was frequently visited by continental acquaintances. When Jane was 15, her mother died in childbirth and Jane was recruited to replace her as hostess at her father's lavish, twice-weekly parties.

Jane became engaged to marry a cousin in the navy, but dissolved the arrangement because of her father's continuing disapproval of the character of her fiancé. At the age

of thirty she found herself unmarried and yet a very desirable marriage prospect because, as was common among
Genevan families, she stood to inherit a full share of her
father's fortune which, on his death, would be divided
equally among all the daughters and sons. The Haldimand
family let it be known among their acquaintances that Jane
was seeking a suitable husband. Several men were considered, including the physician Alexandre Marcet who had
left Geneva to study medicine in Edinburgh in 1793. In
1798 after France annexed Geneva, he decided to relocate
permanently to London. They married in 1799 after a one-
month engagement.

Alexandre's decision to study medicine at the University
of Edinburgh was part of an established tradition of intellectual exchange between the two great Protestant centres of
Edinburgh and Geneva. He was well-connected in Geneva
and quickly established his credentials in the intellectual
milieu of Edinburgh. He carried letters of introduction to
Dugald Stewart from his brother-in-law Pierre Prévost
who was a Professor at the Academy of Geneva. He was
introduced to the Scottish chemist Joseph Black by Jean
de Carro and Louis Odier, both Edinburgh-trained medical
doctors who played a large part in the introduction of the
smallpox vaccine on the continent, and by the natural philosopher and Academy of Geneva Professor Marc-Auguste
Pictet (Bahar 2001, 30-34).

Alexandre trained as a medical doctor but always preferred chemistry to medicine. Unfortunately, he was not
independently wealthy and could devote himself full-time
to that pursuit only after Jane's father died in 1817 leaving
her a very rich woman. As the wife of Alexandre Marcet,

Jane expanded her social activities from her father's guests to include her own, and continued to entertain the growing Swiss expatriate community, visitors from abroad, and the overlapping scientific contacts of her husband, brother and father.

Among the many regular visitors to the home of Jane and Alexandre Marcet was Henry Brougham who would go on to found the Society for the Diffusion of Useful Knowledge in 1827 and convince a somewhat reluctant Jane Marcet to write *John Hopkin's Notions on Political Economy*. Guest lists included Henry Hallam, founder of the Statistical Society, economist Sidney Smith, Humphry Davy, botanist Augustin de Candolle, mathematician HB de Saussure (Lindee 1991, 10; Polkinghorn 1993).

Between 1803 and 1809, Jane gave birth to four children—two boys (one of whom died at 13) and two girls. She was able to employ governesses and tutors, and in their early years arranged for her children an education similar to that she had received. When the Marcets decided to send their eldest son to Cambridge, they enrolled him in Winchester School at the age of twelve. Like his mother before him, he very much disliked the arrangement and made his feelings known by running away from the school on several occasions. Finally, the exasperated Marcets decided to send him to Geneva to live with his uncle where he remained for four years, once again receiving the kind of personalized education he found much more congenial.

Jane Marcet's first book, *Conversations on Chemistry*, was published in 1805 after she attended a lecture series on chemistry given by Humphry Davy. The book was published anonymously because she wanted to avoid an apparent conflict of interest with the professional activities of her husband (Polkinghorn 1993, 24). *Conversations on Chemistry* was tremendously popular, going through at least eighteen British editions and four French editions. At least twenty-three pirated printings of various editions of *Conversations on Chemistry* were published in America, often more than one in the same year by different publishers and sometimes revised by editors for use in classrooms. There was at least one edition printed in Geneva, and one German edition (which sold poorly) in 1839. Twelve American printings of a very similar book, *New Conversations on Chemistry*, by Thomas P. Jones and at least one French plagiarist rounded out its influence. In the absence of international copyright law, Jane had no control over foreign editions and these texts were often attributed to the various editors rather than the original author (Lindee, 14-16). It is difficult to determine precisely how many copies of the work sold; various historians have claimed 160,000 copies in the United States alone (cf. Polkinghorn 34). Lindee has traced that figure to a claim published in 1874 by Sarah Hale,[3] but questions its accuracy (Lindee 16n18).

The book was not written as a textbook although it became one, especially in America where it was widely used in college classes. Rather, Jane conceived of the work as "useful for beginners," and addressed in her preface "the apprehension that such an attempt might be considered by some, either as unsuited to the ordinary pursuits of her sex, or ill-justified by her own imperfect knowledge of the subject" but felt "encouraged by the establishment of those public institutions, open to both sexes, for the dissemination of philosophical knowledge" and argued that, as a beginner herself, she might be better suited to write for others with little formal training in the field. In short, it was a work of popularization aimed at "beginners" and "young persons." Rather than a systematic presentation of ideas, she developed a style in which three characters—the impetuous "Caroline," the serious "Emily" and the tutor "Mrs. B." embark on a series of experiments to discover the principles of the science. Caroline and Emily are thoughtful, intelligent students, notwithstanding Caroline's fascination with explosions, and seem to be about fifteen years old. Caroline's father is said to own a lead mine in Yorkshire, but Emily's family background is unclear (Lindee, p. 11).

These characters, in various combinations, were to reappear in many of Jane's subsequent publications, including *Conversations on Political Economy; in which the elements of that science are familiarly explained,* which began to take shape in Jane's mind as early as 1809 when her younger brother William, who lived with the Marcets, became a Director of the Bank of England. As was the case with her introduction to chemistry, Jane had first been exposed to political economy when she attended a series of public lectures at the Royal Society given by Sidney Smith (Polkinghorn 1993, 41). Names of political economists began to appear on her guest lists more frequently; she entertained the Malthuses, the Ricardos, and James Mill. William Marcet and David Ricardo shared an interest in the appropriate role of the Bank of England in maintaining the value of the currency, and the Marcet home was the site of several informal debates related to the Bullion controversy. The stage seemed set for the creation of *Conversations on Political Economy.* Because of the dramatic market success of her first book,

Longmans was keen to publish such a work and the first edition appeared in 1816.

Jane went on to write texts on a variety of topics including astronomy, botany, mineralogy, physics, the "evidences of Christianity," as well as a number of books for children. Over her lifetime, she published thirty books on a wide variety of topics, most of which went through multiple revisions and editions.

Alexandre Marcet died unexpectedly in 1822, and Jane credited her deep Christian faith, along with her writing, for helping her overcome the subsequent depression. She lived to see her children established and her literary work well respected. She died in London, aged 89, at the home of her daughter and son-in-law.

Geneva Society and Knowledge Brokering

Older views of the popularization of science envision knowledge transfer as a one-way process, in which insights developed by professional "scientists" are simplified for a passive lay audience. This imagined process implies that true science—that is, scientific publication aimed at other professional scientists—is superior to the vulgarized version suitable for amateurs incapable of understanding complexity and subtlety. Professionals, intrigued by the history of their discipline, would for the most part be drawn to their professional predecessors to the relative neglect, or even derision, of popularizers. Alfred Marshall's claim that Jane Marcet, who never imagined herself as other than a popularizer of political economy, presented economic principles "without the conditions required to make them true" (Henderson 1995, 43) reflects this view of popularization.

Recently, some historians of science have begun to question whether knowledge translation should be regarded as a one-way transfer of information from the professional who discovers it, to the amateur who needs merely to understand an issue in broad outline (Myers 2003; Hilgartner 1990; Grundmann and Cavaillé 2000). They dispute the clear distinctions drawn between the two bodies of discourse, and envision the process itself as a reflexive one in which communication flows in all directions, and professional science and scientists are influenced by popular culture, even as that culture is transformed by scientific insights (Barer 2005). According to this view, the popularizer is transformed from someone dependent upon and subordinate to the real scientists, into a knowledge broker—someone who facilitates the creation, sharing and use of knowledge. By definition, the knowledge broker is not engaged in a simple process of knowledge transfer, but rather helps to create the multi-modal network of communications between and among professional scientists and the broader culture.

How does our understanding and evaluation of Jane Marcet's work change if we view it through a lens created by this concept of knowledge brokering? No reader can help but notice the contrast between the intellectual respect shown for Marcet by her contemporaries who included TR Malthus, James Mill, J.-B. Say on the one hand, and the casual dismissal of her work by Marshall and more recent economists on the other. Her contemporaries apparently thought she was doing more than vulgarizing their work.

Marcet was clearly engaged in the work of the knowledge broker—creating and maintaining networks between and among scientists and the larger public. Knowledge sharing made use of the personal and social connections she facilitated by bringing together bankers, scientists, and political economists at her home. It was extended to the popular culture through the many editions of her *Conversations* addressed to the middle classes, and enlarged to include the working classes with her *John Hopkin's Notions on Political Economy* and her cooperation with Henry Brougham and the Society for the Diffusion of Useful Knowledge. Her correspondence with continental thinkers enlarged the worldview of classical economics, and allowed her to introduce J.-B. Say's utility theory in her own work rather than the Ricardian value theory that dominated the classical school. This last highlights the intellectual creativity involved in knowledge brokering. In the same way that creativity is facilitated by networks that bring together disparate social circles, a popular text that juxtaposes elements from distinct theoretical approaches challenges both the lay readers of a text and the professionals upon whose work it is purportedly based.

This evaluation of Marcet's work builds upon Willie Henderson's attempt to place Marcet within an "educational frame," arguing that such a shift in perspective changes her work from "mere capitalist propaganda" to "sophisticated curriculum development" (Henderson 1995, 13). Bette Polkinghorn (1993, 1995, 2000) and Dorothy Thompson (1973) also value Marcet's contributions to economic education. Knowledge brokering contains within it adult education, but the concept extends beyond education in that it values the creation and maintenance of knowledge networks among disciplinary professionals, between professionals in various disciplines, and between the professionals and the educated public—in this case, the bankers, financial experts and policy makers who extend disciplinary expertise into the real world.

If we claim that knowledge brokering includes the serious activity of creating and maintaining social networks, then we must place Jane's *salon* into a historical perspective. Three features of Jane's upbringing suggest that we should take her Geneva heritage seriously. First, she was as well educated as her brothers in the same subjects, which was not typical for English women of her class during the period. Second, on her father's death she stood to inherit an equal share of his fortune, as she would not under the primogeniture arrangements typical in England. Third, she was introduced at a very early age to the elaborate social activities in her parents' home, suggesting that such entertaining was considered a serious business task that had to be maintained even after the premature death of Jane's mother. The social gatherings were not simply entertainment and diversion; they were a mechanism designed to create and maintain social, intellectual and business connections.

Many studies have attempted to place the Huguenot community with its well-developed international network and considerable private wealth drawn from banking and finance into the social, political and ideological framework of the eighteenth century (Bahar 2001; Montandon 1975; Taylor 1981; Tremblay 1988; Pocock 1999). Significantly, well-off Genevan families were personally responsible for the education of their children, and girls were often educated in the same subjects and in the same manner as were their brothers (Bahar 2001, 32; see also Fry and Michaëlis

1997). Jane Marcet benefited from this tradition, and after her mother's death, she undertook some instructional activities for her younger siblings. The exposure of women from well-off families to science was not unique to Geneva, but might be seen as the hallmark of Enlightenment science (Schiebinger 1989, Findlen 1995). It was one of the factors that made the *salons* of Geneva so intellectually stimulating, compared with many of their Parisian counterparts. Women played a significant role in the social networking—the creation of guest lists, the mixing of more and less distinct social circles, the consolidation of social and intellectual connections. At the same time, the core of the community was tightly knit, and the social and intellectual values that governed intellectual life in Geneva persisted as the circle was extended.

Jane Marcet presided at the centre of a vast and intricate web of social, political and intellectual connections. The financial resources of her family allowed her to play the role of hostess, while the intellectual connections of her father, brother and husband created a social base that she extended dramatically through the very real work of the *salonnière*. Significantly, hers was not an English *salon*, but rather one with very elaborate continental branches. This allowed her to place her own work not only within the context of British classical economics, but also to consider how British classical economics fits into the broader context of continental thought. Our reconsideration of Marcet has already elevated her far above that of a "mere propagandist" who promulgates principles without understanding complexity. In fact, we can go further.

The *Conversations on Political Economy*

The first edition of the *Conversations on Political Economy* was published in 1816, and is rightly seen as an exercise in popularization. Marcet's intent was clear:

> I can assure you that the greatest pleasure I derive from success is the hope of doing good by the propagation of useful truths amongst a class of people, who, excepting in a popular familiar form, would never have become acquainted with them (letter to Pierre Prévost, 21 September 1816, Archive de la fondation Augustin de Candolle, Geneva; cited in Polkinghorn 1993, 48).

Are we then to conclude that this dilettante, drawing upon her social connections and attendance at public lectures, simply took the principles established by well-known political economists and presented them in an easy-to-read format for readers of privilege?

The transmission of professional knowledge more broadly through a popular book is relatively straightforward, and has been the focus of most critics who have attempted to place Marcet in context. The contrivance of the governess (Mrs. B) charged with teaching two female students (Emily and Caroline) first appeared in *Conversations on Chemistry* and was carried through many of Marcet's subsequent works. Emily (who does not appear in the *Conversations on Political Economy*) and Caroline have interesting names. Emily is perhaps the feminine counterpart of Rousseau's *Émile* who, on occasion, was accompanied by a rather less serious female student named Caroline. Marcet is, after all, a woman of her time.

How do we understand Hilda Hollis's claim that the gender of Mrs. B and Caroline reinforce an "unfeminist" agenda, by allowing Marcet to dismiss Caroline's objections to the rather austere policy implications of classical economics as "'feminine' and naïve"? Hollis notes that Mrs. B "clearly defers to the male master-thinkers in political economy" and thereby reinforces the professionalization of political economy (Hollis 386). The gender of the student, as Hollis acknowledges, may as easily have been a "protofeminist argument in the line of Wollstonecraft" (386). And there is at least one instance in which neither Caroline nor Mrs. B defers to classical male authority: the value of commodities is determined by "the real intrinsic value which induces people to give money for them. Labour, you will observe, is valuable only if it gives utility to an object" (Marcet 1816). This is vintage Jean-Baptiste Say; it is not Ricardian value theory.

This is not the only instance in which Marcet distinguishes herself from the dominant themes of the British classical school. She, again like J.-B. Say, builds on the optimism of Adam Smith rather than scarcities foreseen by Malthus and Ricardo. She was not convinced that better living conditions would necessarily encourage more births among the working classes, rapidly eroding any momentary improvement in the standard of living. Nor was she certain that there were natural limits to economic growth imposed by resource scarcity. Hers was the classical economics of Adam Smith and J.-B. Say, in which the savings of capitalists support almost limitless growth, rather than the scarcity-based "dismal science" of Ricardo and Malthus.

From the perspective of the present, many might argue that classical economics was defined by its theory of value in which the value of a commodity is determined by its long-run cost of production, that resource scarcity is fundamental to the analysis and follows directly from the theory of rent, and that some kind of a Malthusian population mechanism is central to the story. Marcet is generally praised for popularizing classical political economy and, in particular, for her explanation of rents. Yet she rejects central tenets of the story. What is she popularizing?

We do Marcet a disservice to see her merely as engaged in offering "adults of the wealthy classes ... a sophisticated justification of their wealth in the face of growing unrest and political theories questioning financial inequality" or "the strategic promotion amongst middle- and upper-class adults of the New Poor Law" (Hollis, 380). Part of what she did was to bring the insights of classical economics to bear on social questions, as a counterweight to the "prejudices and popular feeling of uninformed benevolence" (Marcet, vi). But that was only part of the story. Another part of what she did was to bring together the insights of continental thinkers with the writings of the English classical school, and thereby challenge the political economists themselves to decide what was central to the story, and what peripheral. As we see below, they did rise to her challenge and, somewhat ineffectively, attempt to "correct" her excessive praise for continental "errors." She did not take the advice of her English mentors and, as the various editions of the *Conversations on Political Economy* rolled off the presses, Marcet expanded her continental network to include another generation of continental liberals, such as the eminent Rossi.

Jane Marcet, through the agency of her intellectual *salon* and through her books helped consolidate the ideas of bankers such as her brother and those whom we would see as professional political economists like Malthus and Ricardo. She made those ideas accessible, perhaps less to the young people identified as the audience in the book's preface, than to the middle classes—the political actors, bankers and business people who would not take the time to puzzle through Ricardo or Malthus. She challenged the rather insular English classical school to take seriously the ideas of continental economists such as J.-B. Say by inserting those ideas into a popular book, even if she did not attempt to develop a theoretical framework that could accommodate all those disparate elements. Jane preserved her intellectual distance from some of the central tenets of classical economics, but continued the conversation with its masters, sometimes accepting criticism and other times keeping her own counsel. Her participation was active; she was not simply transmitting wisdom created by professionals to unschooled amateurs. The networks she established were certainly constrained; there was, for example, no attempt at this stage to draw the working classes into the conversation. But it is a conversation, and not a lecture transmitted through a translator.

If Marcet was a knowledge broker, as I've claimed, we would expect to find evidence that, through Marcet, the public became aware of the ideas of professionals, but also that professionals were tasked with new challenges presented to them by Marcet, and that Marcet herself played an active role in facilitating that two-way communication. We do find all of this.

Reception and Influence of the *Conversations on Political Economy*

Marcet's *Conversations on Political Economy* went through at least fourteen legal editions[4] and was translated into French (at least twice), Dutch, German and Spanish. It had a measurable impact on at least four distinct audiences. First, there were the "young persons" to whom Marcet explicitly addressed her work. Second, there were the textbook writers and popularizers, including Harriet Martineau, Jean-Baptiste Say, Millicent Garrett Fawcett and others, who drew confidence from her success and took lessons from her style. Third, she was noticed by the great political economists of the nineteenth century, such as Malthus, JS Mill and others. And finally there were the politicians and bankers, the men of affairs with whom she socialized.

Reaching Young Minds

One of the great achievements of Marcet's *Conversations on Chemistry* had been to help ignite a scientific passion in the young Michael Faraday. He entered the shop of a bookseller and bookbinder in 1804 at the age of thirteen, and worked there for the next eight years. During that time, he read the books he was surrounded by and claimed two were particularly helpful. From the *Encyclopedia Britannica* he learned something of electricity, and from Mrs. Marcet's *Conversations on Chemistry* he learned the first principles of that science. In a letter written somewhat later, Faraday recounts his experiences:

> [I]t was in those books I found the beginning of my philosophy...and Mrs. Marcet's *Conversations on Chemistry* which gave me my foundation in that science.... I felt that I had got hold of an ancor [sic] in chemical knowledge, and clung fast to it. Hence my deep veneration for Mrs. Marcet: first, as one able to convey the truth and principle of those boundless fields of knowledge which concern natural things, to the young, untaught, and inquiring mind (Edgar Fahs Smith, *Old Chemistries*, McGraw-Hill Book Company, 1927, pp 67-68).

It was, perhaps, a contrivance when Marcet addressed her *Conversations on Political Economy* to "young persons," and there is no evidence of a Michael Faraday drawn to the study of political economy through Caroline's lessons. Nevertheless, her book did ignite a passion, if not in the hearts of young readers, then in those of their parents who began to see political economy as a very fashionable subject for young ladies to study. The novelist Maria Edgeworth, who was friendly with the Marcets, claimed:

> It has now become high fashion with blue ladies to talk political economy. There is a certain Lady Mary Shepherd who makes a great jabbering on this subject.... Mean time fine ladies now require that their daughters' governesses should teach political economy. Pray Ma'am said a fine Mamma to one who came to offer herself as a governess, "Do you teach political economy?" The governess who had thought she had provided herself well with French Italian Music drawing dancing &c was quite astounded by this unexpected requisition; she hesitatingly answered "No Ma'am I cannot say I teach political economy, but I would if you think it proper try to learn it." "Oh dear no Ma'am. If you don't teach it you wont do for me" (Colvin 1971: 364).

To some extent the "mania" for political economy predates Jane Marcet. In France and Geneva, it was a fashionable topic in intellectual *salons* throughout the last quarter of the eighteenth century. Marcet did, however, give the trend new life and firmly established political economy among the well-off public in Britain. This was a function of style as much as intent; her *Conversations on Chemistry* had the same attraction among intellectual women. Mme de Stael, a well-known *salonniére* in Geneva with whom the Marcets were associated, wrote to tell the Marcets that she had "proposed the study of chemistry in the dialogues of Mrs. Marcet" (de Stael 1816, quoted in Polkinghorn: 30).

Textbook Writers and Popularizers

Marcet's success in reaching impressionable minds attracted the attention of others with similar goals. Marcet has been appreciated as an educator, as a teacher of political economy (Watts and Weiner; Bahar; Henderson; Shackleton). Few, however, have recognized just how profoundly her educational techniques paralleled the developing science of education at the end of the eighteenth century. The use of the student names Caroline and Emily has already alerted us to the potential influence of Rousseau on Marcet. It would, in fact, be far more surprising that someone intent on education during the period should ignore Rousseau. The pervasiveness of Rousseauvian ideas in late eighteenth-century France and Geneva, both faithfully rendered and vulgarized, can hardly be exaggerated. For most educators, however, including Marcet, those ideas reduce to some fairly simple precepts. First, the dialogue format was fundamental in formal classes, and was seen as most useful for teaching children and those who already had a reasonable education. Teaching in dialogue form predates Socrates, and yet the unique realization of that format in the eighteenth century is worth considering. Twenty-first century readers are sometimes surprised to realize that one of the ways the dialogue format appeared in late eighteenth-century France was in the form of a catechism. After the French Revolution, the Roman Catholic Church was no longer the profound influence it might have been earlier, yet at the same time the influence of the Church waned, the popularity of the secular catechism flourished.

Jean-Baptiste Say was among the first to congratulate Marcet for her *Conversations on Political Economy*, and not only partly because Marcet adopted his theory of value rather than looking to Ricardo or Malthus as authorities. He appreciated her less as a political economist, than as a would-be popularizer. He writes, in a letter to Marcet:

> You have worked much more efficiently than I to popularize and to spread extremely useful ideas; and you will succeed Madame, since you have built on the strength of science.... It is not possible to stay closer to the truth with more charm; to clothe such indisputable principles with a more elegant style. I am an old soldier who asks only to die in your light. (Polkinghorn 1985, 167).

More significantly, he requested her permission to translate "sizeable passages from your excellent book," which he did in his *Cours complet d'économie politique pratique* (1828). This affinity between the two writers is not surprising when one considers that much of Say's work, including the *Cours* complet and the *Catéchisme d'économie politique* (1815) were devoted to adult education; the first was addressed to students not dissimilar to the bankers and businessmen that Marcet entertained at her home and hoped to educate through her Conversations, and the second to working class audiences similar to those who would have attended the Mechanics' Institutes for adult education in Britain.

A second form of education, usually directed towards the lower orders, the members of which were commonly believed not to be able to follow a rational presentation of material building from simple to more complex, involved presenting "principles" cloaked in examples from everyday life. Harriet Martineau is a name that frequently comes to mind when considering nineteenth-century popularizers, and she was master of this form. Although the styles of the two women were very distinct at the outset, they were friends and they did share their work. Martineau reports that, when she read Marcet's *Conversations* in 1827, she was surprised to find that she had been teaching political economy "unawares": "it struck me at once that the principles of the whole science might be advantageously conveyed in the same way,—not by being smothered up in a story, but by being exhibited in their natural workings in selected passages of social life" (Martineau *Autobiography* I: 138). This insight led to a change in Martineau's presentation, from more detailed "stories" in which social and economic issues were explored, towards a series of "tales" published in a series entitled *Illustrations of Political Economy* and aimed at the working classes. Each tale was 130 pages long and sold tremendous numbers of copies for 6 pence apiece.

Marcet's *Conversations* was aimed at a very different class than were Martineau's *Illustrations of Political Economy*. The former saw her natural audience as the bankers, men of affairs and politicians who frequented her parties, despite her stated audience of "young persons." The latter, by contrast, intended to influence working class behaviour and selected a style of presentation commonly believed superior for reaching those with little time and less formal education. It is telling that, when she chose to reach a similar audience with her *John Hopkins Notions of Political Economy*, Jane Marcet adopted the very successful style of the irrepressible Harriet Martineau.

The Reactions of Political Economists

Since Jane Marcet insisted on many of J.-B. Say's insights, it is perhaps not surprising that he valued her work greatly. It is, perhaps, more intriguing since Marcet did not mindlessly conform to classical precepts, that she was equally well received by Malthus, Ricardo and others of the English classical school. Malthus's response to Marcet's *Conversations* is of particular interest, because the archive exhibits a telling habit of Jane Marcet who saved her correspondence for posterity, but not without editing it. Marcet censored the archive by cutting out those bits of letters she received that were critical of her work. Polkinghorn notes that in her correspondence there are "about a dozen and a half such letters, all where the writer's position on a point differed from hers" (1993, 54). Malthus writes:

> I own I had felt some anxiety about the success of your undertaking, both on account of its difficulty, and its utility; and I am very happy to be able to say that I think you have overcome the first and consequently insured completely the second.... I am much obliged to you for your explanations on rents, and think you have managed some other difficult subjects remarkably well, particularly the subject of exchanges and bill merchants.... I will only just observe that I think you have given too much sanction to Mr. Say's opinion reflecting utility [rest of text missing]—letter from Malthus to Jane Marcet. August 1816. Marcet collection, cited by Polkinghorn (1993, 54).

Notwithstanding the managed archives, the book was well received by Ricardo, Torrens, McCulloch as well as many non-economists in public life (Polkinghorn 1993, 54-56). None, Polkinghorn notes, mentioned the "young persons" to whom the book was supposedly addressed (1993, 56). McCulloch raised a toast to Marcet at a meeting of the Political Economy Club in Edinburgh, and much later wrote that the *Conversations* was "on the whole, the best introduction to the science that has yet appeared" (McCulloch 1845: 18).

Ricardo, like Malthus, drew to Marcet's attention instances in which she tells a story not entirely in accord with his own, but nevertheless recognized the value of the work in its entirely. He writes to Malthus on 9 March 1817:

> ... Mrs. Marcet will immediately publish a second edition: I have given her my opinion on some passages of her book, and I have pointed out those which I know you would dispute with me. If she begins to listen to our controversy, the printing of her book will be long delayed,—she had better avoid it and keep her course on neutral ground. I believe we should sadly puzzle Miss Caroline and I doubt whether Mrs. B herself could clear up the difficulty (Ricardo [1816-1818] 2004: 140).

Ricardo did indeed offer her criticism and corrections, as did Malthus. The second edition of *Conversations on Political Economy; in which the elements of that science are familiarly explained,* by the author of *Conversations on Chemistry* (London: Longmans) appeared in 1817. The "Advertisement," dated 11 July, says "The Author has availed herself of a few useful hints from her friends, and of some recent valuable publications on political economy." She did expand the coverage, introducing for example a new chapter on foreign trade. She did not eliminate Say's value theory from the exposition, notwithstanding the encouragement of Ricardo and Malthus to do so. In fact, Say's value theory stayed throughout all editions of the text.

Support for *Conversations On Political Economy* grew with each edition, drawing more people, both leading economists whose names are still remembered, and their counterparts in the business world, into the conversation.

The "Conversations" in Public Life

Jane Marcet introduces her *Conversations on Political Economy* with the claim that the book is addressed to "young persons." Joseph Schumpeter accepted at face value that claim in his authoritative *History of Economic Analysis,* and dismissed it as a work fit for "high school girls" (Schumpeter 1954: 477). It was, however, the people in public life that Jane Marcet saw as her natural audience. The success she had in reaching that audience is made evident by the many letters she received from readers across America and Europe thanking her for making an apparently abstruse science comprehensible. To misapprehend that audience is to undervalue the tremendous impact Jane Marcet had in

extending the knowledge of political economy in the nineteenth century well beyond those acquainted with the great
political economists, to members of Parliament and to the
educated classes more generally. She was not writing for
the working classes, as was Harriet Martineau, and while
she would be pleased to attract young persons to a study of
political economy, it seems she was not writing primarily for
their benefit either. Her *Conversations* was aimed at women
and men of the educated classes. Because the book was
written in English, her primary market was in Great Britain
and America. Soon, however, the work was translated into
French, German, Dutch and Spanish, widening that market
to most of Europe. Even if we set aside the liberal "borrowing" from Marcet's *Conversations* by other popularizers at
home and abroad, her reach was profound.

Many certainly hoped that Marcet would reach this market. TB Macaulay wrote in 1825 that "every girl who has
read Mrs. Marcet's little dialogues on political economy
could teach Montagu or Walpole many lessons on finance"
(Macaulay 1851: 3). Perhaps most telling is the reaction of
the great popularizer Henry Brougham to Marcet's *Conversations:* "I have read—tho' not through—with great admiration. It will do a *great* deal of good…" (letter to Jane Marcet
(nd), quoted in Polkinghorn 1993: 55). That the principle
of the *Society for the Diffusion of Useful Knowledge* should
be so extravagant in his praise suggested that Marcet had
captured the requisite style. August de la Rive recognized,
in his 1859 article on Marcet for the *Bibliothèque universelle de Genève*, the phenomenal publishing success of her
venture, a claim that was reiterated by Kenneth Carpenter
in his *Economic Bestsellers before 1850.*

Recognizing better than Schumpeter the true nature of Marcet's audience, de la Rive quotes one letter from Lady Ann Romilly (wife of the legislator and jurist Sir Samuel Romilly) to Maria Edgeworth:

> Haven't you been delighted by Mme. Marcet's book? What an extraordinary work for a woman! Everyone who knows the subject is astonished, and people like me who understand nothing about it, or next to nothing, are delighted by the knowledge they have gained from it. One of our former judges who at 83 reads everything that comes out was impressed and truly regrets that he didn't know everything this book taught him when he was still presiding on the bench. How fortunate it would be for the country if our judges, not to mention our statesmen, knew half of what this work contains. You may say that this is a rather bold statement, but I assure you that is not merely my opinion (de la Rive, 1859: 13).

Marcet's *Conversations on Political Economy* gave new impetus to a fashion already well established, as did her *Conversations on Chemistry.* It would be unwise, however, to assume that she was writing only for the entertainment of society women, just as it would be wrong to assume "high school girls" were her primary market. One need only follow John Stuart Mill on his adventures in Parliament to realize that many with whom he debated were gleaning their primary knowledge of political economy not from Mill's own works or those of David Ricardo, but rather from Jane Marcet's *Conversations.*

Extending the Audience

In all of the examples considered to this point, the primary impetus to communication was a desire on the part of Jane Marcet to clarify the conversation and to bring the insights of political economy to a larger audience that she thought would benefit. To use a crude metaphor, they exemplify a "knowledge-push" model of popularization. In 1833, however, she published a book that was based on a very different metaphor: *John Hopkin's Notions on Political Economy.* This book was created in response to a demand from outside the profession; Marcet's given task was to gather the information necessary to meet the need, package it in an effective form, and deliver it to those who formulated the demand in the first place. This book was based on a "demand-pull" model.

Marcet claimed, in her *Conversations on Political Economy*, that she did not favour teaching political economy to the lower classes. But times had changed. In the autumn of 1830, agricultural riots had broken out in various parts of the country. The Romilly family, into which one of Jane's daughters had married, owned an estate in Glamorgan in South Wales (Polkinghorn 1993, 98). They, and many of their neighbours, feared that the English riots would spread to that area and several of them got together in 1831 to form "The Society for the Improvement of the Working Population in the County of Glamorgan." Marcet's son-in-law, a member of the Society, approached her to write stories for the Society in which the principles of economics could be illustrated for the working population. They apparently believed that the riots were due to erroneous beliefs about the nature of economy and, in particular, false ideas about how wages and profits were determined.

Riots in the countryside were not the only social disruption. In October 1831, supporters of the parliamentary Reform Bill, then under debate in Parliament, and representatives of the city government, confronted one another in the Bristol Riots. After several public buildings were attacked and set afire, the city magistrates called in the cavalry to restore order. The fear of revolution, and particularly civil unrest in London, was very real.

Conversations On Political Economy was never intended to speak to the working classes. One of its ardent supporters, however, was Henry Brougham. He had earlier persuaded Jane Marcet to allow his "Society for the Diffusion of Useful Knowledge" to publish her *Popular Introductions to Natural Philosophy* (1829), based on her *Conversations on Natural Philosophy* (1819). It was, so to speak, a popularization of a popularization. He was instrumental in convincing Marcet to expand the tales she had written at her son-in-law's urging and publish, through his own society, *John Hopkin's Notions on Political Economy*. The purpose of the book was to demonstrate the natural harmony of society, and to teach the poor that their best interests are met in cooperation with the monied members of society. Three themes were central to the book: the harmony of interests between classes, the determinants of wages, and the effects of the Corn Laws.

These tales are interesting for a number of reasons. First, the method of exposition is dramatically different from Marcet's *Conversations*. In fact, her tales are similar in form to Harriet Martineau's *Illustrations of Political Economy* (1832-34), which both women deemed a better method of reaching the lower classes. Both women were writing as contemporaries, and they were friends. Both were acutely aware of audience. Second, although *John Hopkin's Notions* was addressed to the poor, its publication again brought Marcet accolades from professional political economists, most notably Malthus. The book was reviewed by a number of publications including the *Edinburgh Review*,[5] *American Monthly Magazine*,[6] *Dublin University Magazine*.[7] Her *Conversations on Political Economy,* published in 1805 before the massive expansion of journals in the second quarter of the nineteenth century, had never attracted much notice in the journals. Marcet noted that "My John Hopkins has had a very unlooked for success among the great P.E.'s [political economists]...." (letter to Frank Marcet, 8 February 1833, cited Polkinghorn 1993, 108).

John Hopkin's is, of all Marcet's writing, that book best described as "mere capitalist propaganda" and has, perhaps as a consequence, attracted a good deal less attention from historians than her *Conversations On Political Economy*. If, however, we take seriously the claim that Marcet was a significant knowledge broker of the first half of the nineteenth century, then *John Hopkin's* becomes central to the story because it is the best instance in which Marcet used political economy to respond to demands posed by others, for the direct purpose of addressing very real social problems. The exercise was motivated not by Marcet and not by the great political economists, but rather by those who would ultimately use the knowledge to quell political unrest.

It is with this book that Marcet becomes a true knowledge broker.

Conclusion

Jane Marcet, the great nineteenth-century popularizer of political economy, presided at the centre of a vast social and intellectual web. Her task was networking, as was that of the entrepreneur celebrated by her admirer Jean-Baptiste Say, and like all networks, hers transmitted many kinds of information at the same time, and the information flowed in all directions. Marcet's network created social connections among political economists at home and on the continent, and between those economists and the banking, finance, political and business classes that were represented at her parties. At the same time that social ties were consolidated, intellectual connections were established. Marcet was not outside this process. Part of her task was confronting "the great P.E.s" with dissonant perspectives. While Malthus and Ricardo debated with one another over the Corn Laws at Marcet's home, other debates were introduced in Marcet's books. Say's value theory, not consistent with English classical economics, nevertheless found its way into her *Conversations* and stayed there throughout its publication history, notwithstanding the efforts of Malthus and Ricardo to offer corrections. In a world where her *Conversations* would go on to have a much broader readership than any of the productions of the great political economists, this was indeed a challenge.

Envisioning Jane Marcet as a knowledge broker, rather than a popularizer or teacher, makes this information flow central to her work. Historically, she rests between the great female-led continental *salons* of the eighteenth century and the professional knowledge brokers of the twentieth. In the nineteenth century, Marcet helped to define the field.

It is an error to examine Marcet looking for original insights or neglected intellectual contributions to the science of political economy. No one can be an expert in half a dozen fields. But knowledge brokering is portable. That focus explains how she could have such a significant impact on so many fields of study.

Notes

1.   Biographical data on Jane Haldimand Marcet is presented by Polkinghorn in detail in her 1993 biography, and summarized in Polkinghorn (2000). My summary is based on her archival work.
2.   Antoine Haldimand was Swiss, but not from Geneva.

3.   Hale refers to 160 impressions of the work and assumes a mean print run of
      1,000. Lindee found only 32 impressions, including those attributed to Thomas
      P. Jones. No one claims to have a full list of all editions and reprints.
4.   Both Polkinghorn (p. 57) and DL Thomson claim the book went through 16
      editions. I found 14 between the British Library, the Kress and the Library of
      Congress. No doubt there are translations I've missed, and there were certainly
      pirated editions because of the difficulties with international copyright law.
      Because these editions were intended as popularizations, there was perhaps
      less effort put into collecting and preserving every single version in print.
5.   [William Empson] 1833. "Illustrations of Political Economy" *Edinburgh Review*
      May 9. I-39, jointly reviewed Harriet Martineau's *Illustrations* and commented
      on Jane Marcet's *John Hopkin's*.
6.   "Notions on Political Economy" 1833. *American Monthly Magazine*, 387-9.
7.   [Longfield, Mountifort] 1833. "Critical Notices" *Dublin University Magazine*.
      I(5): 468-70.

References

Anon. "Jane Haldimand Marcet," *Journal of Chemical Education* (on-line). <http://
     jchemed.chem.wisc.edu/JCEWWW/Features/eChemists/Bios/Marcet.html>
     Accessed 30 December 2006.
Bahar, Sara 2001. "Jane Marcet and the limits to public science," *British Journal of
     the History of Science* 34: 29-49.
Barer, Morris. 2005. "Evidence, Interests and Knowledge Translation: Reflections of
     an Unrepentant Zombie Chaser," *Healthcare Quarterly* 8(1).
Bodkin, Ronald G 1999. "The Issue of Female Agency in Classical Economic Thought:
     Jane Marcet, Harriet Martineau and the Men," *Gender Issues*, Fall.
Carpenter, Kenneth. 1975. *Economic Bestsellers Before 1850*. **11.** Cambridge MA:
     Kress Library.
Colvin, Christina (ed.) 1971. *Maria Edgeworth: Letters from England, 1813-1844.*
     Oxford: Clarendon Press.
De la Rive, August. 1859. « Mme. Marcet » *Bibliothèque universelle de Genève.*
De Stael, Mme. 1816. Letter to Alexander Marcet. Marcet Collection, Archive Guy
     de Pourtal s. Etoy, Switzerland. [cited in Polkinghorn 1993]
[Empson, William] 1833. "Illustrations of Political Economy" *Edinburgh Review*
     May 9. I-39
Findlen, P. 1995. "Translating the New Science: women and the circulation of knowl-
     edge in Enlightenment Italy," *Configurations* 2: 167-206.
Fry, CR and Michaëlis, J. (eds) 1997. *En attendant le prince charmant.* Genève.
Gates, Barbara T. and Shteir Ann B. (eds) 1997. *Natural Eloquence: Women Reinscribe
     Science.* Madison: University of Wisconsin Press.
Grundmann, R. and Cavaillé, J.-P. 2000. "Simplicity in Science and its Publics,"
     Science as Culture 9: 353-89.
Hale, Sarah Josepha Buell. 1874. *Woman's Record; or Sketches of Distinguished
     Women From the Creation to A.D. 1868, arranged in four eras.* New York.
Henderson, Willie 1994. "Jane Marcet's *Conversations on Political Economy*: a new
     interpretation," *History of Education* 23(4): 423-37.
--- 1995. *Economics as Literature.* London: Routledge.
Hilgartner, S. 1990. "The Dominant View of Popularization: Conceptual Problems,
     Political Uses," *Social Studies of Science* 20: 519-39.

Hollis, Hilda 2002. "The Rhetoric of Jane Marcet's Popularizing Political Economy," *Nineteenth-Century Contexts* 24(4): 379-96.

Langer, Gary F. 1987. *The Coming of Age of Political Economy, 1815-1825.* New York: Greenwood Press.

Lindee, M. Susan. 1991. "The American Career of Jane Marcet's Conversations on Chemistry, 1806-1853," *Isis* 82(1): 8-23.

[Longfield, Mountifort] 1833. "Critical Notices" *Dublin University Magazine.* I(5): 468-70.

Macaulay TB. 1851. *Critical and Historical Essays.* London: Longman, Brown, Green, Longmans.

McCulloch, JR. [1845] 1938. *The Literature of Political Economy.* [reprint] London: London School of Economics and Political Science.

Marcet, Jane. 1816. *Conversations on Political Economy.* London: Longmans.

Martineau, Harriet. 1832-34. *Illustrations of Political Economy.* London: C. Fox.

Montandon, C. 1975. *Le Développement de la science à Genève aux XVIIIe et XIXe Siècles; le cas d'une communauté scientifique.* Vevey.

Myers, Gregory A. 2003. "Discourse studies of scientific popularization: questioning the boundaries," *Discourse Studies* 5(2): 265-79.

Neeley, Kathryn A. 1992. "Woman as Mediatrix: Women as Writers on Science and Technology in the Eighteenth and Nineteenth Centuries," *IEEE Transactions on Professional Communication* 35(4): 208-216.

"Notions on Political Economy" 1833. *American Monthly Magazine*, 387-9

Pocock, JGA. 1999. *Barbarism and Religion*, 2 vols., 50-72. Cambridge.

Polkinghorn, Bette 1993. *Jane Marcet: An Uncommon Woman.* Aldermaston: Forestwood Publications.

--- 1995. "Jane Marcet and Harriet Martineau: motive, market experience and reception of their works popularizing classical political economy." In *Women of Value*, ed. MA Dimand, RW Dimand and EL Forget. Cheltenham: Edward Elgar Publishing, pp. 71-81.

--- 2000. "Jane Haldimand Marcet," in *A Biographical Dictionary of Women Economists*, ed. RW Dimand, MA Dimand and EL Forget. Cheltenham: Edward Elgar Publishing, pp. 281-85.

--- 1986. "An Unpublished Letter from Malthus to Jane Marcet, January 22, 1833," *The American Economic Review* 76(4): 845-47.

--- 1985. "A Commiunication: An Unpublished Letter of J.B. Say," *Eastern Economic Journal* 9: 167-70.

Ricardo, D. [(1816-1818)] 2004. *The Works and Correspondence of David Ricardo, vol. VII.* Edited by Piero Sraffa with the collaboration of MH Dobb. Originally published by Cambridge University Press (1951) Indianapolis: The Liberty Fund.

Schiebinger, L. 1989. *The Mind Has No Sex? Women in the Origins of Modern Science.* Cambridge MA: 37-66.

Shackleton, JR. 1990. "Jane Marcet and Harriet Martineau: Pioneers of Economics Education." *History of Education*, v19 n4 p283-97 Dec 1990.

Sockwell, WD. 1994. *Popularizing Classical Economics: Henry Brougham and William Ellis.* London and Basingstoke: Macmillan.

Schumpeter, Joseph. 1954. *A History of Economic Analysis.* New York: Oxford University Press.

Taylor, SB. 1981. "The Enlightenment in Switzerland," in *The Enlightenment in National Context*, eds. R Porter and M. Teich. Cambridge, 72-89.

Thomson, DL. 1973. *Adam Smith's Daughters.* Jericho, NY: Exposition Press.

Tremblay, J. 1988. *Les savants genevois dans l'europe intellectuelle: du XVIIe au milieu du XIXe siècle*, Genève

Watts, R. and Weiner, G. 2004. "WOMEN , WEALTH and POWER: Women And Knowledge Production Producers and Consumers: Women enter the Knowledge Market." Presented at the annual conference of the Women's History Network, Hull, England, 3-5 September 2004.

PREFACE

In offering to the Public this small work, in which it is attempted to bring within the reach of young persons a science which no English writer has yet presented in an easy and familiar form, the author is far from inferring, from the unexpected success of a former elementary work, on the subject of Chemistry, that the present attempt is likely to be received with equal favour. Political Economy, though so immediately connected with the happiness and improvement of mankind, and the object of so much controversy and speculation among men of knowledge, is not yet become a popular science, and is not generally considered as a study essential to early education. This work, therefore, independently of all its defects, will have to contend against the novelty of the pursuit with young persons of either sex, for the instruction of whom it is especially intended. If, however, it should be found useful, and if, upon the whole, the doctrines it contains should appear sound and sufficiently well explained, the author flatters herself that this attempt will not be too severely judged. She hopes it will be remembered that in devising the plan of this work, she was in a great degree obliged to form the path she has pursued, and had scarcely any other guide in this popular mode of viewing the subject than the recollection of the impressions she herself experienced when she first turned her attention to this study; though she has subsequently derived great assistance from the kindness of a few friends, who revised her sheets as she advanced in the undertaking.

As to the principles and materials of the work, it is so obvious that they have been obtained from the writings of the great masters who have treated this subject, and more particularly from those of Dr. Adam Smith, of Mr. Malthus, M. Say, M. Sismondi, Mr. Ricardo, and Mr. Blake, that the author has not thought it necessary to load these pages with repeated acknowledgments and incessant references.

It will immediately be perceived by those to whom the subject is not new, that a few of the most abstruse questions and controversies in Political Economy have been entirely omitted, and that others have been stated and discussed without any positive conclusion being deduced. This is a defect unavoidably attached not only to the author's limited knowledge, but also to the real difficulty of the science. In general, however, when the soundness of a doctrine has appeared well established, it has been stated conscientiously, without any excess of caution or reserve, and with the sole object of diffusing useful truths.

It has often been a matter of doubt among the author's literary advisers, whether the form of dialogues, which was adopted in the Conversations on Chemistry, should be preserved in this Essay. She has, however, ultimately decided for the affirmative; not that she particularly studied to introduce strict consistency of character, or uniformity of intellect, in the remarks of her pupil,—an attempt which might have often impeded the elucidation of the subject; but because it gave her an opportunity of introducing objections, and placing in various points of view, questions and answers as they had actually occurred to her own mind,—a plan which would not have suited a more didactic composition. It will be observed, accordingly, that the colloquial form is not here confined to the mere intersection of the argument by questions and answers, as in common school-books; but that the questions are generally the vehicle of some collateral remarks contributing to illustrate the subject; and that they are in fact such as would be likely to arise in the mind of an intelligent young person, fluctuating between the impulse of her heart and the progress of her reason, and naturally imbued with all the prejudices and popular feelings of uninformed benevolence.

CONVERSATION I

INTRODUCTION

ERRORS ARISING FROM TOTAL IGNORANCE OF POLITICAL ECON-
OMY. —ADVANTAGES RESULTING FROM THE KNOWLEDGE
OF ITS PRINCIPLES.— DIFFICULTIES TO BE SURMOUNTED
IN THIS STUDY.

MRS. B.

WE differ so much respecting the merit of the passage you mentioned this morning, that I cannot help suspecting some inaccuracy in the quotation.

CAROLINE

Then pray allow me to read it to you; it is immediately after the return of Telemachus to Salentum, when he expresses his astonishment to Mentor at the change that has taken place since his former visit; he says, "Has any misfortune happened to Salentum in my absence? the magnificence and splendour in which I left it have disappeared. I see neither silver, nor gold, nor jewels; the habits of the people are plain, the buildings are smaller, and more simple, the arts languish, and the city is become a desert"—"Have you observed," replied Mentor with a smile, "the state of the country that lies round it?"—"Yes," said

Telemachus; " I perceive that agriculture is become an honourable profession, and that there is not a field uncultivated."—"And which is best," replied Mentor, "a superb city, abounding with marble, gold, and silver, with a sterile and neglected country; or a country in a state of high cultivation, and fruitful as a garden, with a city where decency has taken place of pomp? A great city full of artificers, who are employed only to render manners effeminate, by furnishing the superfluities of luxury, surrounded by a poor and uncultivated country, resembles a monster with a head of enormous size, and a withered, enervated body, without beauty, vigour, or proportion. The genuine strength and true riches of a kingdom consist in the number of people, and the plenty of provisions; and innumerable people now cover the whole territory of Idomeneus, which they cultivate with unwearied diligence and assiduity. His dominions may be considered as one town, of which Salentum is the centre: for the people that were wanting in the fields, and superfluous in the city, we have removed from the city to the fields."

Well—must I proceed, or have I read enough to convince you that Mentor is right?

MRS. B.

I still persist in my opinion; for though some of the sentiments in this passage are perfectly just, yet the general principle on which they are founded, that town and country thrive at the expense of each other, is quite erroneous; I am convinced, on the contrary, that flourishing cities are the means of fertilising the fields around them. Do you see any want of cultivation in the neighbourhood of London? or can you name any highly improved country which does not abound with wealthy and populous cities? On the other hand, what is more common than to observe decayed cities environed by barren and ill-cultivated lands? The purple and gold of Tyre during the prosperity of the Phoenicians, far from depriving the fields of their labourers, obliged that nation to colonise new countries as a provision for its excess of population.

CAROLINE

That is going very far back for an example.

MRS. B.

If you wish to come down to a later period, compare the ancient flourishing state of Phoenicia with its present wretchedness, so forcibly described by Volney in his travels.

CAROLINE

Has not this wretchedness been produced by violent revolutions, which during a course of ages have impoverished that devoted country, and does it not continue in consequence of the detestable policy of its present masters? But in the natural and undisturbed order of things, is it not clear that the greater number of labourers a sovereign should, after the example of Idomeneus, compel to quit the town in order to work in the country, the better that country would be cultivated?

MRS. B.

I do not think so; I am of opinion, on the contrary, that the people thus compelled to quit the town would not find work in the country.

CAROLINE

And why not?

MRS. B.

Because there would already be as many labourers in the country as could find employment.

CAROLINE

In England that might possibly be the case, but would it be so in badly cultivated countries?

MRS. B.

I think it would.

CAROLINE

Do you mean to say, that if a country which is ill culti-vated were provided with a greater number of labourers, it would not be improved? You must allow that this requires some explanation.

MRS. B.

It does so, and perhaps even more than you imagine; for you cannot well understand this question without some knowledge of the principles of political economy.

CAROLINE

I am very sorry to hear that, for I confess that I have a sort of antipathy to political economy.

MRS. B.

Are you sure that you understand what is meant by po-litical economy?

CAROLINE

I believe so, as it is very often the subject of con-versation at home; but it appears to me the most uninteresting of all subjects. It is about custom-houses, and trade, and taxes, and bounties, and smuggling, and paper-money, subjects which I cannot listen to without yawning. Then there is a perpetual reference to the works of Adam Smith, whose name is never uttered without such veneration, that I was induced one day to look into his work on Political Economy to gain some information on the subject of corn, but what with forestalling, regrating, duties, drawbacks, and limiting prices, I was so overwhelmed by a jargon of unintelligible terms, that after running over a few pages, I threw the book away in despair, and resolved to eat my bread in humble ignorance. So if our argument respecting town and country relates to political economy, I believe that I must be contented to yield the point in dispute without understanding it.

MRS. B.

Well, then, if you can remain satisfied with your ignorance of political economy, you should at least make up your mind to forbear from talking on the subject, since you cannot do so to any purpose.

CAROLINE

I assure you that requires very little effort; I only wish that I was as certain of never hearing the subject mentioned, as I am of never talking upon it myself.

MRS. B.

Do you recollect how heartily you laughed at poor Mr. Jourdain in the *Bourgeois Gentilhomme,* when he discovered that he had been speaking prose all his life without knowing it?—Well, my dear, you frequently talk of political economy without knowing it. It is but a few days since I heard you deciding on the very question of the scarcity of corn; and it must be confessed that your verdict was in perfect unison with your present profession of ignorance.

CAROLINE

Indeed I only repeated what I had heard from very sensible people, that the farmers had a great deal of corn; that if they were compelled to bring it to market, there would be no scarcity; and that they kept it back with a view to their own interest, in order to raise the price. Surely it does not require a knowledge of political economy to speak on so common, so interesting a subject as this first necessary of life.

MRS. B.

The very circumstance of its general interest renders it one of the most important branches of political economy. Unfortunately for your resolution, this science spreads into so many ramifications, that you will seldom hear a conversation amongst liberal-minded people without some reference to it. It was but yesterday that you accused the Birmingham manufacturers of cruelty and injustice towards their workmen, and asserted that the rate of wages should be proportioned by law to that of provisions; in order that the poor might not be sufferers by a rise in the price of bread. I dare say you thought that you had made a very rational speech?

CAROLINE

And was I mistaken? You begin to excite my curiosity, Mrs. B.; do you think I shall ever be tempted to study this science?

MRS. B.

I do not know; but I have no doubt that I shall convince you of your incapacity to enter on most subjects of general conversation, whilst you remain in total ignorance of it; and that however guarded you may be, that ignorance will be betrayed, and may frequently expose you to ridicule. During the riots of Nottingham I recollect hearing you condemn the invention of machines, which, by abridging labour, throw a number of workmen out of employment. Your opinion was founded upon mistaken principles of benevolence. In short, my dear, so many things are more or less connected with the science of political economy, that if you persevere in your resolution, you might almost as well condemn yourself to perpetual silence.

CAROLINE

I should at least be privileged to talk about dress, amusements, and such lady-like topics.

MRS. B.

I have heard no trifling degree of ignorance of political economy betrayed in a conversation on dress. "What a pity," said one lady, "that French lace should be so dear; for my part I make no scruple of smuggling it; there is really a great satisfaction in cheating the custom-house." Another wondered she could so easily reconcile smuggling to her conscience; that she thought French laces and silks, and all French goods, should be totally prohibited; that she was determined never to wear any thing from foreign countries, let it be ever so beautiful; and that it was shameful to encourage foreign manufactures whilst our own poor were starving.

CAROLINE

Surely you can have no fault to find with the latter opinion? It appears to me to be full of humanity and patriotism.

MRS. B.

The benevolence of the lady I do not question; but without knowledge to guide and sense to regulate the feelings, the best intentions will be of little use. The science of political economy is intimately connected with the daily occurrences of life, and in this respect differs materially from that of chemistry, astronomy, or any of the natural sciences; the mistakes we may fall into in the latter sciences can have little sensible effect upon our conduct, whilst our ignorance of the former may lead us into serious practical errors.

There is scarcely any history or any account of voyages or travels that does not abound with facts and opinions, the bearings of which cannot be understood without some previous acquaintance with the principles of political economy: besides, should the author himself be deficient in this knowledge, you will be continually liable to adopt his errors from inability to detect them. This was your case in reading Telemachus. Ignorance of the principles of political economy is to be discovered in some of the most elegant and sensible of our writers, especially amongst the poets. That beautiful composition of Goldsmith, the Deserted Village, is full of errors of this description, which, from its great popularity, are very liable to mislead the ill informed.

CAROLINE

I should almost regret to learn any thing which would lower that beautiful poem in my estimation.

MRS. B.

Its intrinsic merit as a poem is quite sufficient to atone for any errors in scientific principles. Truth is not, you know, essential to poetic beauty; but it is essential that we should be able to distinguish between truth and fiction.

CAROLINE

Well, after all, Mrs. B., ignorance of political economy is a very excusable deficiency in women. It is the business of Government to reform the prejudices and errors which prevail respecting it; and as we are never likely to become legislators, is it not just as well that we should remain in happy ignorance of evils which we have no power to remedy?

MRS. B.

When you plead in favour of ignorance, there is a strong presumption that you are in the wrong. If a more general knowledge of political economy prevented women from propagating errors respecting it, in the education of their children, no trifling good would ensue. Childhood is spent in acquiring ideas, adolescence in discriminating and rejecting those which are false; how greatly should we facilitate this labour by diminishing the number of errors imbibed in early youth, and by inculcating such ideas only as are founded in truth!

CAROLINE

Would you teach political economy to children?

MRS. B.

I would wish that mothers were so far competent to teach it, that their children should not have any thing to unlearn; and if they could convey such lessons of political economy as Miss Edgeworth gives in her story of the Cherry Orchard, no one I should think would esteem such information beyond the capacity of a child.

CAROLINE

I thought I remembered that story perfectly, but I do not recollect in it a single word relative to political economy.

MRS. B.

The author has judiciously avoided naming the science, but that little tale contains a simple and beautiful exposition of the division of labour, the merit of which you would more highly appreciate if you were acquainted with its application to political economy. You would perhaps also allow children to hear the story of King Midas, whose touch converted every thing into gold.

CAROLINE

Is that also a lesson of political economy? I think, Mrs. B., you have the art of converting every thing you touch into that science.

MRS. B.

It is not my art, but the real nature of things. The story of King Midas shows, that gold alone does not constitute wealth, and that it is valuable only as it bears a due proportion to the more immediately useful productions of the earth.

CAROLINE

But children will not be the wiser for such stories, unless you explain their application to political economy. You must give them the *moral* of the fable.

MRS. B.

The *moral* is the only part of a fable which children never read; and in this they are perfectly right, for a principle abstractedly laid down is beyond their comprehension. The application will be made as they advance in life. Childhood is the period for sowing the seed, not forcing the fruit; you must wait the due season if you mean to gather a ripe and plentiful harvest.

CAROLINE

Well, my dear Mrs. B., what must I do? You know that I am fond of instruction, and that I am not afraid of application. You may recollect what pleasure I took in the study of natural philosophy and chemistry. If you could persuade me that political economy would be as interesting, and not more difficult, I would beg of you to put me in the way of learning it. Are there any lectures given on this subject? or could one take lessons of a master? for as to studying scientific books, I am discouraged by the difficulty of the terms: when the language as well as the subject is new, there are too many obstacles to contend with at first setting out.

MRS. B.

The language of a science is frequently its most difficult part, but in political economy there are but few technical terms, and those you will easily comprehend. Indeed, you have already a considerable stock of information on this subject, but your notions are so confused and irregular, such a mixture of truth and error, that your business will rather be to select, separate, and methodize what you already know, than to acquire new ideas. It is not in my power to recommend you a master on this subject; it has hitherto been taught only in public lectures at the universities, and in London, by Mr. Macculloch, who, both by his writings and his clear method of teaching, has greatly contributed to the progress of the science.

Political economy has within these few years been much cultivated; besides the celebrated treatise of Adam Smith, who may be considered as the father of this science, several very excellent works have been since published, by Mr. Say, Mr. Ricardo, Mr. Malthus, Mr. Sismondi, Mr. Senior, and others; but it is true that they are not easy for beginners.

CAROLINE

But what then am I to do, Mrs. B.? I cannot attend those lectures, and I fear I shall never have courage to undertake the study of treatises which you allow to be difficult.

MRS. B.

Perhaps I may be able to smooth the way for you. It has been my good fortune to have passed a great part of my life in a society where this science has been a frequent topic of discussion, and the interest I took in it has induced me to study its principles in the works of the best writers on the subject; but I must tell you fairly, that I did not commence my studies by opening these works at random, or by consulting Adam Smith on an insulated point, before I had examined his plan, or understood his object I knew that in order to learn I must begin at the beginning, and. if you are of opinion that my experience can be of any service to you, and if you will be content to receive an explanation in a familiar manner of what has been discussed or investigated by men of acknowledged talent and learning, I will attempt to guide you through the first elements of the science, without, however, presuming to penetrate into its abstruse parts.

CAROLINE

Well, then, I am quite decided to make the attempt; you are but too good to me, Mrs. B., to allow me again to become your pupil. You have so much indulgence, however, that I am never afraid of exposing my ignorance by my inquiries, though I fear I shall put your patience to a severe test.

CONVERSATION II

INTRODUCTION—*continued*

DEFINITION OF POLITICAL ECONOMY. — RISE AND PROGRESS OF
SOCIETY. —CONNECTION BETWEEN POLITICAL ECONOMY-
AND MORALITY.—DEFINITION OF WEALTH.

CAROLINE

I have been thinking a great deal of political economy
since yesterday, my dear Mrs. B., but I fear not to much purpose: at least I am no farther advanced than to the discovery
of a great confusion of ideas which prevails in my mind on
the subject. This science seems to comprehend every thing,
and yet I own, that I am still at a loss to understand what it
is. Cannot you give me a short explanation of it, that I may
have some clear ideas to begin with?

MRS. B.

I once heard a lady ask a philosopher to tell her in a few
words what is meant by political economy. Madam, replied
he, you understand perfectly what is meant by household
economy, you need only extend your idea of the economy
of a family to that of a whole people—of a nation, and you
will have some comprehension of the nature of political
economy.

CAROLINE

Considering that he was limited to a few words, do you not think that he acquitted himself extremely well? But as I have a little more patience than this lady, I hope you will indulge me with a more detailed explanation of this universal science.

MRS. B.

Political economy treats of the nature, the production, and the distribution of wealth; it teaches us the causes which promote or prevent its increase, and their influence on the happiness or misery of society.

In a country of savages, you find a small number of inhabitants spread over a vast tract of land. Depending on the precarious subsistence afforded by fishing and hunting, they are subject to frequent dearths and famines, by which great numbers are destroyed; they rear but few children, for want cuts them off in their early years; the aged and infirm are often put to death rather from motives of humanity than of cruelty; for the hunter's life requiring a great extent of country, and long and perilous excursions in quest of food, they would be wholly incapable of following the young and robust, and would die of hunger, or become a prey to wild beasts.

If these savages apply themselves to pasturage, their means of subsistence are brought within narrower limits, requiring only that degree of wandering necessary to provide fresh food for their cattle. Their flocks ensuring them a more easy subsistence, their families begin to increase; they lose in a great measure their ferocity, and a considerable improvement takes place in their character.

By degrees the art of tillage is discovered, a small tract of ground becomes capable of feeding a greater relative number of people; the necessity of wandering in search of food is superseded; families begin to settle in fixed habitations, and the arts of social life are introduced and cultivated.

In the savage state, scarcely any form of government is established; the people seem to be under no control but that of their military chiefs in time of war.

The possession of flocks and herds in the pastoral state introduces property; laws then become necessary for its security; the elders and leaders of these wandering tribes therefore begin to establish laws, to violate which is to commit a crime, and to incur a punishment. This is the origin of social order; and when in the third state the people settle in fixed habitations, the laws gradually assume the more regular form of a monarchical or republican government. Every 'thing now wears a new aspect; industry-flourishes, the arts are invented, the use of the metals is discovered; labour is subdivided, every one applies himself more particularly to a distinct employment, in which he becomes skilful. Thus, by slow degrees, this people of savages, whose origin was so rude and miserable, become a civilised people, who occupy a highly cultivated country, intersected by fine roads, leading to wealthy and populous cities, and carrying on an extensive trade both at home and with other countries.

CAROLINE

This is a very pleasing outline of the history of the rise and progress of civilisation; but I should like to see it a little more filled up.

MRS. B.

The subject you will find hereafter sufficiently developed; for the whole business of political economy is to study the causes which have thus co-operated to enrich and civilise a nation. This science is, therefore, essentially founded upon history,—not the history of sovereigns, of wars, and of intrigues; but the history of the arts, of trade, of discoveries, and of civilization. We see some countries, like America, increase rapidly in wealth and prosperity, whilst others, like Egypt and Syria, are impoverished, depopulated, and falling to decay: when the causes which produce these various effects are well understood, some judgment may be formed of the measures which governments have adopted to contribute to the welfare of their people; whether such or such a branch of commerce should be encouraged in preference to others; whether it be proper to prohibit this or that kind of merchandise; whether any peculiar encouragement should be given to agriculture; whether it be right to establish by law the price of provisions or the price of labour, or whether they should be left without control; and so on.

You see, therefore, that political economy consists of two parts,—theory and practice; the science and the art. The science comprehends a knowledge of the facts which we have enumerated: the art relates more particularly to legislation, and consists in doing whatever is requisite to contribute to the increase of national wealth, and avoiding whatever would be prejudicial to it. Mistakes in theory lead to errors in practice. When we enter into details we shall have occasion to observe that governments, misled by false ideas of political economy, have frequently arrested the natural

progress of wealth when it was in their power to have ac-
celerated it.

CAROLINE

But since the world was originally a rude wilderness, and
yet has arrived at the improved state of civilisation in which
we now find it, the errors of governments cannot have been
very prejudicial.

MRS. B.

The natural causes which tend to develop the wealth and
prosperity of nations are more powerful than the faults of
administration, which operate in a contrary direction. But
it is nevertheless true that these errors are productive of a
great deal of mischief; that they check industry and retard
the progress of improvement. Under bad governments particular classes of people are favoured, others discouraged
and oppressed: prosperity is thus unequally shared, and
riches unfairly distributed. You look very grave, Caroline;
do you already begin to grow tired of the subject?

CAROLINE

Oh no; I think thus far I have understood you: but before we proceed you must allow me to mention an objection which, I confess, distresses me; if it is well founded
I shall be quite at variance with the maxims of political
economy, and that science will no longer retain any interest
for me. I find that you are constantly talking of wealth; of
the causes which produce it; of the means of augmenting
it. To be rich, very rich, richer than other people, seems
to be the great aim of political economy. Whilst religion
and morality teach us that we should moderate the thirst
of gain for inordinate love of wealth is the source of all

crimes. Besides that, it is very evident that the richest people are not always the happiest. Now, if wealth does not conduce to the happiness of individuals, how can it constitute that of nations? A poor but virtuous people is surely happier than a rich and vicious one. What remarkable examples do we not see of this in history. We are taught to admire the Greek republics, who despised the pomp and luxury of wealth. And then the Romans; during the early part of their history they were poor and virtuous, but the acquisition of wealth depraved their character, and made them slaves. Now political economy appears to me to induce the love of riches, and to consider it as the only end to be attained by government.

MRS. B.

This is a most alarming attack upon political economy! When, however, you understand it better, you will find that your censure is unfounded. At present you must take my word for it, as I cannot show you the benefits arising from just principles of political economy before you are acquainted with the principles themselves; but I can assure you that they all tend to promote the happiness of nations, and the purest morality. I do not pretend to deny that wealth, like almost every other human good, is liable to abuse; and the Greeks and Romans may, perhaps, in a great measure, owe their degradation to the ill use which they made of their ill-gotten wealth; for it should be observed, that their riches were obtained by rapine and plunder, and did not arise from the gradual and natural growth of industry, in which case alone they spread happiness around, creating new desires by offering new gratifications. But history acquaints us more with the sovereign than with the people. In order to be able to form a just estimate of the morals and manners of a country, we must avail ourselves also of the information of travellers, and from their account we shall generally find, that the poorer societies of mankind are proportionally miserable in their condition, ferocious in their manners, and vicious in their morals.

That wealth is not sufficient to constitute the happiness of a people I most readily admit; it is but one among a number of causes which conduce to it. Social happiness is the result of a pure religion, good morals, a wise government, and a general diffusion of knowledge; without such advantages wealth can never be enjoyed. But these are subjects upon which we can touch only incidentally; they constitute the science of general politics and legislation, and our attention is to be particularly directed to political economy, which is but a branch of it, and treats especially of the means of promoting social happiness so far as relates to the acquisition, possession, and use of the objects which constitute wealth. Do you think that the labouring classes possess a sufficiency of these objects; and if not, is it not our duty to study how they may get more? for without increasing the general wealth of the community the state of the lower classes cannot be improved. Besides, poverty but too frequently leads to crime. Theft is never so prevalent as in a season of scarcity and distress; an increase of wealth, therefore, among the lower classes must be considered as tending to improve their moral character, as well as to increase their physical comforts. Then, so far from exciting illiberal feelings, political economy tends to moderate all unjustifiable ambition, by showing that the surest means of increasing national prosperity are peace, security, and justice; that jealousy between nations is as prejudicial as between individuals; that each finds its advantage in reciprocal benefits; and that far from growing rich at each other's expense, they mutually assist each other by a liberal system of commerce. Political economy is particularly inimical to the envious, jealous, and malignant passions; and if ever peace and moderation should flourish in the world, it is to enlightened views of this science that we should be indebted for the miracle.

But, my dear Caroline, I suspect that there is some error in your idea of riches. What do you call riches?

CAROLINE

To be rich is to have a great income; to be able to spend a great deal more than other people.

MRS. B.

You speak of the riches of individuals; of comparative wealth. A rich man in one class of society might be poor in another. But this is not the definition that I asked for. What do you understand by riches in general—in what does wealth consist?

CAROLINE

Oh, I suppose, you mean money?—I should say that wealth consists in gold and silver.

MRS. B.

Consider what would be the situation of a country which possessed no other wealth than money. Do you recollect in what estimation Robinson Crusoe held his

bag of gold, when he was wrecked upon a desert island?

CAROLINE

True: but in an island which is not desert, money will
purchase whatever you want.

MRS. B.

Then I should say that the things which we are desirous
to procure with money, such as land, houses, furniture,
clothes, food, &c., constitute riches, as well as the money
by which they are obtained.

CAROLINE

Certainly: these are clearly the things which constitute
real wealth; for unless we could procure the necessaries of
life with gold and silver, they would be of no more use to
us than lead or iron.

MRS. B.

We may therefore say that wealth comprehends every
article of utility, convenience, or luxury. This includes
every object of our wishes which can become an article of
commerce; such as landed estates, houses, the products of
agriculture, those of manufactures, provisions, domestic
animals, in a word, whatever has value, and can contribute
to the welfare and enjoyment of man.

CAROLINE

Why should you confine your definition of wealth to
things that can become articles of commerce?

MRS. B.

Because there are many countries where the earth

spontaneously produces things which can neither be consumed nor sold; and however valuable such things would
be to us, could we obtain them, they cannot, under those
circumstances, be considered as wealth. The herds of wild
cattle, for instance, which feed on the rich pastures called
the Pampas, in South America, are of this description. Many
of those extensive tracts of land are uninhabited, and the
cattle that range at large over them are of no value there.
Parties of hunters occasionally make incursions, and destroy
some of them for their hides and fat, whilst the flesh is either left to putrefy on the ground, or is used as fuel to melt
the fat for the purposes of tallow, which being transported
to places where it can be sold and consumed, it acquires
value, and becomes wealth.

CAROLINE

This can be the case only in wild and uncultivated
countries; in those which are civilised, any land yielding
unsaleable produce would be converted by the proprietor
to some other use.

MRS. B.

I have heard that the fruit of many of the vineyards in
France was not gathered some years ago, the grapes being at that time so much reduced in value in consequence
of a decree prohibiting the exportation of French wines,
that the price at which they could be sold would not pay
the expense of gathering them. In England, also, when all
kinds of colonial produce were excluded from the continent of Europe, coffee is said to have been thrown into the
sea, because it would not pay the charges on being landed.
You see, therefore, that the effects of war, or other circum-

stances, may for a time, in any country, destroy the value of commodities.

CAROLINE

How very much you have already extended my conception of the meaning of wealth! And yet I can perceive that all these ideas were floating confusedly in my mind before. In speaking of wealth, we ought not to confine ourselves to the consideration of the relative wealth of individuals, but extend our views to whatever constitutes riches in general, without any reference to the inequality of the division.

MRS. B.

The confusion has arisen from the common practice of estimating riches by money, instead of observing that wealth consists in such commodities as are useful or agreeable to mankind, of which gold and silver constitute but a very small portion.

CONVERSATION III

ON PROPERTY

LABOUR THE ORIGIN OF WEALTH.—LEGAL INSTITUTION OF
PROPERTY.—OF LANDED PROPERTY.—SECURITY THE RE-
SULT OF PROPERTY.—OBJECTIONS TO LANDED PROPERTY
ANSWERED.—ORIGIN OF NATIONS IN A SAVAGE PASTORAL
LIFE.—THEIR PROGRESS IN AGRICULTURE.—CULTIVATION
OF CORN.—RECAPITULATION.

CAROLINE

WELL, my dear Mrs. B., since you have reconciled me to
wealth, and convinced me that the poor can obtain a com-
petence only when the nation is wealthy, I begin to grow
impatient to learn what are the best means of obtaining this
desirable object

MRS. B.

Do not leave every thing to me, Caroline; I have told you
that you were not without some general notions of political
economy, though they are but ill arranged in your mind.
Endeavour, therefore, to unravel the entangled thread, and
discover yourself what are the principal causes of the production of wealth in a nation.

CAROLINE

Let me see: gold and silver are dug out of the mines, but I know they do not alone constitute wealth; houses are built by men; corn, and the produce of the earth result from agriculture; manufactures are produced by industry. All wealth, therefore, seems to me to proceed from *labour.*

MRS. B.

It is very true that labour is a most essential requisite to the creation of wealth, and yet it does not necessarily ensure its production. The labour of the savage who possesses no wealth is often more severe than that of our common ploughman, whose furrows teem with riches. The long and perilous excursions of savages in search of prey; the difficulty which, from want of skill, they must encounter in every process of industry, in constructing the simplest habitations, fabricating the rudest implements;—all concur to increase their toil. Labour is the lot of man; whether in a barbarous or a civilised state, he is destined to earn his bread by the sweat of his brow. But how is it that in the one case labour is productive of great wealth, whilst in the other it affords barely the necessaries of life?

CAROLINE

The skill and ardour of the savage are absorbed in the chase, and when he is compelled to undertake some simple domestic industry, such as the construction of a hut, or the fabrication of weapons, he works neither with the activity and zeal nor with the steady perseverance of men in civilized society. Savages, you know, are proverbially noted for their idleness.

MRS. B.

Inducements must then be found to rouse them from that idleness; motives to awaken their industry and habituate them to regular labour. Men are naturally disposed to indolence; all exertion requires effort, and efforts are not made without an adequate stimulus. The activity we behold in civilised life is the effect of education; it results from a strong and general desire to share not only in the necessaries of life, but in the various comforts and enjoyments with which we are surrounded. The man who has reaped the reward, as well as undergone the fatigues of daily exertion, willingly renews his efforts, as he thus renews his enjoyments. But the ignorance of a savage precludes all desires which do not lead to the immediate gratification of his wants; he sees no possessions which tempt his ambition—no enjoyments which animate his desires; nothing less than the strong impulse of want rouses him to exertion; and, having satisfied the cravings of hunger, he lies down to rest without a thought of the future.

CAROLINE

But if the desires of savages are so few and so easily satisfied, may not their state be happier than that of the labouring classes in civilised countries, who wish for so much, and obtain so little?

MRS. B.

The brutish apathy which results from gross ignorance can scarcely deserve the name of content, and is utterly unworthy that of happiness. Goldsmith, in his Traveller, justly as well as beautifully observes, that

"Every want that stimulates the breast
Becomes a source of pleasure when redress'd."

Besides, it is only occasionally that a savage can indulge in this state of torpid indifference. If you con* suit any account of travels in a savage country, you will be satisfied that our peasantry enjoy a comparative state of affluence and even of luxury.

But let us suppose a civilised being to come among a tribe of savages, and succeed in teaching some of them the arts of life—he instructs one how to render his hut more commodious, another to collect a little store of provisions for the winter, a third to improve the construction of his bows and arrows; what would be the consequences?

CAROLINE

One might expect that the enjoyment derived from these improvements would lead their countrymen to adopt them, and would introduce a general spirit of industry.

MRS. B.

Is it not more probable that the idle savages would, either by force or fraud, wrest from the industrious their hard-earned possessions; that the one would be driven from the hut he had constructed with so much labour, another robbed of the provisions he had stored, and a third would see his well-pointed arrows aimed at his own breast? Here then is a fatal termination to all improvement. Who will work to procure such precarious possessions, which expose him to danger instead of ensuring their enjoyment?

CAROLINE

But these evils would be prevented if laws were made for the protection of property.

MRS. B.

True; but the *right* of property must be established before it can be protected; for nature has given mankind every thing in common, and property is of human institution. It takes place in such early stages of society that one is apt to imagine it of natural origin; but until it has been established by law, no man has a right to call any thing his own.

CAROLINE

What, not the game he has killed, the hut he has built, or the implements he has constructed? These may be wrested from him by force; but he who thus obtains them acquires no right to them.

MRS. B.

When a man has produced any thing by his labour, he has, no doubt, in equity the fairest claim to it; but his right to separate it from the common stock of nature, and appropriate it to his own use, depends entirely upon the law of the land.

In the case of property in land, for instance, it is the law which decrees that such a piece of ground shall belong to Thomas, such another to John, and a third to James ; that these men shall have an exclusive right to the possession of the land and of its produce; that they may keep, sell, or exchange it; give it away during their lives, or bequeath it after their deaths, And, in order that this law should be respected, punishments are enacted for those who should transgress it. It is not until such laws have been made for the institution and protection of property, of whatever description it be, that the right of property is established.

CAROLINE

You astonish me! I thought that properly in land had always existed; I had no idea that it was a legal institution, but imagined that it had originated from the earliest period of the world. We read that in the time of the ancient patriarchs, when families became too numerous, they separated; and that those who went to settle elsewhere fed their flocks, and occupied the land without molestation. There was no one to dispute their right to it; and after their deaths the children inhabited and cultivated the hind of their fathers.

If we were to found a colony in a desert island, every man would cultivate as much ground as he wanted for his own use, and each having an equal interest in the preservation of his possessions, property would thus be established by general agreement, without any legal institution.

MRS. B.

This general agreement is a kind of law; a very imperfect one it is true, and which was perhaps originally founded on the relative strength of individuals. If one man attempts to carry off the cattle or the fruits of another, the latter opposes force to force; if he is stronger or better armed, he either kills his antagonist or drives him away; if weaker, he is despoiled, or he calls in his neighbours to his succour, shows them the common danger, and may induce them to unite with him in taking vengeance on the aggressor.

Many incidents of this nature must occur before regular laws are instituted; that is to say, before a public authority is established, which shall protect individuals against those who attack them, and punish the offenders. It is then only that a man can say, "This is my field; this is my house; this seed which I cast into the ground will bring forth an abundant provision for me and my family; these trees which J plant will every year yield us fruit, which we alone shall have a right to gather."

CAROLINE

I now comprehend perfectly the advantage of such laws—it is *security:* before they were established, the strong might wrest every thing from the weak; and old men, women, and children who had no means of defence were exposed to their rapine and violence. The idle and improvident, when in want of subsistence, became the natural enemies of the laborious and industrious. So that without this law the men who had toiled hardest would be most likely to fall victims to those who had done nothing. In a word, the wasps would devour the honey of the bees.

MRS. B.

Yes, *security* is the grand point; it is security which stimulates industry, and renders labour productive; every step towards security is a step towards civilisation, towards wealth, and towards general happiness.

CAROLINE

All this is very true; yet an objection to the institution of property in land has just occurred to me, which appears of considerable importance. Before land became private property, the earth, you say, was possessed in common by all mankind; every one had an equal claim to it. But the law which institutes landed property takes it from mankind at large, to give it to a few individuals; in order, therefore, to make some men rich, it makes others poor. Now what right has the law to dispossess some in order to enrich others? It should be just, before it is generous.

This objection, however, does not extend to any other than landed property; nothing is more fair than that men should gather the fruits of their labour; that they should possess the houses they have built, the goods they have fabricated; but the land, it appears to me, cannot become private property without injury to others, who are thus deprived of their natural right to it.

MRS. B.

You would then secure to every one the possession of the wealth he may acquire, though you would refuse him the means of producing it? You would make him master of his house, but take away the ground on which it stands; protect his harvests, but not allow him the property of a field on which he may raise his crops?

CAROLINE

I must confess that you have placed my objection rather in a ludicrous point of view; but that is not enough, Mrs. B.; you must show me where the error lies, before I can consent to relinquish it. If it is necessary for the encouragement of industry that land should become private property, justice requires that it should be equally divided amongst all those who have a natural claim to it?

MRS. B.

In countries newly occupied, grants of land are usually made to those who are willing to reclaim it from a state of nature; it is in cases of conquest only that land has been arbitrarily partitioned by the conqueror. Such was the fate of Europe when over-run by the northern barbarians, who, by their division of land, laid the foundation of the feudal system.

But whatever may have been the original causes of the division of land, and whether or not it were equally apportioned at first, it is impossible to prevent inequality from arising afterwards.

CAROLINE

Yet we read of laws having been instituted in several countries to preserve this equality, and in some instances with considerable success. In Rome, frequent attempts were made to this effect; and the Spartans, during a long series of years, rigorously persevered in the equal division of landed property.

MRS. B.

And what were the consequences of this attempt? At Rome, the laws to prevent inequality of landed property proved ineffectual; in Sparta they produced a community of warriors, who tyrannised with cruelty over a population of slaves, and who were not possessed of a single virtue unallied to military glory.

Both the virtues and vices of mankind tend to destroy this equality; the laborious, the intelligent, and skilful, will raise plentiful harvests. Nature thus rewards their exertions. The possessions of the idle, the careless, and the ignorant, will, on the contrary, gradually degenerate. Nature has annexed this penalty to their neglect. Shall we then counteract so wise a dispensation of Providence, by giving to the idle the reward of industry, and making the industrious bear a punishment due to the idle?

CAROLINE
Yet poverty frequently arises from sickness and misfortune, which render men unable to work; and, under such circumstances, it is hard to suffer the penalty incurred by idleness.

MRS. B.
True; but you must consider also, that the in-equality of condition, and the vicissitudes of human life, give rise to the exercise of almost every virtue; patience, resignation, fortitude, on the part of the afflicted; benevolence, compassion, generosity, charity, on that of the more prosperous of the community—feelings which purify and refine the enjoyment of wealth, arid are amongst its highest gratifications.

Nature, for equally wise purposes, has dispensed her bleating with various degrees of munificence: in some instances she bestows them with unbounded and inexhaustible profusion. It is thus that she has given us light and air, which are alike possessed and enjoyed by all. No one ever thought of converting these elements into private property; and if food were as easily obtained, and the human frame as readily supplied with nourishment as it is with the air we breathe, no one would ever have conceived the idea of separating from the common stock, and converting into private property, either the food he required or the land on which it was produced.

CAROLINE
How delightful that would be! Labour would no

longer be required; and mankind would be transformed into a race of contemplative philosophers, whose only occupation would be to study and admire the works of nature!

MRS. B.

It is dangerous to trust to your judgment when it leads you to conclusions so different from the established course of nature. We must bear in mind that the dispensations of Providence are always wise and good, and, though it is not always in our power to trace their beneficial effects, in the present instance they appear sufficiently obvious. Were mankind not under the necessity of labouring for a subsistence, so far from becoming philosophers, I am inclined to think that they would ever have remained a race of indolent savages, scarcely raised above the brute creation. What motive would they have had for exertion, what incentive to awaken their faculties, and rouse them from the apathy of indolence so natural to man? The necessity of regular industry to secure subsistence appears to be the first step towards the developement of their faculties, both physical and mental. But we have observed that men will not be induced to cultivate the earth to long as it is possessed in common, when the idle may reap the harvest sown by the hand of industry. Property in land is therefore of necessity a preliminary step to cultivation, and we have seen that cultivation could not take place were the earth unlimited in extent and powers of production. Let us then reflect, that when nature conferred this blessing upon us with a more sparing hand than she has bestowed the other elements, it was a doubtless with a view of rousing the latent faculties of man, and calling them into action; it was in order to raise him from a state of animal nature, in which he is assimilated to the beasts that perish, and urge him through a progressive course of improvement, during which new ideas are successively formed; the character is developed by reason, the mind strengthened by trials, chastened by adversity, elevated by piety, softened by social affections, enlarged by science, refined by literature, and brought at length to that state in which we discern the traces of a being destined for immortality.

CAROLINE

I am glad we arrive at the same satisfactory conclusion, the happiness of our fellow-creatures, by a safer road than that in which my imagination had first wandered. There remains no rational doubt in my mind of the advantages resulting from the division of land, and the accumulation of landed property; nor am I disposed to murmur at the larger share you have assigned to the more industrious and better part of mankind. I see that soon after the division of land these will infallibly become the most considerable possessors; that their property should be secured to them and to their heirs, and that in their hands it will be the most highly cultivated, and yield the greatest produce.

MRS. B.

The institution of property in land augments the wealth, not only of the proprietors but likewise of all other classes of men.

Lands may be considered as the instrument by which alone wealth is created; and we have just seen that the security of its possession gives life and vigour to industry: it is this security which raises the condition of our peasantry so much above that of a savage people who possess the land in common.

CAROLINE

An institution of such evident and general utility cannot then be considered as unjust.

MRS. B.

Certainly not. It is by the test of general utility that the justice of all laws should be tried; for there are none which do not impose some restraint on the natural liberty of man, and which, in that point of view, might not be deemed objectionable. But, without the control of laws, we have seen that neither the lives, the property, the reputation, nor even the liberty of men, are secure: we sacrifice therefore some portion of that liberty to the law; and, in return, it secures to us the remainder, together with every blessing which security can give. Blackstone, in his Commentaries, says, "Every man, when he enters into society, gives up a part of his natural liberty, as the price of so valuable a purchase; and in consideration of receiving the advantages of mutual commerce, obliges himself to conform to those laws which the community has thought proper to establish. For no man who considers a moment would wish to retain the absolute and uncontrolled power of doing whatever he pleases; the consequence of which is, that every other man would also have the same power, and there would be no security to individuals in any of the enjoyments of life: political, therefore, or civil liberty, which is that of a member of society, is no other than natural liberty, so far restrained by human laws (and no farther) as is necessary and expedient for the general advantage of the public.

That constitution or form of government, that system of laws, is alone calculated to maintain civil liberty, which leaves the subject entire master of his own conduct, except in those points wherein the public requires some direction or restraint."

CAROLINE

You have completely removed all my scruples respecting the institution of landed property, Mrs. B.; let us now, therefore, return to the progress of wealth and civilisation.

MRS. B.

We must not proceed too rapidly; for the progressive steps in the history of civilisation are extremely slow, and we must learn to view the developement of human intellect and the progress of human industry in successive and almost insensible degrees.

Civilised nations generally originate from the settlement of a colony; they seldom arise from a savage state. It was in this state we found the Indians on the discovery of America; they were mere hunters; and so long as men behold an unlimited space before them, in which they may wander without obstacle or control, it is difficult to conceive any circumstances which should lead them to adopt a settled mode of life, and apply themselves to tillage.

In countries abounding with large plains, the pastoral mode of life has prevailed; but for this purpose there must have been established property in cattle, though the land were possessed in common. Such was the ease with the ancient Scythians, who inhabited the vast plains of Tartary, and with the modern Tartars and Arabs; who, to this day, are wandering tribes, and, like the patriarchs of old, live in tents, and travel about with their flocks and herds in search of pasture.

The indolence to which men are naturally disposed is necessarily a great obstacle to the introduction of agriculture; for it requires a considerable degree of foresight and knowledge, and a firm reliance on the security of property, to labour at one season in order to reap the fruits at another. We may suppose agriculture to be a progressive step from pastoral life; that a tribe of shepherds may have met with enemies in their wandering excursions, and the apprehensions of losing their flocks may have induced them to settle; they would probably choose a spot defended by nature from attacks of wild beasts, or the incursions of savage neighbours. Thus Cecrops pitched upon the rock on which the citadel of Athens is founded to build a town. Or they may have been tempted by the attractions of some fruitful spot, under the protection of a neighbouring government able to defend them. Volney, in his account of the wandering tribes in Syria, says, "As often as they find peace and security, and a possibility of procuring sufficient provisions in any district, they take up their residence in it, and insensibly adopt a settled life and the arts of cultivation." These arts they must have attained by very slow degrees: they observed that fruit-trees may be multiplied; that nutritious plants may be propagated; that there are seeds which reproduce every year; and that a great variety of animals may be tamed and domesticated. Thus supplied with a new fund of subsistence, their children are better fed, their families increase, and age and infancy are protected and provided for.

But these people are yet acquainted with only the first elements of agriculture; how many fortunate chances must have occurred before they reached the important era of the cultivation of corn! Wild corn has nowhere been found; and the Greeks imagined that a divinity descended on earth, to introduce it, and to instruct them in the cultivation of this valuable plant. Athens, Crete, Sicily, and Egypt, all claim the merit of being the original cultivators of corn; but whoever are the people to whom we are indebted for this important discovery, or whatever are the means by which it was accomplished, there is none which has had so great an influence on the welfare of mankind. Feeble as it appears, this plant can resist the summer's heat and the winter's cold. It flourishes in almost every climate, and is adapted, not only for the food of man but for that of a great variety of domestic animals, and it yields by fermentation a pleasant and salubrious beverage. The grain will keep many years, and affords such a durable means of subsistence that danger could no longer be apprehended in trusting to futurity, and plenty was secured during the most unproductive seasons.

But the cultivation of this inestimable plant cannot be undertaken without considerable funds, fixed habitations, implements of husbandry*, domestic animals; in a word, establishments which could neither be created

---

* These are at first of a very rude and imperfect construction, la some parts of India, the plough of a Hindoo, even to this day, is formed of a crooked stick very inartificially sharpened, and not unfrequently drawn by his wife. The use of domestic animals in agriculture is another step towards civilisation; but no farming establishment whatever could either be created or maintained without the institution of property.

nor maintained without the institution of property. Savages have no corn, no cultivation, no domestic animals; they consume and destroy every thing without ever considering reproduction;—and how different are the results! We now see millions of men and animals inhabiting an extent of country which would scarcely have sufficed for the maintenance of two or three hundred savages.

CAROLINE

Let us rest a little, my dear Mrs. B. I am almost bewildered with the number and variety of ideas that you have presented to my mind. I wonder that these things have not occurred to me before; but I have been so accustomed to see the world in its present improved state, that my attention was never drawn to the many obstacles and difficulties it must have encountered, and the laborious progressive steps it must have made, before society could have attained its present state of perfection.

MRS. B.

Perfection I comparatively speaking I suppose you mean; for it is not long since you were making lamentable complaints of the actual state of society ; in which indeed I could not entirely agree with you, though I think that we are still far removed from perfection. But let us continue to trace the progress of wealth and civilisation up to their present state, before we begin to find any fault with existing institutions.

CAROLINE

I think I have now a very clear idea of the important consequences which result from the establishment of property. It puts an end to the wandering life of barbarians, induces men to settle, and inures them to regular labour; it gives them prudence and foresight; teaches them to embellish the face of the earth by cultivation; to multiply the useful tribes of animals and nutritious plants; and, in short, it enables them so prodigiously to augment the stock of subsistence, as to transform a country which contained but a few poor huts and a scanty population into a great and wealthy nation.

CONVERSATION IV

ON PROPERTY—*continued*

EFFECTS OF INSECURITY OF PROPERTY.—EXAMPLES FROM
VOLNEY'S TRAVELS.—OBJECTIONS RAISED AGAINST CI-
VILISATION.—STATE OF BOETICA, FROM TELEMACHUS.—
OBJECTIONS TO COMMUNITY OF GOODS.—ESTABLISH-
MENT OF JESUITS IN PARAGUAY.—MORAVIANS.—STATE
OF SWITZERLAND.—ADVANTAGES RESULTING FROM THE
ESTABLISHMENT AND SECURITY OF PROPERTY.

MRS. B.

Now that we have traced the rise and progress of civilisation to the security of property, let us see whether
the reverse, that is to say, insecurity of property in a
civilised country, will not degrade the state of man, and
make him retrace his steps till he again degenerates into
barbarism.

CAROLINE

Are there any examples of a civilised people returning
to a savage state? I do not recollect ever to have heard of
such a change.

MRS. B.

No, because when property has once been instituted,

the advantages it produces are such that it can never be totally abolished; but in countries where the tyranny of government renders it very insecure, the people invariably degenerate, the country falls back into poverty and a comparative state of barbarism. We have already noticed the miserable change in the once wealthy city of Tyre. Egypt, which was the original seat of the arts and sciences, is now sunk into the most abject degradation; and if you will read the passages I have marked for you in Volney's Travels, you will find the truth of this observation very forcibly delineated.

CAROLINE *reads.*

"When the tyranny of a government drives the inhabitants of a village to extremity, the peasants desert their houses, and withdraw with their families into the mountains, or wander in the plains. It often happens that even individuals turn robbers in order to withdraw themselves from the tyranny of the laws, and unite into little camps, which maintain themselves by force of arms; these, increasing, become new hordes and new tribes. We may say, therefore, that in cultivated countries the wandering life originates in the injustice or want of policy of the government."

MRS. B.

This, you see, is very much to the point: but here is another passage equally applicable.

CAROLINE *reads.*

"The silks of Tripoli are every day losing their quality from the decay of the mulberry trees, of which scarcely any thing now remains but some hollow trunks. Why not plant new ones? That is an European observation. Here they never plant; because, were they either to build or plant, the Pacha would say this man has money, and it would be extorted from him."

Besides, where there is so little actual security, what reliance can be placed on futurity? What reason would the proprietors have to hope that the mulberry trees would ever repay them for the trouble and expense of planting them? Yet I wonder that the government of the country should not, for its own sake, encourage the industry of its subjects.

MRS. B.

In the wretched government of the Turks, every thing is so insecure, from the life and property of the sovereign to that of the lowest of his subjects, that no one looks to futurity, but every man endeavours to grasp at and enjoy what is immediately within his reach. The following passage will show you what sufferers they all are by such a mistaken system of policy.

CAROLINE *reading*.

"In consequence of the wretchedness of the government, the greater part of the pachalics are impoverished and laid waste. In the ancient registers of imports, upwards of 3,200 villages were reckoned in that of Aleppo, but at present the collector can scarcely find 400. Such of our merchants as have resided there 20 years have themselves seen the greater part of the environs of Aleppo become depopulated. The traveller meets with nothing but houses in ruins, cisterns rendered useless, and fields abandoned. Those who cultivated them are fled into the towns, where the population is absorbed, but where at least the individual conceals himself among the crowd from the rapacious hands of despotism. In other countries the cities are in some measure the overflow of the population of the country; in Syria, they are the effect of its desertion. The roads in the mountains are extremely bad, as the inhabitants are so far from levelling them, that they endeavour to render them more rugged, in order, as they say, to cure the Turks of their desire to introduce their cavalry.

"The Pacha may applaud himself for penetrating into the most secret sources of private property, but what are the consequences? The people, denied the enjoyment of the fruits of their labour, restrain their industry to the supply of their necessary wants; the husbandman sows only to prevent himself from starving, the artificer labours only to maintain his family; if he makes any savings, he strives to conceal them. The people live therefore in poverty and distress, but at least they do not enrich their tyrants, and the rapacity of despotism is its own punishment."

MRS. B.

The degeneracy of the mighty Persian and Indian monarchies, since the conquest of those countries by the Mahometans, is also clearly deducible from the insecurity of property, and affords the most tremendous examples of national decline. Trott, in his History of Hindostan, informs us that during the disastrous times of the latter monarchs of India, the cruelties and oppressions of the agents of government were such, that the farmers burnt their houses, utensils, and crops, and took refuge in the woods and mountains, where those who could neither excite charity nor maintain themselves by the sword, perished through want.

CAROLINE

What a melancholy picture this is, my dear Mrs. B.! it is, I think, even more painful to contemplate than the wretchedness of savages; for to their actual misery these people must add the regret of having known better times.

MRS. B.

Dr. Clarke's Travels abound with similar instances of insecurity of property, and legal oppression, which subvert society, and degrade the human species. "In Circassia," he observes, that " the sower scattering seed, or the reaper who gathers the sheaves, are constantly liable to an assault; and the implements of husbandry are not more essential to the harvest than the carbine, the pistol, and the saber."

Speaking of the Isle of Cyprus, he says: — "The soil every where exhibited a white marly clay, said "to be exceedingly rich in its nature, although neglected. The Greeks are so oppressed by their Turkish masters, that they dare not cultivate the land; the harvest would instantly be taken from them if they did. Their whole aim seems to be, to scrape together barely sufficient, in the course of the whole year, to pay their tax to the governor. The omission of this is punished by torture or by death: and in case of their inability to supply the impost, the inhabitants fly from the island. So many emigrations of this sort happen during the year, that the population of Cyprus rarely exceeds 60,000 persons, a number formerly insufficient to have peopled "one of its towns."

You have made me sensible of the advantages of civilisation; but yet I confess that my mind is not fully satisfied. Is there no medium between a savage life and the extreme inequality of condition which we see in the present state of society? can we not have conveniences without luxuries; plenty without superfluity? I think I have met with an example of such a people, Mrs. B.; but I dare not venture to mention my authority, as you have once before rejected it.

If you allude to Telemachus, there are many sound doctrines of political economy in that work; though it must be acknowledged that it is not free from error. But let me hear the sentiments of Fenelon on this subject.

Do you remember that delightful picture which he draws of the inhabitants of Boetica? There is an irresistible charm in the description of their happiness; and, if fabulous, it is certainly meant at least to delineate what ought to constitute the happiness of nations: equality, community of goods, but few arts and few wants; an ignorance or contempt of luxury, and manners perfectly conformed to the simplicity of nature. I must read you the passage, and you will tell me whether it is not a satire on political economy:—

"They live in common, without any partition of lands: the head of every family is its king. They have no need of judges, for every man submits to the jurisdiction of conscience. They possess all things in common; for the cattle produce milk, and the fields and orchards fruit and grain of every kind in such abundance, that a people so frugal and temperate have no need of property. They have no fixed place of abode; but when they have consumed the fruits, and exhausted the pasturage, of one part of the paradise which they inhabit, they remove their tents to another: they have, therefore, no opposition of interest, but are connected by a fraternal affection, which there is nothing to interrupt. This peace, this union, this liberty, they preserve by rejecting superfluous wealth and deceitful pleasure: they are all free, they are all equal.

"Superior wisdom, the result either of long experience or uncommon abilities, is the only mark of distinction among them; the sophistry of fraud, the cry of violence, the contention of the bar, and the tumult of battle, are never heard in this sacred region, which the gods have taken under their immediate protection: this soil has never been distained with human blood, and even that of a lamb has rarely been shed upon it. When we first traded with these people, we found gold and silver used for ploughshares, and, in general, employed promiscuously with iron. As they carried on no foreign trade, they had no need of money; they were, almost all, either shepherds or husbandmen; for as they suffered no arts to be exercised among them, but such as tended immediately to answer the necessities of life, the number of artificers was consequently small: besides, a greater part, even of those that live by husbandry, or keeping of sheep, are skillful in the exercise of snob arts as are necessary to manners so simple and frugal."

MRS. B.

This, ray dear Caroline, is a representation of what the poets call the Golden Age, and requires only truth to make it perfect. If it were an historical account, all the conclusions you deduce from it would be just; but it is fiction, which, you must allow, makes an essential difference.

Supposing that the earth yielded spontaneously all that is now produced by cultivation; still, without the institution of property, it could not be enjoyed; the fruit would be gathered before it was ripe, animals killed before they came to maturity; for who would protect what was not his own? or, who would economise when all the stores of nature were open to him? There would be a strange mixture of plenty, waste, and famine.

In this country, for instance, where the only common property consists in hedge-nuts and black-berries, how seldom are they allowed to ripen! In some parts of Spain, where the beauty of the climate produces a considerable quantity of good wild fruit, it is customary for the priest to bestow a blessing upon it before any is allowed to be gathered; and this ceremony is not performed till the fruit is considered to be generally ripe; by which means it is prevented from being prematurely gathered. It is with, the same view that our game-laws prohibit shooting, till the season when the birds have attained their full growth.

CAROLINE

But though the Boeticans had all their goods in

common, they were not without laws for protecting them.

MRS. B.

If the earth were possessed in common, who would get about cultivating this or that spot of ground? Government must allot to every man his daily task, and say to the one, You must work in this spot; to another, You must work in that. Would these men labour with the same activity and zeal as if they tilled their own ground, or received wages equivalent to their exertions? Certainly not. Such a system would transform independent men into slaves, into mere mechanical engines. There would be no inequality of condition, it is true; but the earth would not yield one tenth part of its actual produce, the population would necessarily be diminished in the same proportion, and if all escaped the distresses of poverty, none would enjoy the acquisition of riches; an enjoyment, which, when derived from the exercise of our talents and our industry, is a just and virtuous feeling; it raises men not Only in the scale of wealth, but in that of the power of doing good, of enlarging the sphere of human knowledge, with all the inestimable benefits which result from it.

There have, however, really existed establishments founded on a community of goods. That of the Jesuits in Paraguay was of this description. The influence of religion enabled these priests to exercise a despotic away over the poor Indians whom they had converted to Christianity; it must be allowed that they tempered their power by a patriarchal care of their docile subjects. Such a species of government might perhaps be well adapted to a tribe of ignorant uncivilised Indians, but it would never make a free, a happy, an independent, and a wealthy people. There is, indeed, still existing a sect of the same description, called Moravians; but it is their religious tenets alone which enable them to keep up such an artificial system of community, and it should be compared rather to a convent of monks and nuns, than to a great nation.

I must again repeat it, and cannot too strongly urge you to bear in mind, that the industry of man requires the stimulus of exclusive possession and enjoyment; and will always be proportioned to the personal advantage which he derives from it.

CAROLINE

I find I must give up the point of community of goods; but still I cannot help thinking that the great inequality of conditions which exist in the present state of society is a serious evil.

In Switzerland, where there is much less inequality of fortune than in this country, I have often admired and almost envied the innocent and simple manners of the people. They seem not to know half our wants, nor to suffer half our cares.

MRS. B.

The Swiss are generally governed by mild and equitable laws, which render them a virtuous and a happy people; and if they are not a rich and populous nation, it proceeds not from any want of industry, but from the obstacles opposed both to agriculture and trade by the nature of their country; for they are, on the contrary, uncommonly active and enterprising. I have often seen men carry on their shoulders baskets of manure up steep ascents inaccessible to beasts of burden and this for the purpose of cultivating some little insulated spot of ground, which did not appear worth any such labour. The country-women wear their knitting fastened round their waists, in order to have it at hand to fill up every little interval that occurs in their domestic employments. If a Swiss woman goes to fetch water from the fountain, or faggots from the wood, her burden is skillfully poised on her head, whilst her fingers busily ply the needles. But, industrious as they are, the resources of the country are too limited to enable a father of a family to provide for all his children; some of them are therefore obliged to emigrate, and seek their fortune in a foreign land, which offers greater resources to their industry. Hence the Dumber of Swiss merchants, governesses, shop-keepers, and servants, that are to be met with in almost all countries. Would not these people be happier if they found means of exercising their industry and their talents in a country to which they are all so much attached, and which they have so much reason to love? In the energy of youthful vigour, men may often quit their own country, and live happily in a foreign land; but inquire of the parents who are on the point of separating from their children as soon as they have attained the hopeful age of manhood, whether their country would be less happy for offering them the means of employment and maintenance at home.

The Swiss cannot afford to support a standing army for the defence of their territory; they are therefore under the necessity of engaging their troops in the service of foreign potentates, in order to provide for a part of their population, and to have a resource by calling them home in times of danger. Would not these soldiers be happier in defending their own country, than in shedding their blood as mercenaries in the cause of foreigners? We hare a remarkable proof of it in the effect which their patriotic songs are said to produce on them. When these simple airs recall to their minds their beloved and regretted country, it either drives them to desertion, or renders their lives miserable; and, so deep is the impression made by these national airs, that it was found necessary to forbid their being sung by the troops in foreign service.

CAROLINE

There is no withstanding your attacks, Mrs. B. You drive me from all my strong holds. I expected to have found a safe asylum in the mountains of Switzerland; but I see that I must once more take refuge in London, where I am sure you will admit that the contrast between the luxuries of the rich and the wretchedness of the poor is shocking to every person of common feeling.

MRS. B.

If the wretchedness of the poor were the effect of the luxuries of the rich, I should certainly agree with you on that point; but I believe it to be otherwise. However, as the people, whose progress towards wealth and civilisation we have been tracing in our two last conversations, are yet far from being sufficiently advanced in their career to be guilty of any great excess in luxury, we must patiently follow them in their advancement in knowledge and the acquisition of wealth before we treat of the subject of luxury.

CONVERSATION V

ON THE DIVISION OF LABOUR

MRS. B.

We have ascertained that the establishment and security of property were the chief causes of the emancipation of mankind from the shackles of sloth and ignorance; but there are other subordinate causes which tend greatly to promote the progress of industry and civilisation. The first of these is the introduction of *exchange* or *barter.*

We observed, that when men found they could place a reliance on the security of their possessions, they laboured with redoubled activity, and, far from being satisfied with a scanty and temporary maintenance, they provide for the future, they accumulate a little store, not only of the necessaries but of the comforts and conveniences of life. The one has a stock of arrows for the chase, another of provisions for the winter, a third of clothes or ornaments for his person.

They will remain in undisturbed possession of this little property; but those who can no longer obtain it by force or fraud will endeavour to procure it by other means. In the hunting season, they will apply to the fabricator of arrows; but they will not go to him with empty hands; they must be provided with something to offer in exchange for the arrows, something which they think will tempt him to part with them: whilst those who have nothing to give in return will wish in vain to obtain them.

Here, then, is a new incitement to a spirit of industry. Whoever has accumulated more than he wants of any commodity, may find means of exchanging the surplus for something that will gratify other desires. As objects of desire increase, the wish to possess and the effort to obtain them increase also; and the industry of man is exerted either in producing them himself, or in producing something by means of which he may obtain them. Thus the torpid apathy and languid indolence of a savage yields to the curiosity, the admiration, the desire, the activity, and industry of a civilised being.

The man, for instance, who first cultivates a little spot of ground, may be said to produce in time a general harvest; not only by introducing the art of tillage, but by the powerful impulse which it gives to industry in general. He cannot himself consume the whole produce of his little garden, but he exchanges the surplus for other things of which he stands in need.

CAROLINE

Besides, he would not have had sufficient time to bestow on the cultivation of his garden, if he had been, at the same time, obliged to provide for all his other wants.

MRS. B.

Very true; those therefore who mean to partake of the fruits of his garden must contribute towards the supply of those other wants; some will bring him fish from the river, others game from the woods: when his immediate necessities are supplied, he will be induced to exchange his vegetables for articles of conveniency, such as baskets to contain his fruit, or some of the rude implements of husbandry; or he may finally be tempted to part with some for mere luxuries, such as rare shells, feathers, and other personal ornaments. His neighbours will therefore be eager to produce or procure articles, which, either from necessity, conveniency, or merely from pleasure, will induce the gardener to part with the produce of his garden: for this purpose invention will be stimulated, new commodities will be fabricated, skill will be acquired, and a general spirit of industry developed.

CAROLINE

So far the introduction of barter seems to answer a very useful purpose; but when once industry is roused, why should not every one exert his abilities to supply his own wants, and gratify his desires, without the intervention of barter? If a man happens to be possessed of a superfluous quantity of any commodity, it is no doubt desirable to exchange it for something more wanted: but it seems to me to be an unnatural and circuitous mode of proceeding, to produce something which we do not want, in order afterwards to exchange it for something which we do want.

MRS. B.

Would you then have the baker kill his own meat

as well as bake his own bread, brew his own beer, build his own house, and make his own clothes, instead of procuring these various articles in exchange through the sale of his bread.

CAROLINE

Oh no; it would be impossible to undertake so many occupations; and then he can do one thing better than he can do many: but this separation of trades and employments cannot take place in a savage state.

MRS. B.

No, but it begins to operate as soon as barter is introduced; and it is to this circuitous mode that we owe all our improvements in skill and dexterity; the advantages of which are much more important than you imagine.

When barter became common, it was soon discovered that the more a man confined himself to any one single branch of industry, to the fabrication of bows and arrows for instance, the greater the skill and dexterity he acquired in that particular art; so that be could make bows and arrows not only quicker, but of better workmanship, than another man who followed a variety of pursuits.

CAROLINE

Now I begin to understand the advantage that results from barter, independently of its inspiring a spirit of industry and a taste for a variety of enjoyments. The artist who has acquired a superior degree of excellence in the fabrication of bows and arrows, would gain more, by confining himself entirely to that occupation and exchanging his merchandise for whatever else he was desirous of obtaining, than by taming his attention to a variety of pursuits.

MRS. B.

No doubt he would, provided he were sure of being able to dispose of all *the* bows and arrows he could make: for it would be useless to fabricate more than he could sell or exchange; and as no one could become a purchaser unless he had something to offer in return, a long period of time must elapse before the progress of industry would create a sufficient number of purchasers to enable an individual to earn a livelihood by the fabrication of bows and arrows.

It is therefore only in a more advanced stage of society that the demand for commodities is so great that men find it advantageous to devote themselves wholly to one particular art.

Adam Smith observes, that "in lone houses and very small villages, which are scattered about in so desert a country as the Highlands of Scotland, every farmer must be butcher, baker, and brewer for his own family. In such situations we can scarcely expect to find even a smith, a carpenter, or a mason within less than twenty miles of another of the same trade. The scattered families that live eight or ten miles distant from the nearest of them, must learn to perform for themselves a great number of little pieces of work, for which, in more populous countries, they call in the assistance of these workmen."

This separation of employments, which, in political economy, is called the *division of labor,* can take place only in civilised countries. In the flourishing states of Europe we find men not only exclusively engaged ill the exercises of one particular art, but that art subdivided into numerous branches, each of which forms a distinct occupation for different workmen.

Here is a beautiful passage in Adam Smith, the merits of which you will now be able to appreciate.

"Observe the accommodation of the most common artificer or day-labourer in a civilised and thriving country, and you will perceive that the number of people of whose industry a part, though but a small part, has been employed in procuring him this accommodation, exceeds all computation. The woollen coat, for example, which covers the day-labourer, coarse and rough as it may appear, is the produce of the joint labour of a great multitude of workmen. The shepherd, the sorter of the wool, the wool comber or carder, the dyer, the scribbler, the spinner, the weaver, the fuller, the dresser, with many others, must all join their different arts in order to complete even this homely production. How many merchants and carriers, besides, must have been employed in transporting the materials from some of those workmen to others who often live in a very distant part of the country! How much commerce and navigation in particular, how many ship-builders, sailors, sail-makers, rope-makers, must have been employed in order to bring together the different drugs made use of by the dyer, which often come from the remotest corners of the world! What a variety of labour too is necessary in order to produce the tools of the meanest of those workmen! To say nothing of such complicated machines as the ship of the sailor, the mill of the fuller, or even the loom of the weaver, let us consider only what a variety of labour is requisite in order to form that very simple machine, the shears with which the shepherd clips the wool. The miner, the builder of the furnace for heating the ore, the feller of the timber, the burner of the charcoal to be made use of in the smelting-house, the brickmaker, the bricklayer, the workmen who attend the furnace, the millwright, the forger, the smith, must all of them join their different arts in order to produce them. Were we to examine, in the same manner, all the different parts of his dress and household furniture, the coarse linen shirt which he wears next his skin, the shoes which cover his feet, the bed which he lies on, and all the different parts which compose it, the kitchen-grate at which he prepares his victuals, the coals which he makes use of for that purpose, dug from the bowels of the earth, and brought to him by a long sea and a long land carriage, all the other utensils of his kitchen, all the furniture of his table, the knives and forks, the earthen or pewter plates upon which he serves up and divides his victuals, the different hands employed in preparing his bread and his beer, the glass window which lets in the heat and the light, and keeps out the wind and rain, with all the knowledge and art requisite for preparing that beautiful and happy invention, without which these northern parts of the world could scarce have afforded a very comfortable habitation, together with the tools of all the different workmen employed in producing those different conveniences; if we examine, I say, all these things, and consider what a variety of labour is employed about each of them, we shall be sensible that without the assistance and co-operation of many thousands, the very meanest person in a civilised country could not be provided, even according to what we very falsely imagine the easy and simple manner in which he is commonly accommodated. Compared, indeed, with the more extravagant luxury of the great, his accommodation must no doubt appear extremely simple and easy, and yet it may be true, perhaps, that the accommodation of an European prince does not always so much exceed that of an industrious and frugal peasant, as the accommodation of the latter exceeds that of "many an African king, the absolute master of the "lives and liberties of ten thousand naked savages."

CAROLINE

It is very true, certainly; and it reminds me of an observation of Dr. Johnson in the Rambler, "That not a washerwoman sits down to breakfast without tea from the East Indies, and sugar from the West."

I now comprehend your reference to the little story of the cherry orchard: it was by dividing amongst the children the different parts of the process of plaiting straw, that they succeeded so much better than the boy who was left to perform the whole of his plait alone.

MRS. B.

I will point out to you some examples remarked by Adam Smith in illustration of the benefits derived from the division of labour. That of the pin manufactory I shall give you in his own words. He observes, that "a workman not educated to this business, nor acquainted with the use of the machinery employed in it, could scarce, perhaps, with his utmost industry, make one pin in a day; and certainly could not make twenty. But in the way in which this business is now carried on, not only the whole work is a peculiar trade, but it is divided into a number of branches, of which the greater part are likewise peculiar trades. One man draws out the wire, another straightens it, a third cuts it, a fourth points it, a fifth grinds it at the top for receiving the head. To make the head requires two or three distinct operations; to put it on is a peculiar business, to whiten the pins is another; it is even a trade by itself to put them into the paper; and the important business of making a pin is, in this manner, divided into about eighteen distinct operations, which, in some manu- factories, are all performed by distinct hands, though in others the same man will sometimes perform two or three of them. I have seen a small manufactory of this kind where ten men only were employed, and where some of them consequently performed two or three distinct operations: but though they were very poor, and therefore but indiffer- ently accommodated with the necessary machinery, they could, when they exerted themselves, make among them about twelve pounds of pins in a day. There are in a pound upwards of four thousand pins of a middling size. Those ten persons, therefore, could make among them upwards of forty-eight thousand pins in a day. Each person, therefore, making a tenth part of forty-eight thousand pins, might be considered as making four thousand eight hundred pins in a day. But if they had all wrought separately and independently, and without any of them having been educated to this peculiar business, they certainly could not each " of them have made twenty, perhaps not one pin in "a day; that is, certainly, not the two hundred and fortieth, perhaps not the four thousand eight hundredth part of what they are at present capable of performing, in consequence of a proper division and "combination of their different operations."

CAROLINE

These effects of the division of labour are really wonderful!

MRS. B.

The instance which Adam Smith quotes in proof of the dexterity acquired by men, whose labour is reduced to one simple operation, is also very remarkable. After observing that a man unaccustomed to a black-smith's forge can with difficulty make three hundred nails in a day, he says that a common blacksmith can forge one thousand; but that he has seen boys who have been brought up to the art of nail-making exclusively, acquire such a degree of dexterity as to complete two thousand three hundred in a day.

CAROLINE

The difference is prodigious: but I can conceive it when I observe with what awkwardness a man handles the tools of an art with which he is unacquainted, whilst they are used with ease and dexterity by those who are accustomed to them.

MRS. B.

Then we must consider that when a man's whole attention and talents are turned to one particular object, there is a much greater probability of his discovering means of improving his workmanship, or facilitating and abridging his labour, than if his mind were engaged in a variety of pursuits. It is most frequently to workmen, that we are indebted for improvements in the process and instruments of labour.

Another advantage derived from the division of labour is the regular and uninterrupted manner in which it enables the work to proceed. A labourer who has many diversified occupations not only loses time in going from one to another, but also in settling himself to his different employments; and, to use a common expression, as soon as his *hand is in,* he must quit his work to take up another totally different Thus he must go from his plough to his loom, from his loom to his forge, from his forge to his mill,—but no—there could be neither plough, nor loom, nor forge, nor mill, before a division of labour had taken place; for no man could either find time or acquire skill to construct such machines, unless they could bestow the whole of their labour and attention upon them.

The construction of machines, therefore, we may consider as a refined branch of the division of labour. Their effect in facilitating and abridging labour is almost incredible. How easy, for instance, the operation of grinding corn is rendered by so simple a machine as a wind-mill, or a water-mill I Were this to be done by manual labour, by bruising it between stones, it would be almost an endless task: the hand-mill, which is still in general use in India and many other countries, requires both time and labour; whilst in the wind-mill, or the water-mill, the natural motion of the air, or water, performs nearly the whole of the work.

CAROLINE

But the cotton-mills we have lately seen are a much more wonderful *example* of the effect of the machinery.

In these a steam-engine sets all the wheels and spindles in motion, and performs the work of hundreds of people.

MRS. B.

The great efficacy of machinery in the hands of man depends upon the art of compelling natural agents, such as wind, steam, and water, to perform the task which he would otherwise be obliged to execute himself; by which means labour is very much abridged, a great deal of human effort is saved, and the work is often accomplished in a more uniform and accurate manner.

We noticed the skill that could be acquired in the art of forging nails: but the utmost efforts of manual labour fall far short of machinery. A machine has been invented in the United States of America for the purpose of cutting nails out of iron, the operation of which is so rapid that it forms 250 perfect nails in the space of one minute, or 15,000 in an hour.

CAROLINE

The metals, I suppose, could not have been brought into use, till a considerable progress had been made in the division of labour?

MRS. B.

Certainly not; for it requires the exclusive labour of a great number of men to work a mine. The Mexicans and Peruvians in America, though they had made some progress towards civilisation, had never sought for gold in the bowels of the earth, but contented themselves with what they could pick up in the beds of rivers. In Britain, the Cornish mines were worked in very ancient times; and it is even supposed that the Phoenicians bad introduced this art among the ancient Britons, with whom they are said to have trafficked for tin and other metals.

CAROLINE

I am perfectly satisfied that the division of labour is a necessary step towards the accumulation of national wealth: but may it not have an injurious effect on the mental faculties of individuals? A man who is confined to one simple mechanical operation, however great the facility and perfection be may acquire in the performance of it, is shut out from all other improvement; his mind will never be roused to exertion by difficulty, interested by variety, or enlightened by comparison. His ideas will be confined within the narrow limits of his monotonous employment, and his rational powers will become so degraded as to render him scarcely superior to the machinery at which he works. Whilst a common husbandman, whose occupations are diversified, and but little aided by machinery, acquires knowledge by experience in his various employments, and, having a much wider range of observation, enjoys a corresponding development of intellect.

MRS. B.

The knowledge of a ploughman is often remarkably distinct in his limited sphere: but yet I have usually found, that in conversing upon general topics with a ploughman and with a mechanic, the latter has discovered more intelligence, and that his mind has appeared more active and accustomed to reflection. I conceive this to be owing to the facility which the arts afford of bringing men together in society. They are carried on in town, where neighbourhood renders social intercourse much more easy than in scattered hamlets in the country. When they meet together they talk over each other's concerns, read the newspapers, and discuss the politics of the parish, or of the state. This observation is particularly applicable to manufactories, where a number of persons generally work together in the same room, and' their employment seldom prevents conversation. Social intercourse, in whatever class of the community it takes place, cannot fail to promote the diffusion of knowledge; the lower orders of people become acquainted with the comforts and conveniences which have been acquired by the more skilful and industrious; they learn to appreciate the value, and are stimulated to acquire the means of obtaining them; a mode of instruction which we have observed to be the most essential step towards dispelling ignorance, and exciting industry.

CAROLINE

But is there not some danger that the advantages obtained in the improvement of the mind by this state of constant intercourse amongst the lower classes in manufacturing towns will be more than counterbalanced by the corruption of morals? How much more vice appears to prevail amongst the poor in crowded cities, than in the cottages of the peasantry!

MRS. B.

You should consider the difference of the population; there are often a greater number of people collected together in a manufacturing town, than there are scattered over a space of thirty square miles of country: were their morals, therefore, the same, vice would appear much more conspicuous in the town than in the country. The comparative amount of crimes among a given number of people is, however, generally admitted, by those who have the best opportunity for information, to be greater among the agricultural than the manufacturing classes. If a peasant be viciously inclined, his coarse and uncultivated feelings do not shrink from the commission of open violence, robbery, and murder. The more developed mind of the vicious townsman revolts from such brutality: the address and skill he has acquired by constant intercourse with his fellow-species addicts him more to petty frauds and thefts. It has been observed, both in France and Italy, that the most heinous crimes have been perpetrated by the peasantry; and by a comparative view, lately taken in England between a manufacturing and an agricultural district of equal population, the amount of crimes in the latter greatly preponderated.

CAROLINE

You astonish me! and yet we are taught to consider a pastoral life as a picture of simplicity and innocence.

MRS. B.

But this picture is drawn by the poet, who paints it, not from the life, but from the enchanting yet delusive image formed by his imagination. There is more simplicity in the country, I doubt not; but that a superior state both of talent and of virtue should accompany a superior state of civilisation is equally to be expected and desired.

CAROLINE

Yet you must allow that we hear much more of the

vices than of the virtues of manufacturing towns and great cities.

MRS. B.

Because crimes, from being amenable to the laws, are necessarily made known, whilst virtue seldom receives any public testimony of approbation. Every act of fraud or violence is sounded in our ears, whilst the humanity, the sympathy for sufferings, the sacrifices which the poor make to relieve each other's distresses, are known only to those who enter into their domestic concerns. This has been frequently noticed by medical men who have attended the lower classes of people in sickness at their own houses.

CAROLINE

Yet, upon the whole, do you not think that the situation of the poor in the country is better than it is in towns?

MRS. B.

They have each their advantages and disadvantages, and I should imagine that good and evil are pretty equally balanced between them. If the inhabitants of towns are better informed, and can more easily acquire some of the comforts of life, the inhabitants of the country are more vigorous and healthy, more cleanly, and they have the advantage of a more constant and regular demand for the produce of their labour, which is not so liable to be affected by the casualties of war, fashion, and other causes, which often occasion great distress to manufacturers.

But should you still entertain any apprehension that the division of labour may check and repress the intellectual improvement of the lower classes, I should consider this as amply compensated by its prodigious effect in the multiplication of wealth; a circumstance which not only increases the comforts of the poor, but by facilitating the means of acquiring knowledge, ultimately promotes its diffusion among all classes of men. It is to the division of labour that we are indebted for improvements in the processes of art, and amongst others for the invention of printing, which has proved such wonderful means of extending knowledge of every description.

We have now, I think, brought our savages to a considerable degree of advancement in civilisation; I would wish you briefly to recapitulate the causes which have produced this happy change, and at our next interview we will continue to trace their progress.

CAROLINE

Labour seems to be the natural and immediate cause of wealth: but it will produce little more than the necessaries of life, until its benefits are extended by the establishment of such a government as can give security to property. The spirit of industry will then be rapidly developed. The surplus produce of one individual will be exchanged for that of another. The facilities thus offered to barter will naturally introduce the division of labour or of employment; and will soon give rise to the invention of machinery, the merits of which we have just discussed.

MRS. B.

Extremely well, Caroline. We shall now take leave of this improved state of society for the present, with a conviction, I hope, that we leave mankind both better and happier than in its barbarous state.

CONVERSATION VI

ON CAPITAL

MRS. B.

In tracing the progress of society towards civilisation, we noticed the happy effects resulting from the security of property and the division of labour. From this period we may also date the diversity of ranks, and the general distinction between rich and poor.

CAROLINE

And all the evils that arise from inequality of condition. This, alas! is the dark side of the picture.

MRS. B.

So far from viewing the diversity of rank and condition as an evil, I consider it as productive of much general benefit, as it is that state of society best calculated to stimulate the industry, and bring into action the various faculties of mankind. If it does not exist in a savage state, it is because indigence is universal; for no one being able to acquire more than what is necessary for his immediate maintenance, every one is poor. When civilisation takes place, the advantages arising from the security of property and the division of labour enable an industrious and skilful man to acquire more wealth than will suffice to gratify his wants or desires. By continued exertion, this surplus produce of his industry in the course of time accumulates, and he becomes rich; whilst the less industrious, who acquires merely a daily subsistence, remains poor, or accumulates nothing, and the idle are reduced to positive indigence.

CAROLINE

I cannot perceive what advantage arises from the accumulation of wealth, for it must either be spent or hoarded; if spent, the hard-working man is eventually no richer than his less industrious neighbour; and if hoarded, the accumulation is of no use to any one.

MRS. B.

Your dilemma is put with some ingenuity, but you must at least allow, that where more is spent, there is a greater scope for enjoyment; and in regard to hoarding, I hope you are not recurring to your notions about riches and money, and forget that the wealth of which we have been speaking consists of exchangeable commodities, either agricultural or manufactured, many of which are not of a nature to be kept, were men inclined to hoard them. A much better mode of disposing of them has been devised; one which not only secures, but augments them.

CAROLINE

Indeed! What can that be?

MRS. B.

This you will hardly understand without some previous explanation.

In civilised society men cannot, as in a state of nature, obtain a subsistence by hunting, or from the spontaneous produce of the earth; because the wilderness has been destroyed by cultivation, and the land has become private property.

CAROLINE

And when the land is occupied by the rich, there seems to be no resource left for the poor?

MRS. B.

What do you suppose the rich do with their wealth?

CAROLINE

The poor, I am sure, partake but little of it; for the sums the most charitable give away are but trifling compared to what they spend upon themselves.

MRS. B.

I am far from wishing that the poor should be dependent on the charity of the rich for a subsistence. Is there no other mode of partaking of their wealth but as beggars?

CAROLINE

Not that I know of, unless by stealth. Oh no, I guess now—you mean they may earn it by their labour?

MRS. B.

Certainly. The poor man may be supposed to say to the rich one, "You have more than you want, whilst I am destitute. Give me some little share of your wealth for a subsistence; I have nothing to offer in exchange but my labour; but with that I will undertake to procure you more than you part with— if you will maintain me, I will work for you."

CAROLINE

But is ft not usual to pay wages to labourers instead of maintaining them?

MRS. B.

It is in effect the same; for the wages purchase a maintenance; the money merely represents the things of which the labourer stands in need, and for which he may exchange it.

CAROLINE

The labourer may then be supposed to say to the rich man, "Give me food and clothing, and I by my labour will produce for you other things in return."

MRS. B.

Precisely; the rich man exchanges with the labourer the produce or work that is already done, for work that is yet to be done. It is thus that he acquires a command over the labour of the poor, and increases his wealth by the profits he derives from it.

CAROLINE

This is a resource for the poor, I own; but not enough to satisfy me entirely, for they are left at the mercy of the rich, and if these did not choose to employ them, they would starve.

MRS. B.

True; but what could the rich do without their assistance?

CAROLINE

Their wealth would furnish them a plentiful subsistence.

MRS. B.

At first it might, but in time it would be consumed. Their harvests and their cattle would be eaten, their clothes worn out, and their houses fallen into decay.

CAROLINE

But you know that the harvests are annually reproduced, new clothes are purchased, and houses repaired or rebuilt: riches easily obtain all these things.

MRS. B.

And who is it that re-produces the harvests? Who manufactures new clothes, and builds new houses, but the poorer classes of men?

CAROLINE

That is very true; I was indeed aware that it was necessary to employ labourers for this purpose; but I did not consider that it created reciprocity of benefit, by rendering the poor in a great measure independent of the will of the rich.

MRS. B.

The rich and poor are necessary to each other; it is precisely the fable of the belly and the limbs; without the rich the poor would starve; without the poor the rich would be compelled to labour for their own subsistence.

CAROLINE

And this, I suppose, is what you alluded to, when you said that the rich had a means of securing their wealth without hoarding it?

MRS. B.

Yes; the labouring classes consume and re-produce it; and when a man abstains from spending the whole of his wealth, but saves a part of it, in order to turn it to profit by the employment of labourers, that wealth is called *capital.* You have heard of capital before no doubt?

CAROLINE

Oh yes; a man of fortune is said to be a man of capital: I always considered these as synonymous terms.

MRS. B.

So they are; and you may have heard also that to spend a capital is very ruinous; that it should be placed in some profitable line, so as to yield an income; that is to say, it must be employed to set labourers to work, and the profit derived from their labour is called revenue or income.

CAROLINE

If capital is employed in paying the wages of labourers, it is spent and consumed by them, and is lost to the capitalist as much as if he spent it himself.

MRS. B.

No; capital employed is consumed, but not destroyed; it is at least no more destroyed than the seed sown in the ground, which is re-produced with increase. Thus the capital consumed by labourers is re-produced with increased value in the articles of their workmanship. If the labourer raise corn for twenty loaves of bread whilst his wages are equivalent to the value of tea, if he manufactures cloth for two coats whilst his wages are equal to the price of one, the second coat and the second ten loaves of bread will be the profit, and constitute part of the income of his employer. It is thus that the employment of capital produces an income.

CAROLINE

Yet I have some scruple as to the mode of obtaining this income. If the labourer can by his industry produce more than the value of his wages, it seems but fair that he should keep the whole of his earnings; He is surely a great discouragement to his industry to be obliged to yield part of them to his employer.

MRS. B.

If the labourer re-produced for the capitalist commodities equal in value to his wages, the *income* would be only equivalent to the *out-going*; he would restore therefore exactly what the capitalist had advanced him, the latter being neither a loser nor a gainer by the bargain; any further, at least, than that, by reproduction, perishable produce is made to last Now it is evident that no capitalist would consent to such an agreement. When therefore the poor man applies to the rich one for a maintenance, offering his labour in return, he does not say—for the food you give me during the present year, I will produce an equal quantity of food next year—because he knows that he would not be employed on such terms; he must induce the capitalist, by the prospect of some advantage, to exchange food that is already produced for something that is yet to be produced. He therefore says —for the food you give me now, I will raise you a greater or more valuable supply next year.

CAROLINE

It appears to me a hardship, notwithstanding, that after the rich have engrossed the whole property of the land, nothing being left to the poor beyond their own labour, that they should not be allowed to reap the whole of the advantages it affords. If I were a legislator, I should be disposed to establish a law compelling the capitalist to allow the labourer the whole of the profit arising from his work. Such a regulation would surely tend to improve the condition of the poor. You smile, Mrs. B.; I am afraid that you do not approve of my plan.

MRS. B.

I would suggest an addition to it, which is, a law to compel the capitalist to employ the labourers; for on your terms none would give them work. The farmer, were he obliged to pay the husbandmen the value of the crop they raised, would derive no profit from their sale; he would, therefore, leave his fields uncultivated, the land would lie waste, and the husbandmen starve. Manufacturers for the same reason would discharge their workmen, merchants their clerks; in a word, industry would be paralysed; and were you to devise a system of certain and inevitable ruin to a country, I do not think you could adopt a more efficacious mode of promoting your design.

CAROLINE

So much for the wisdom of my laws! I certainly ought to have foreseen these consequences, since, as you observed before, the inducement for the rich to employ the poor is the advantage the former derive from it.

MRS. B.

Undoubtedly. The profits the rich derive from the employment of their capital constitute their income; without such income the capital, it is true, might, by our compulsatory laws, be re-produced annually; but yielding no income, the capitalist would gradually consume it in the maintenance of his family; he would every year become poorer, and his means of employing labourers would annually diminish.

CAROLINE

This is an idea which often perplexed me when I was a child. I thought that in proportion as my father spent his money he must be impoverished; but now I understand that wealth is reproduced and augmented by the labour of the poor.

MRS. B.

And observe, that an income can be obtained by no other means than by the employment of the poor.

So far from considering the profits which the capitalist derives from his labourers as an evil, I have always thought it one of the most beneficent ordinations of Providence, that the employment of the poor should be a necessary step to the increase of the wealth of the rich.

Thus the rich man has the means of augmenting his capital, not by hoarding, but by distributing it among his labourers, who consume it, and reproduce another and a larger capital—hence have they obtained the name of *productive labourers.*

CAROLINE

When a man, therefore, becomes possessed of a capital, whether by accumulation of his savings or by inheritance, it is no longer requisite for him to work for a maintenance, as others will labour for him?

MRS. B.

It depends on the amount of his capital, and the extent of his desires. If it will yield an income sufficient to maintain him and his family with the degree of comfort or affluence which satisfies his ambition, he may live in idleness; if not, he will work himself; or at least superintend his labourers. This is the case with the farmer, the merchant, the master-manufacturer, each of whom superintends his respective concerns.

Do you understand now, that no productive enterprise can be undertaken without capital? Capital is necessary to pay labourers, to purchase materials to work upon, instruments to work with; in short, to defray the whole expense attached to the employment of labourers.

CAROLINE

But a man may undertake a productive enterprise without employing labourers: for instance, if he gathers mushrooms on a common, he requires no capital for that purpose; no tools are used; the earth produces mushrooms spontaneously, and every one has a right to gather them. The same may be said of nuts and wild strawberries.

MRS. B.

These are small remnants of the resources of a savage state, in which subsistence is derived from the spontaneous produce of the earth: but the employments which require no capital are very inconsiderable, and occur only during a short season of the year.

CAROLINE

There is one, which appears to me of great importance— fishing. Fishermen are in no want of capital; the fish costs them merely the trouble of catching. Oh no! I am mistaken; I forgot the nets and the boats that are necessary for fishing; besides, the men must have something to subsist on, when the weather will not allow them to venture on the water.

But there is another case, Mrs. B.; I have known persons who were worth nothing, and yet who set up in business on credit.

MRS. B.

That is no exception; for credit is the employment of the capital belonging to another.

CAROLINE

Well, it is a melancholy reflection that one must always possess something in order to gain more. He then who has nothing to begin with has no means of escaping from poverty.

MRS. B.

Poverty is a word of vague signification. If you mean to express by it a state of positive indigence, the labourer who earns a subsistence from day to day cannot come under that description. But if you use the word poverty in opposition to wealth, that is to say, to the possession of capital, labourers, though usually in that state, are not necessarily condemned to it. A healthy and hard-working man may, especially if he be skilful, often get more wages than are necessary to maintain him; now he may spend this surplus at the public-house, or in some other mode of indulgence. But if he is of a provident disposition, he will abstain from spending it, or consuming it; but will lay it aside as the beginning of a little capital, which by additional savings accumulates.

CAROLINE

That is true. Thomas, our under-gardener, who is a very intelligent, industrious man, was saying the other day to one of his fellow-labourers, that as soon as he had laid by a little money to begin the world with he intended to marry. But it seems to me that if my father would give him a cottage, and an acre or two of ground, he might raise vegetables for market, and by these means support himself and his family.

MRS. B.

In that case your father would supply the capital. The cottage and the land is a capital, but they will not do alone. Thomas would besides require garden tools to work with, and an assistant, if not several, to prepare the ground. Then he must not only subsist himself, but maintain his family, till the produce of his garden can be brought to market In the course of three or four years, from the earnings of daily labour, he may have amassed a little capital sufficient to enable him to undertake this; he will then no longer be a labourer for hire, but will work on his own account It is thus every thing has a beginning; the largest fortunes have often had no greater origin.

Now, supposing Thomas to be able to rent an acre of land when he is worth £100 he may rent ten acres when he is worth £1,000, but he cannot rent more; he cannot increase his farm, beyond his means of paying for it; his industry, therefore, is limited by the extent of his capital.

CAROLINE

I do not quite understand that.

MRS. B.

Let us imagine a tradesman, a shoemaker for instance, to be master of a capital which will enable him to maintain ten workmen, and that the following year he finds that he has gained £100 by the profits derived from their labour. This £100 constitutes his income; if he spend it, his capital remains what it was before: but if he adds it to his capital it will enable him to maintain and provide work for a greater number of journeymen. Let us say that he can now employ twelve instead of ten men; these will make him a greater quantity of shoes, and the additional profits arising from their sale, will, if added to his capital, still further increase his means of employing workmen. Thus the demand for labour, or, in other words, employment for the poor, will ever increase with the increase of capital, and be limited only by its deficiency.

CAROLINE

But we must not forget that the master shoemaker and his family are to be maintained out of these profits; the whole of them cannot, therefore, be added to his capital.

MRS. B.

Certainly not. The expenses of his family consume, in general, by far the greater part of a man's income; but, if he is prudent, he will lay aside as much as can be spared, and these savings will enable him to enlarge and improve his business, of whatever description it may be.

CAROLINE

Thus a farmer would be able to extend and improve the cultivation of his farm by increasing the number of his labourers—and a merchant proportionally to extend his commercial dealings—so that the richer a man becomes, the more it will be in his power to increase his wealth?

MRS. B.

Yes; the second thousand pounds is often acquired with less difficulty than the first hundred.

CAROLINE

That is hard upon those who have nothing. The rich have too many advantages over the poor.

MRS. B.

The man who accumulates a large fortune by his industry injures no one; on the contrary, he confers a benefit on the community. You will understand this better by-and-by. In the mean time I must observe to you, that happiness, so far as it is dependent on wealth, consists less in the possession of riches, than in the pleasure of acquiring them. Every degree of increasing prosperity is attended with its enjoyment Your gardener, who saves his earnings with the prospect of settling at the end of two or three years, has probably more satisfaction in the anticipation of his future wealth than he will have in the possession of it; as long as he continues making annual additions to his capital, the same source of enjoyment will be preserved, but will never excite so strong an interest as at first. Merchants will tell you that their first gains gave them greater pleasure than all their subsequent accumulations. Nature has wisely attached happiness to the gradual acquisition, rather than to the actual possession of wealth, thus rendering it an incitement to industry; and we shall hereafter see that this progressive state of prosperity is most conducive also to the happiness of nations.

CONVERSATION VII

ON *CAPITAL—continued*

OF FIXED CAPITAL—DISTINCTION BETWEEN FIXED AND CIRCU-
LATING CAPITAL—EXAMPLES OF THE DIFFERENT KINDS OF
CAPITAL.—OF SLAVES.—FIXED CAPITAL AND CIRCULAT-
ING CAPITAL EQUALLY BENEFICIAL TO THE LABOURING
CLASS.—MACHINERY ADVANTAGEOUS TO THE LABOURING
CLASSES.—QUOTATION FROM MACPHBRBON ON THE AD-
VANTAGES OP MACHINERY.—QUOTATION FROM MR. SAY'S
TREATISE ON POLITICAL ECONOMY.

MRS. B.

I HAVE some further remarks to make to you on the nature
of capital.

A land-owner, when he increases his wealth by savings
from his income, may probably, instead of employing the
whole of his additional capital on husbandmen, find it more
advantageous to lay out some part of it on workmen to build
barns and outhouses, to store his crops and shelter his cattle;
he may plant trees to produce timber, build cottages, and
bring into cultivation some of the waste land on his farm.

A manufacturer also may employ part of his capital in
enlarging his machinery or augmenting his implements of
industry.

CAROLINE

But the capital laid out in buildings, tools, and
machinery will not yield a profit like that which is

employed in the payment of workmen, the produce of whose labour is brought to market?

MRS. B.

Not so immediately; but the farmer and manufacturer would not lay out their capital in this way, did they not expect to reap a profit from it. If a farmer has no barn or granary for his corn, he will be compelled to sell his crops immediately after the harvest, although he might probably dispose of them to greater advantage by keeping them some time longer. So a manufacturer, by improving or enlarging his machinery, can, with less labour, perform a greater quantity of work, and his profits will be proportionate.

CAROLINE

No doubt if he employ machines instead of men, he will have no wages to pay, and the whole will be profit.

MRS. B.

Thus, for instance, when a manufacturer can afford to establish a steam-engine, and use a stream of vapour as a substitute for the labour of men and horses, he saves the expense of more than half the number of hands he before employed.

The capital laid out in this manner is called *fixed capital;* because it becomes fixed, either in land, in buildings, in machinery or implements of art; it is by keeping this capital in possession, and using it, that it produces an income. Whilst the capital employed in the maintenance of productive labourers, whose work is sold and affords an immediate profit, is distinguished by the name of *circulating capital.*

The produce of a farm, or the goods of a manufacturer, afford no profit until they are brought to market, and sold or exchanged for other things. This description of capital is, therefore, constantly circulating. It is transferred first from the master to the labourer, in the form of wages and raw materials; then from the labourer it is returned to the master, in the form of produce or workmanship of increased value; but the latter does not realise his profits until this produce is sold to the public, by which it is consumed.

CAROLINE

I think I understand the difference between fixed and circulating capital perfectly. A farmer derives profit from his implements of husbandry by their use, while kept in his possession; and from his crops by parting with them. But to which kind of capital should the farming cattle be referred?

MRS. B.

It depends upon the nature of the cattle. The value of the labouring cattle is fixed capital, like the implements of agriculture; thus, the horses which draw the plough, as well as the plough itself, are fixed capital. But sheep and oxen intended for market are circulating capital.

CAROLINE

But should the plough be drawn by oxen, Mrs. B., how would you settle the point then? for whilst they labour for the farmer they are fixed capital; but when they are sold to the butcher they become circulating capital.

MRS. B.

They alternately belong to each of these descriptions

of capital; because the farmer makes his profit, first by keeping, and afterwards by selling them.

CAROLINE

I do not understand why you should call the maintenance of labouring, *men* circulating capital, whilst you consider that of labouring *cattle* as fixed capital: they appear to me to be exactly similar.

MRS. B.

The maintenance of cattle as well as that of labourers is circulating capital; that maintenance is in both cases consumed and reproduced with advantage; it is therefore by parting with it that profits are derived. But the value of the cattle themselves is fixed capital; and if labourers, like cattle, were purchased, instead of being hired, thus becoming the property of their employers, they also would be fixed capital.

CAROLINE

And this was formerly the case with the poor Africans in the West Indies?

MRS. B.

Yes, and with slaves of every description. Even the peasantry of Russia and Poland are in general considered as fixed capital, because their state of vassalage is such as to amount to slavery, the proprietors of the land having a right to their labour without remuneration: and the value of an estate in Russia is not estimated by the number of acres, but the number of slaves upon it; in the same manner as a West Indian plantation was estimated previous to the emancipation of the negroes. A similar state of vassalage prevailed throughout most parts of Europe some centuries ago; but in later times the progress of civilisation has been such, that I believe every country, excepting Russia and Poland, has emancipated the labouring classes; experience having proved that the more free and independent men are, the more industrious they become, and the better the land is cultivated.

CAROLINE

I thought at first that I understood the difference of fixed and circulating capital perfectly; but I find upon reflection, that I am at a loss to determine to which kind of capital several articles of property belong. For instance, does the money laid out in the improvement of land constitute fixed or circulating capital?

MRS. B.

The money laid out on waste land to bring it into a state fit for cultivation, such as inclosing, draining, ditching, preparing the soil, &c. is fixed capital; and so is that which is employed in the improvement of land already cultivated. If it is the proprietor who lays out capital on land which he lets, he receives in remuneration an increase of rent; if the farmer, he makes greater profits. But the money laid out in the regular course of cultivation, such as ploughing, sowing, reaping, & c., consists, as we have before observed, partly in fixed and partly in circulating capital

CAROLINE

I must say that I prefer the employment of wealth in the form of circulating, rather than in that of fixed capital. Granaries, barns, machinery, especially, may be advantageous to the proprietors, but they must be injurious to the labouring classes; for the more a man lays out as fixed capital, the less remains to be employed as circulating capital, and therefore the fewer labourers he can maintain.

MRS. B.

You must always remember that the greatest good you can do the labouring classes, is to increase the consumable produce of the country. Whilst plenty of the necessaries of life is raised, it signifies little to whom it belongs; for whoever may be the proprietors of this wealth, they can derive no advantage from it but by employing it; that is to say, by maintaining with it productive labourers. The more abundant, therefore, this wealth is, the greater the number of people who will be employed.

Now it is evident that whatever tends to improve or facilitate labour, increases the productions of the country; and if fixed capital should eventually occasion the raising a greater produce than circulating capital, it must be more beneficial to the labourers as well as to the capitalist.

CAROLINE

So it appears; and yet I cannot understand how this operates with regard to machinery. We cannot substitute the powers of nature for human industry, and make a steam engine perform the work of men, without throwing people out of work. How then can the poor derive any benefit from inventions and improvements which prevent their being employed?

MRS. B.

It may appear paradoxical, but it is nevertheless true, that whatever abridges and facilitates labour will *eventually* increase the demand for labourers.

CAROLINE

Or, in other words, to turn people out of work is the most certain means of procuring them employment!—This is precisely the objection I was making to the introduction of new machinery.

MRS. B.

The invention of machinery, I allow, is often attended with much partial and temporary inconvenience and hardship; but on the other hand, the advantages resulting from it are almost incalculable both in extent and duration.

CAROLINE

To the rich that may be the case, but it appears to me that the poor derive injury instead of benefit from machinery, since it turns them out of work.

MRS. B.

When, for instance, the machine for weaving stockings was first invented, it was considered as a severe hardship on those who had earned a maintenance by knitting them; but the superior facility with which stockings were made in the loom, rendered them so much cheaper, that those, who before were unable to purchase them, could now indulge in the comfort of wearing them, and the prodigious increase of demand for stockings enabled all the knitters to gain a livelihood by spinning the materials that were to be woven into stockings.

CAROLINE

That was a resource in former times, but household spinning is scarcely ever seen since Arkwright's invention of machinery for spinning. Where are the spinners now to find employment? The improvement in machinery drive these poor workmen from one expedient to another, till I fear at last every resource will be exhausted.

MRS. B.

You admit that the products and consequently the wealth of the country is much increased by the use of machinery?

CAROLINE

No doubt; but how can the poor partake of it unless they are employed? that is the question I am anxious to have answered.

MRS. B.

It is evident that if the poor do not partake of these increased productions there will be more than the rich can possibly consume; more cottons fabricated at Manchester, more broad-cloth at Leeds, and more hardware at Birmingham: what then will the rich do with this surplus of commodities?

CAROLINE

Indeed I cannot tell.

MRS. B.

They will lay aside that portion of it which they do not want for their own consumption, in order to employ it as capital; that is to say, to set the labouring classes to work, either to produce other commodities, or even perhaps to restore them to the very manufacture from which they have been discarded.

CAROLINE

Of what advantage then is machinery if the same number of hands are required in the manufacture as before?

MRS. B.

The advantage is, that the machinery and the work-men conjointly do perhaps twenty times as much work as was previously performed by manual labour alone; so that there is twenty times as much clothing and of all the commodities which constitute the necessaries and conveniences of life produced. Now, all these things, being, by the aid of machinery, made at much less expense, will fall in price; this enables a greater number of persons to become purchasers; the demand for them therefore increases, and the manufacture must be extended to meet the increased demand; so that it frequently happens that more hands are eventually employed in manufactures than were before employed in manual labour.

CAROLINE

That is a very satisfactory explanation, for I see now that by the use of machinery the poor not only get work, but a greater portion of these cheap commodities.

MRS. B.

There is therefore no danger of the rich benefiting by machinery to the injury of the poor; the interests of both coincide, and the augmentation of wealth in consequence of the introduction or improvement of machinery, to whatever extent it may be carried, is enjoyed by all.

CAROLINE

Yes; wherever there is an increase of capital the poor in some way or other will find employment, and the low price of commodities produced by machinery will certainly better their condition.

MRS. B.

In countries possessed of great wealth we see prodigious works undertaken. Roads cut through hills, canals uniting distant rivers, magnificent bridges, splendid edifices, and a variety of other enterprises which give work to thousands, independently of the usual employment of capital in agriculture, manufactures, and trade. What is the reason of all this? It is in order that the rich may employ their capital; for in a secure and free government no man will suffer any part of it to lie idle; the demand for labour is therefore proportioned to the extent of capital. Industry, we have already observed, knows no other limits. The capitalist who employs a new machine is no doubt the immediate gainer by it; but it is the public who derive from it the greatest and most lasting advantage. It is they who profit by the diminution of price of the goods fabricated by the machine; and, singular as it may appear, no class of the public receives greater benefit from the introduction of those processes which abridge manual labour, than the working classes, as it is they who are most interested in the cheapness of the goods.

CAROLINE

But, Mrs. B., I have heard that the workmen complain that they are not paid so much for the work they produce as they were before the use of machinery?

MRS. B.

That is very true, nor would it be fair to pay workmen the same for work executed by manual labour as for that in which machinery has performed a part, and enabled the workmen to complete it in one quarter of the time that they would otherwise have required. Ask the workman what are now his daily earnings, and you will find that they are much greater than formerly, though certainly not increased in proportion to the quantity of work he performs.

CAROLINE

But that does not seem fair?

MRS. B.

Perfectly fair; for as it is the machinery which performs the greater part of the work it is but just that it should have some share of the wages, and so it has, for the fixed capital which the manufacturer invests in machinery may be considered as wages paid to it.

CAROLINE

The manufacturer therefore divides his capital into two parts, one of which is fixed in machinery and the other circulating in the payment of wages.

MRS. B.

Yes; and when labourers complain of machinery they know not what they do; could they see its results in a true point of view, they would find that a great portion of them owe to it, not only their maintenance but their very existence; for many of those who gain a livelihood by machinery would not have been called into existence at all, did not the wonderful power of natural agents working gratuitously in machinery provide for their support.

CAROLINE

Well, Mrs. B., I must confess myself vanquished,

and beg pardon of Mr. Watts for having ventured to doubt the beneficial effects of his steam-engine, and of Sir Richard Arkwright for having found fault with his mechanical improvements.

MRS. B.

I will read you a passage in Macpherson's History of Commerce, which will show you the degree of estimation in which the inventions of Arkwright were held by that writer.

"If Mr. Arkwright made a great fortune, he certainly deserved it; for the advantages he conferred upon the nation were infinitely greater than those he acquired for himself; and far more solid and durable than a hundred conquests. Instead of depriving the working poor of employment by his vast abridgment of labour, that very abridgment has created a vast deal of work for more hands than were formerly employed; and it was computed that in 1785, about 25 years after the invention of his spinning jennies, half a million of people were employed in the cotton manufactures of Lancashire, Cheshire, Derby, Nottingham, and Leicester. And it is but justice to the memory of Sir Richard Arkwright to say, that be was unquestionably one of the greatest friends to the manufacturing and commercial interests of this country, and to the interest of the cotton planters in almost all parts of the world, and that his name ought to be transmitted to future ages, along with those of the most distinguished benefactors of mankind."

CAROLINE

This is indeed a magnificent eulogium of Sir Richard Arkwright, yet not more so than he appears to deserve. But, Mrs. B., is it not possible for manufacturers to produce too great a quantity of goods? I mean more than is wanted.

MRS. B.

That there should be too much of any given commodity frequently happens. There may be too much woolen or linen cloth in the market, or too many hats or shoes. This is called a glut; for as the commodity is oat of proportion to other commodities, the whole of it will not find equivalents to be given in exchange, and the surplus will remain unsold. But that there should be a general glut, that we should have too much of every thing, is an absurd idea; and could not possibly take place, unless all men were agreed in the opinion that they had a sufficiency of wealth, and did not wish for more. Now, I believe that you will scarcely find a single individual who is perfectly satisfied with that portion of the good things of this life which he actually possesses, and would refuse to partake of a universal superabundance of the articles of wealth.

CAROLINE

But it is not all men who can profit by such a super-abundance.

MRS. B.

You have just learned how those who have nothing to offer in exchange but their labour become partakers of increased production; a general superabundance would ensure them an ample participation; but it is useless to trace consequences from a case which cannot possibly occur.

I shall conclude my observations on the benefits

arising from machinery, by reading to you some remarks on the invention of printing, extracted from Mr. Say's excellent treatise on Political Economy.

"Au moment où elle fut employée one foule de copistes dûrent rester inoccupés, car on peut estimer qu'un seul ouvrier imprimeur fait autant de besogne que 200 copistes. Il faut donc croire que 199 ouvriers sur 200 restèrent sans ouvrage. Hé bien, la facilité de lire les ouvrages imprimés, plus grande que pour les ouvrages manuscrits, le bas prix auquel les livres tombèrent, l'encouragement que cette invention donna aux auteurs pour en composer un bien plus grand nombre, soit d'instruction, soit d'amusement; toutes ces causes firent, qu'au bout de très peu de temps, il y eut plus d'ouvriers imprimeurs employés, qu'il n'y avoit auparavant de copistes. Et si à présent on pouvoit calculer exactement non seulement le nombre des ouvriers imprimeurs, mais encore des industrieux que l'imprimerie fait travailler, comme graveurs de poinçons, fondeurs de caractères, relieurs, libraires, on trouveroit, peut-être, que le nombre des personnes occupées par la fabrication des livres est cent fois plus grand que celui qu'elle occupoit avant l'invention de rimprimerie."

CAROLINE

And the number of readers must have increased in a still greater proportion. You may recollect observing, in our conversation on the division of labour, that the invention of printing was a circumstance most favourable to the diffusion of knowledge.

But a considerable increase would not, in the case of every commodity produced by machinery, be required?

MRS. B.

Certainly not. It is not a necessary consequence of the invention of machinery that more hands should be required in the manufacture where it is applied; the additional quantity of the commodity produced by the same number of hands will in some instances be sufficient to supply the increased demand. But supposing even that no augmentation of the commodity should be required, and that a certain number of hands should be dismissed in consequence of the abridgment of labour, the capital thus economised, by being applied to some other purpose, is an advantage both to the proprietor and the public, and eventually affords employment for the labourers thrown out of work.

Thus you see that capital, whether fixed or circulating, invariably promotes the increase of the produce of the country; we may, therefore, I think, define capital to be any accumulated produce which tends to facilitate future productions. And the capital of a country is composed of the aggregate property of all its inhabitants.

CONVERSATION VIII

ON WAGES AND POPULATION

EXTREME LIMIT OF WAGES.—WAGES REGULATED BY THE PRO-
PORTION WHICH CAPITAL BEARS TO POPULATION.—SMALL
CAPITAL CREATES SMALL DEMAND FOR LABOUR, LOW
WAGES, AND GREAT PROFIT TO THE CAPITALIST.—IN-
CREASE OF CAPITAL CREATES GREATER DEMAND FOR
LABOUR, HIGHER WAGES, AND LESS PROFIT TO THE CA-
PITALIST.—NECESSITY OF RAISING SUBSISTENCE BEFORE
OTHER WORKS ARE UNDERTAKEN.—HOW WAGES ARE
LOWERED BY THE INCREASE OF POPULATION WITHOUT
AN INCREASE OF CAPITAL,—EFFECT OF SCARCITY OF
PROVISIONS ON WAGES.—EFFECT OF RAISING WAGES
DURING A SCARCITY.—OF A MAXIMUM PRICE OF PRO-
VISIONS.—EFFECT OF DIMINUTION OF POPULATION BY
SICKNESS ON THE RATE OF WAGES.—IT IS NOT WORK BUT
FUNDS THAT CREATE A DEMAND FOR LABOUR.—WAGES
IN IRELAND. —WAGES IN TOWN AND COUNTRY.—IMMATE-
RIAL CAPITAL.

MRS. B.

IN our last conversation I think we came to this conclusion, that capital is almost as beneficial to the poor as
to the rich; for though the property of the one, it is by its
nature destined for the maintenance of the other.

CAROLINE

It comes to the labourer in the form of wages; but
since we must allow the capitalist a profit on the

work of the latter, I should like very much to know what proportion that profit bears to the wages of the labourer?

MRS. B.

It varies extremely, but the wages of the labourer can never be permanently less than will afford him the means of living, otherwise he could not labour.

CAROLINE

On the other hand, they can never be equal to the whole value of the work he produces; for if his master made no profit by him he would not employ him.

MRS. B.

Such then are the two extremes of the wages of labour, but they admit of many intermediate degrees of variation. If besides furnishing subsistence for himself, the wages of the labourer would not enable him to maintain a wife and bring up a family, the class of labourers would gradually diminish, and the scarcity of hands would then raise their wages, which would enable them to live with more comfort and rear a family: but as the capitalist will always keep wages as low as he can, the labourer and his family can seldom command more than the necessaries of life.

CAROLINE

By the necessaries of life do you mean such things only as are indispensably necessary for its support?

MRS. B.

No; I mean such food, clothing, and general ac-commodation, as the climate and custom of the country have rendered essential to the preservation of the life, health, and decent appearance of the lowest classes of the people. Fuel, for instance, and warm clothing, are necessary articles in this country; but they are not so in Africa. Civilisation and the progress of wealth and manufactures have greatly extended the scale of necessaries; the use of linen is now considered as necessary by all classes of people, and shoes and stockings, in England at least, almost equally so. Houses with glazed windows and a chimney are become necessaries; for if our poor were deprived of such accommodation it would very materially increase mortality amongst them. In Ireland the peasantry bring up their children in a mud cabin, the door of which answers also the purposes of window and chimney.

CAROLINE

Then would it not be better that the labouring classes here should, like the Irish, accustom themselves to hardships and inconveniences, rather than indulge in a degree of comfortable accommodation, the privation of which, in a season of distress, is attended with so much misery?

MRS. B.

No: I would on the contrary wish rather to extend than contract the scale of the necessaries of life. There is more health, more cleanliness, more intellect, and more happiness, in an English cottage than in an Irish cabin. There is more strength, vigour, and industry in an English peasant, who feeds on meat, bread, and vegetables, than in an Irish one, who subsists on potatoes alone.

CAROLINE

No doubt I would wish the lower classes every comfort which they can afford; but as their wages will not always allow them such gratifications, I thought it might be better that they should not be accustomed to them.

MRS. B.

By lowering the scale of the comforts and accommodations of the poor, you not only diminish their enjoyments, but deprive them of a resource in seasons of distress. If their usual fare is confined to the bare necessaries of life, they cannot be reduced lower: and when a scarcity occurs, a famine must ensue. This is the case with the Hindoos, who subsist almost wholly on rice; when this supply fails, they perish by thousands.

CAROLINE

It is then most desirable that the rate of wages should be such as to afford the lower classes something beyond a mere subsistence; but what is it that determines the rate of wages?

MRS. B.

It depends upon the proportion which capital bears to the labouring part of the population of the country.

CAROLINE

Or, in other words, to the proportion which subsistence bears to the number of people to be maintained by it?

MRS. B.

Yes; it is this alone which regulates the rate of wages, when they are left to pursue their natural course. It is this alone which creates or destroys the demand for labour. In order to render it more clear to you, let us simplify the question by examining it on a small scale;—let us suppose, for instance, that we have founded a colony in a desert bland; that the settlers have divided the land amongst them, and cultivated it for their own subsistence; and that being both proprietors and labourers, they reap the whole reward of their industry. Thus situated, should a ship be wrecked on the coast, and some of the crew effect their escape to shore, what would ensue? They would furnish a supply of labourers, who would be dependent on the original settlers for maintenance and employment.

CAROLINE

But if those settlers have not raised a greater quantity of subsistence than is necessary for their own use, how can they maintain the new-comers? Without capital, you know, they cannot employ labourers.

MRS. B.

You are perfectly right. But it is probable that the most industrious of them will have raised somewhat more subsistence than is necessary for their immediate consumption. They will possess some little stock in reserve which they will use as capital, and which will enable them to maintain and employ at least a few of the shipwrecked crew. Yet as these poor destitute men will all be anxious to share in this little surplus, each will offer his labour in exchange for the smallest pittance that will support life. Thus the capital of the island being inadequate to the maintenance of its population, the competition amongst the labourers to get employment will render wages extremely low, and the capitalist will derive a high profit from the industry of his labourers. A small capital, therefore, creates but a small demand for labour.

CAROLINE

By demand for labour do you mean the demand of the poor for work, or of the capitalist for workmen?

MRS. B.

Certainly the latter. It is the capitalist who demands labour of the poor; the poor demand wages of the capitalist, and as wages can be obtained only by work, they ask for work; but that is not what in political economy is meant by the demand for labour; and it is necessary you should keep this distinction in mind.

CAROLINE

I think it should be called the demand for labourers, and then no confusion could arise.

MRS. B.

That is true; for the demand for labour means the demand for labourers by those who have the means of paying them for their work, whether it be in the form of wages, maintenance, or any other kind of remuneration.

But what will happen in our colony, when the labourers shall have richly repaid their employers by the fruit of their industry?

CAROLINE

By raising a more plentiful harvest they would of course have a more plentiful subsistence.

MRS. B.

The harvest, you must observe, belongs, not to the men who produced it but to their employers; how, therefore, does it follow of course that the labourers obtain a larger share of it?

CAROLINE

I suppose, that their masters having more capital are willing to bestow a large proportion of it on their labourers.

MRS. B.

I believe that the capitalist will always make as high a profit as he can upon the work of his labourers; and that when his capital increases, he will choose rather to increase the number of his workmen than the rate of their wages. But the power of employing more labourers increases the demand for labour; and this, as I shall explain to you, eventually raises the wages or reward of labour.

The capital of the settlers will probably be so muck augmented by the industry of the labourers, that there will no longer be any difficulty in maintaining the new-comers. The possessors of this increased capital will be eager to procure the services of the labourers; one perhaps to build a hut, another to fence a field, a third to construct a boat, and so on. For the surplus capital, unless employed, will yield no profit; the com-petition therefore will no longer be amongst the labourers to obtain work, but amongst the masters to obtain workmen; and this will necessarily raise the price of wages, and consequently diminish the profits of the capitalist.

CAROLINE

Oh, that is very clear. If John offers a man a shilling a day to work at his house, and Thomas gives eighteen-pence to those who will build his boat, while James pays two shillings for fencing his field, wages must rise to two shillings a day; for if John and Thomas did not give as much as James, the latter would monopolise all the labourers.

MRS. B.

You see therefore that it is the additional capital produced by the labour of these men, which by increasing the demand for labour raises their wages. Thus, whenever capital for the maintenance of labourers abounds, the capitalist must content himself with smaller profits, and allow his workmen a more liberal remuneration.

CAROLINE

Oh, that is charming! that is exactly what I wish. But, Mrs. B., if, during the second year, our colonists employ their labourers in building houses and fencing fields, instead of cultivating them, subsistence will again fall short, and the labourers will be reduced to their former necessitous condition; unless, having once experienced such distress, they guard against it in future.

MRS. B.

That does not depend on the choice of the labourers, who must do the work they are hired to perform, of whatever nature it may be. But their employers will be careful to provide for their maintenance, for they know that those who should neglect to make such a provision for their future services would be deprived of them. They cannot work without subsistence, nor will they work without an ample subsistence whilst any of the colony has it to offer them. If John therefore does not raise so great a harvest as James, he will not be able, the following year, to employ so many workmen. Each landed proprietor therefore will take care to direct the labour of his workmen towards raising the requisite subsistence, before he employs them in any other description of labour: it is for this subsistence that there will be the greatest demand, demand which regulates supply.

Now let us suppose that the shipwrecked crew had brought wives with them, and reared families: would that have affected the rate of wages?

CAROLINE
Their wages would remain the same; but as they would have to maintain their wives and children as well as themselves, they would not fare so well.

MRS. B.
And if there were not food enough for them all, the most weakly of the children would die, not precisely of hunger, but of some of those diseases which want of sufficient and proper food engenders. It is evident, therefore, that a labourer ought not to marry unless his wages are adequate to the maintenance of a family; or unless he has, like your gardener, some little provision in store to make up the deficiency.

Let us make another supposition. If, after several years of prosperity, a hurricane was to make such devastation amongst the crops of our colonists as to reduce the harvest to one half what it was the preceding year; what effect would this have on the wages of labour?

CAROLINE
It would unquestionably reduce them, for the stock of subsistence would be diminished; but in what manner the reduction would take effect I do not clearly see.

MRS. B.
In order to trace its consequences step by step we may suppose that John, finding his capital will not maintain more than one half of the number of labourers he before employed, reluctantly discharges the

other half. These poor men wander about the colony seeking work; but, instead of finding any, they meet only with companions in distress, who have lost their employment for similar reasons; thus, without resource, they return to their masters, and entreat to be employed on lower terms. John, who had discharged these men, not for want of work to give them but for want of funds to pay them, is happy, in his reduced circumstances, to employ labourers at lower wages. He therefore makes a new agreement with them, and determines to discharge those whom he had originally retained in his service, unless they will consent to work for him on the same terms. These men, aware of the difficulty of finding employment elsewhere, are compelled by necessity to accept the conditions, and thus wages are reduced to one half their former rate throughout the colony.

CAROLINE

It appears as evident as possible. I have only one objection to make, which is, that though this may be the case in our colony, it certainly is not so in other places. Wages, so far from being reduced, are, I believe, frequently raised during a scarcity; at least there are great complaints amongst the poor if that be not done.

MRS. B.

In countries where money is used it is unnecessary to make any reduction in the rate of wages during a scarcity, because the high price of provisions occasioned by a scarcity produces a similar effect. If you continue to pay your labourer the same wages when the articles of provision on which he subsists have doubled in price, his wages are less efficient by one half, because he can procure with them only one half of what he did before the scarcity.

CAROLINE

But this is a kind of imposition upon the poor labourers, who, I suppose, are at least as ignorant as I am of political economy, and are not aware that a shilling can purchase more at one time than it can at another, and therefore during a scarcity continue to work at the usual rate of wages for want of knowing better.

MRS. B.

Knowledge, in this instance, would only teach them that they must bear with patience an unavoidable evil The alternative for capitalists, when capital is diminished, is to reduce, either the number of their labourers or the rate of their wages—or rather, I should say, the remuneration of their labour; for the money-wages frequently remain the same. Now, is it not more equitable to divide the maintenance amongst the whole of the labouring class, than to feed some of them amply, whilst the remainder starve?

CAROLINE

No doubt it is; but would it not, in this instance, be allowable for the legislature to interfere, and oblige the capitalist to raise the rate of wages in proportion to the rise of price of provisions, so as to afford the labourers their usual quantity of subsistence? I think the rate of wages ought to be regulated by the price of bread, as that is the principal subsistence of the poor; so as to enable them to purchase the same quantity of bread whatever its price may be.

MRS. B.

Or, in other words, that every man may eat his usual quantity of bread, however deficient the harvest is in its produce; for unless you could find means to increase the quantity of subsistence, it will avail nothing to raise the rate of wages.

CAROLINE

Very true; yet two shillings will purchase twice the quantity of bread that one will; is not that true also Mrs. B.? and yet these truths appear incompatible.

MRS. B.

One of them must therefore be an error; two shillings would not purchase twice the quantity of bread that one did if wages were doubled, because provisions would continue to rise in price in proportion to the advance on wages.

CAROLINE

But I would prohibit the farmer from raising the price of his corn and his cattle, and then there would be no necessity for the butcher and the baker raising the price of meat and bread. It is not just that the farmer, when he has a bad crop, should throw his misfortune on the public, and be the only person who does not suffer from it; which is the case if he raises the price of his produce in proportion to its scarcity.

MRS. B.

The farmer consumes as well as produces provisions; and as a consumer he partakes of the evil of the advance of price. If he sell his corn for twice the usual price, what he consumes at home stands him in the same value, for such is the price it would fetch at market.

But supposing it were possible to prevent the rise in price during a scarcity, what consequences would ensue? Keep in mind the important point, that the harvest has yielded but half its usual product; that whilst the wages of labour and the price of provision! undergo no alteration, the labourers purchase am consume the usual quantity of food, and at the end of six months....

CAROLINE

You need not finish the sentence, Mrs. B.; at the end of six months the whole stock of provisions would be consumed, and the people who excited my commit aeration would be starved.

MRS. B.

This would infallibly be the case were such a measure persevered in; but though it has often been attempted by sovereigns more benevolent than wise to set limits to the price of provisions, the consequences soon became so formidable as to compel the legislature to put a stop to a remedy which was as ineffectual at it was pernicious. "In the year* 1315 England was afflicted by a famine, grievous beyond all that ever were known before, which raised the price of provisions far above the reach of the people of middling " classes. The parliament, in compassion to the general distress, ordered that all articles of food should be sold at moderate prices, which they took upon themselves to prescribe. The consequence was, that all things, instead of being sold at or under the maximum price fixed by them, became dearer than before, "or were entirely withheld from the market Poultry

* Macpherson's Annals of Commerce

were rarely to be seen. Butchers' meat was not to be found at all. The sheep were dying of a pestilence, and all kinds of grain were selling at most enormous prices. Early the next year the parliament, finding their mistake, left provisions to find their own price."

Thus you see that the rise in the price of provisions is the natural remedy to the evil of scarcity. It is the means of husbanding the short stock of food, and making it last Out to the ensuing harvest, and it diminishes the scarcity, by inducing dealers in corn to import it from foreign countries; but government should never interfere, either with the price of provisions or the rate of wages; they will each find their respective level if left uncontrolled.

But to return to our colony. What effect would it produce on wages, were some contagious malady to carry off one half of the labourers?

CAROLINE

It would increase the demand for the labour of those which remained, and consequently raise their wages.

MRS. B.

We may generally state, therefore, that when the number of labourers remains the same, the rate of wages will increase with the increase of capital, and lower with the diminution of it; while if the amount of capital remain stationary, the rate of wages will fall as the number of labourers increase, and rise as the number of labourers diminish; or, as mathematicians would express it, the rate of wages varies directly as the quantity of capital, and inversely as the number of labourers.

Macpherson mentions that "a dreadful pestilence,

which originated in the eastern regions, began its ravages in England in the year 1348, and is said to have carried off the greater part of the people, especially in the lower ranks of life. The surviving labourers took advantage of the demand for labour and the scarcity of hands to raise their prices. The king, Edward III, thereupon enacted the statute of labourers, which ordained that all men and women under 60 years of age, whether of free or servile condition, having no occupation or property, should serve any person of whom they should be required, and should receive only the wages which were usual before the year 1346, or in the five or six preceding years, on pain of imprisonment, the employers being also punishable for giving greater wages. Artificers were also prohibited from demanding more than the old wages; and butchers, bakers, brewers, &c. were ordered to sell their provisions at reasonable prices. The 'servants having no regard to the said ordinance, but to their ease and singular covetise,' refused to serve unless for higher wages than the law allowed them. Therefore the parliament, by another statute, fixed the yearly and daily wages of agricultural servants, artificers, and labourers, the payment of threshing corn by the quarter, and even the price of shoes. They also forbad any person to leave the town in summer wherein he had dwelt in the winter, or to remove from one shire to another.

"Thus were the lower classes debarred by laws, which in their own nature must be inefficient, from making any effort to improve their situation in life."

CAROLINE

I had always imagined that a great demand for

labour was occasioned by some great work that was, to be executed, such as digging a canal, making new roads, cutting through hills, &c.; but it seems that the demand for labour depends, not so much on the quantity of work to be done as on the quantity of subsistence provided for the workmen.

MRS. B.

Work to be performed is the immediate cause of the demand for labour; but however great or important is the work which a man may wish to undertake, the execution of it must always be limited by the extent of his capital; that is to say, by the funds he possesses for the maintenance or payment of his labourers. The same observation applies to the capital of a country, which is only an aggregate of the capital of individuals; it cannot employ more people than it has the means of maintaining. All the waste land capable of cultivation in the country might be called work to be done; but one must have, not only labourers to do that work, but a sufficient quantity of subsistence to support them. In our conversation on capital we observed, that in countries of large capital great works were undertaken, such as public buildings, bridges, iron railways, canals, &c. All these things are a sign of redundance of wealth.

CAROLINE

In Ireland I understand that the wages of common labourers are much lower than in England: is it on account of the capital of that country being less adequate to the maintenance of its population?

MRS. B.

That is, no doubt, one of the principal causes of the

low price of labour in that country; but there are many other causes which affect the price of labour, arising from the imperfection of its government. The Irish are far less industrious than the English. Arthur Young, in his Travels through Ireland, observes, that "husbandry-labour is very *low-priced,* but not *cheap.* Two shillings a-day in Suffolk is cheaper than six-pence a-day in Cork. If a Huron would dig for two-pence a-day, I have little doubt but that it might be dearer than the Irishman's sixpence."

CAROLINE

But, Mrs. B., the price of labour does not only vary in different countries, but very considerably in different parts of the same country. In purchasing some cutlery a few days ago, I was shown country and town made knives and forks, apparently the same, yet the difference in price was considerable. Upon enquiring the cause, I was informed that it was owing to wages being so much higher in London than in the country.

MRS. B.

And if you had enquired the cause of the higher rate of wages of London workmen, you would have heard that it was on account of their being better workmen: the ablest artificers generally resort to London, as the place where their skill will be most duly appreciated, and where their employers can best afford to reward it.

It is but just to remunerate labourers according to their ability. Your head-gardener does less work than any of the men under him; yet he has the highest wages, on account of the skill and experience he has acquired. A working silversmith or a watchmaker has on this account higher wages than a tailor or a carpenter.

Where skill is not requisite, the hardest and most disagreeable kinds of labour are best paid; this is the case with blacksmiths, iron-founders, coal-heavers, &c.

A consideration is also bad for arts of an unwholesome, unpleasant, or dangerous nature; such as painters, miners, gunpowder makers, and a variety of other analogous employments.

CAROLINE

And physicians and lawyers, Mrs. B., who devote their time and talents to the service of their employers, are they not skilled labourers of a superior class? I am sure they receive the highest wages; and it appears to me, that the man who exerts his mental faculties is a labourer equally with him who exerts his bodily powers, only of a higher quality, as strength of mind is superior to strength of body.

MRS. B.

I do not quite agree with you there. The cultivation of the mental powers, such as are required in a learned lawyer, a skilful physician, or a distinguished artist, is attended with very considerable expense; and this expensive education should, I think, be considered as a capital which is fixed in the human mind; the remuneration received by such persons would then be reckoned as the profits of that fixed capital, and not as wages.

CAROLINE

This is quite a new sort of fixed capital, and by what name do you distinguish it from the common fixed capital?

MRS. B.

It is sometimes called intellectual, sometimes immaterial capital, to distinguish it from that which is of a material nature. Mr. Senior observes, "There appears no reason to doubt that, as civilisation advances, every person will receive an education which will materially increase his power of production. Brutes and machinery can effect almost every thing that is to be effected by mere bodily exertion. Whatever requires mind will be dope better in proportion as the mind has received earlier or more judicious cultivation; even in our present state of civilisation, which, high as it appears by comparison, is far short of what may easily be conceived, or even of what may confidently be expected, the intellectual and moral capital of Great Britain far exceeds all her material capital, not only in importance but even in productiveness. The families that receive mere wages probably do not form a fourth of the community, and the comparatively large amount of the wages even of these is principally owing to the capital and skill with which their efforts are assisted and directed by the more educated members of the society. Those who receive mere rent, even using that word in its largest sense, are still fewer; and the amount of rent, like that of wages, principally depends on the knowledge by which the gifts of nature are directed and employed. The bulk of the national income is profit, and of that profit, the portion which is mere interest, or material capital, probably does not amount to one third; the rest is the result of personal capital, or, in other words education."

CAROLINE

This is a fine eulogium on intellectual capital.

But you observe, Mrs. B., that Mr. Senior gives it two other epithets; he calls it moral and personal capital.

MRS. B.

It is personal, because it is vested in the person who possesses it; and it is moral, because the progress of intellect has a powerful tendency to the improvement of virtue.

CAROLINE

Then it appears that a want of knowledge is as great an obstacle to the progress of a country as a want of wealth?

MRS. B.

Yes; for it is knowledge that will point out the means, and enable the people to procure wealth. The most fertile soil, the finest climate, nay, even the most intelligent people, without that knowledge, which is procured by education, will ever remain poor. This is strongly exemplified in Ireland, and is so powerfully described by Mr. Senior that I shall give it you in his own words. "It is not on the accidents of soil or climate or on the existing accumulation of the material instruments of production, but on the quantity and the diffusion of this immaterial capital that the wealth of a country depends. The climate, the soil, and the situation of Ireland have been described as superior, and certainly are not much inferior to our own. Her poverty has been attributed to the want of material capital; but were Ireland now to exchange her native population for seven millions of English, north countrymen, they would quickly create the capital that is wanted. And were England, north of

Trent, to be peopled exclusively by a million of families
from the west of Ireland, Lancashire, and Yorkshire would
still more rapidly resemble Connaught Ireland is physically
poor because she is morally and intellectually poor, because she is morally and intellectually uneducated; and
while she continues uneducated, while the ignorance and
violence of her population render persons and property
insecure, and prevent the accumulation and prohibit the
introduction of capital, legislative measures, intended
solely and directly to relieve her poverty, may not indeed
be deemed ineffectual, for they may aggravate the disease
the "symptoms of which they are meant to palliate, but
undoubtedly will be productive of no permanent benefit
Knowledge has been called power; it is far more certainly
wealth. Asia Minor, Syria, Egypt, and the northern coast
of Africa, were once among the richest, and are now among
the most miserable countries in the world, simply because
they have fallen into the hands of a people without a sufficiency of the immaterial sources of wealth to keep up the
material ones."

CAROLINE

Well, Mrs. B., I am so highly gratified with this account
of immaterial capital, that the other quite sinks in importance before it

MRS. B.

You must not, however, forget that, however delightful is the possession of knowledge in all its various branches to those who are in affluence, the greatest importance of immaterial capital to the poorer
classes is the means it affords them of creating material

capital; the enjoyment of plenty of food and good clothing is more essential to their happiness than the refined gratifications resulting from the pursuits of the fine arts, science, or literature.

CONVERSATION IX

ON WAGES AND POPULATION — *continued*

HIGH WAGES NOT INVARIABLY ACCOMPANYING GREAT CAPI-
TAL.—GREAT CAPITAL AND LOW WAGES IN CHINA.— SMALL
CAPITAL AND HIGH WAGES IN AMERICA.—ADVANTAGES
OF NEW-SETTLED COUNTRIES.—POVERTY THS NATURAL
CHECK TO POPULATION.—GREAT POPULATION ADVANTA-
GEOUS ONLY WHEN RESULTING FROM PLENTY.—INCREAS-
ING WEALTH PREFERABLE TO ANY STATIONARY CAPITAL.—
MISTAKE IN ENCOURAGING POPULATION.—POPULATION OF
MANUFACTURING TOWNS.—INDUSTRY.— PIECE-WORK.

CAROLINE

I HAVE been reflecting a great deal on our last conversation, Mrs. B.; and the conclusions I have drawn from
it are, that the greater the capital a country possesses, the
greater number of people it can maintain, and the higher
the wages of labour will be.

MRS. B.

The greater the stock of subsistence the more people may
be maintained by it, no doubt; but your second inference
is not a tall a necessary conclusion. China is a very rich
country, and yet wages are, I believe, nowhere so low. The
accounts which travellers give of the miserable state of the
inferior classes are painful to hear; and their poverty is not

the result of idleness, for they run about the streets with took in their hands, begging for work.

CAROLINE

That is owing to the immense population of China; so that, though the capital of the country may be very considerable, still it is insufficient for the maintenance of all its inhabitants.

MRS. B.

You should therefore always remember that the rate of wages does not depend upon the absolute quantity of capital, but upon its quantity relative to the number of people it is to maintain. This is a truth which, however simple, is continually lost sight of, and hence arise errors without number in political economy. If China had ten times the wealth it actually possesses, and its population were at the same time tenfold as numerous, the people would not be better fed.

America, on the other hand, is a country of very small capital, and yet wages are remarkably high there.

CAROLINE

How do you account for that; for the demand for labour, you know, can be only in proportion to the extent of capital?

MRS. B.

The capital of America, though small when compared with those of the countries of Europe, is very considerable in proportion to the number of people to be maintained by it. In America, and in all newly-settled countries as yet thinly inhabited, the wages of labour are high, because capital increases with prodigious rapidity. Where land is plentiful and productive, and the labourers to cultivate it scarce, the competition amongst the landholders to obtain labourers is so great as to enable this class to raise their demands; and the higher the wages the labourer receives the sooner he has it in his power to purchase a piece of land and become land-holder himself. Thus the class of labourers is continually passing into the class of proprietors, and making room for a fresh influx of labourers, both from the rising generation and from emigrations from foreign countries.

CAROLINE

America has then the double advantage of high wages and low price of land; no wonder that it is so thriving a country.

MRS. B.

The progress of wealth and improvement is nowhere so rapid as in the settlement of a civilised people in a new country; provided they establish laws for the security of their property, they require no other incitement to industry. In the new settlements of America, where the experienced farmer with his European implements of husbandry is continually encroaching on the barren wilderness, want is almost unknown, and a state of universal prosperity prevails. We may form some judgment of the rapid increase of their capital by that of their population. The facility with which the Americans acquire a maintenance sufficient to bring up a family encourages early marriages, and gives rise to numerous families; the children are well fed, thriving, and healthy; you may imagine how small are the proportion that die in comparison to the number born, when I inform you that in the United States their population doubles itself in about 23 years!

CAROLINE

But does not such an immense increase of population reduce the rate of wages?

MRS. B.

No; because their capital increases in a still greater proportion; and as long as that is the case, wages, you know, will rise rather than fall. But observe that what I have said relative to America refers only to the United States of that country, which have the advantage of a free government protecting the property of all classes of men. In the Spanish settlements, where the government is of a very different description, the condition of the people is far less flourishing. The population of Mexico, one of the finest provinces of Spanish America, does not double itself in less than 48 years.

CAROLINE

Yet I do not well understand why the poor should be worse off in England where there is a large capital, than in America where there is a small one.

MRS. B.

Because you are again forgetting the fundamental rule which I have laid down for you, that capital must always be considered with reference to the number of people to be employed and maintained by it.

England and all the old-established countries of Europe no longer afford the same facility for the growth of capital that a newly-settled country does, and if the population goes on augmenting without a proportional increase of wealth, the wages of labour will fall instead of rising, and the condition of the poor be deteriorated.

CAROLINE

But how is it possible for population to exceed the means of subsistence? People cannot live without eating.

MRS. B.

No; but they may live upon a smaller portion of food than is requisite to maintain them in health and vigour; children may be born without their parents having the means of providing for their sustenance. Population under such circumstances not only cannot increase but it will gradually decline.

When such a state becomes permanent the country is falling to decay, and we find this to be the case in many eastern countries, where the government is despotic and industry discouraged by the insecurity of property.

CAROLINE

But in those which are advanced in civilisation and in which property is secure, such as England, this cannot happen, for so far from falling to decay, oar wealth and prosperity is yearly increasing.

MRS. B.

That is true; and though our population increases also, we may be sure that our wealth makes the greatest progress, as a greater share of it falls to the lot of every one. Our ancestors had neither linen, nor shoes and stockings, and the furniture of the house of a nobleman in the middle ages was scarcely so good as that of a cottage is at the present day. Excess of population can, therefore, be only accidental and temporary in a flourishing country.

CAROLINE

Well! I declare I always thought that a great

population was the cause of wealth. All rich, thriving countries are populous; great cities are populous; wealth, which you esteem so advantageous to a country, encourages population; and population in its turn promotes wealth, since labourers produce more than they consume. You recollect how rich our colony became by the acquisition of the labour of the shipwrecked crew: their first arrival was attended with some inconvenience, it is true; but I should say, as you do with respect to machinery, the inconvenience is small and temporary, the advantage both durable and extensive.

MRS. B.

A great population is highly advantageous to a country where there is a capital which will afford wages sufficient for a labourer to bring up his children in health and comfort; for population is not usually increased by the acquisition of a number of able labourers, (as was the case in our colony,) but by the birth of helpless infants, who depend entirely upon their parents for subsistence. If this subsistence is not provided, the children are born merely to languish a few years in poverty, and to fall early victims to disease, brought on by want and wretchedness. Under such circumstances they can increase neither the strength, the wealth, nor the happiness of the country; on the contrary, they weaken, impoverish, and render it more miserable; they consume without reproducing, they suffer without enjoying, and they give pain and sorrow to their parents without ever reaching that age when they might reward their paternal cares. Yet such is the lot of many poor children wherever population exceeds the means of subsistence, and I fear but too often occurs even in this country.

CAROLINE

What a dreadful reflection this is! But you do not suppose that there are any children actually starved to death?

MRS. B.

I hope not; but the fate of those unfortunate infants is scarcely less deplorable who perish by slow degrees for want of proper care and a sufficiency of wholesome food. A large family of young children would require the whole of a mother's care and attention; but that mother is frequently obliged to leave them to obtain by hard labour their scanty meal. Want of good nursing, of cleanliness, of fresh air, and of wholesome nourishment, engenders a great variety of diseases, which either carry them off, or leave them in such a state of weakness, that they fall a sacrifice to the first contagious malady which attacks them. It is to this state of debility, as well as to the want of medical advice and judicious treatment, that must be attributed the mortality occasioned by the small-pox and measles amongst the lower classes of children, so much greater than in those of the upper ranks of society.

Nor are the fatal effects of an excess of population confined to children. A sick man, who might be restored to health by medical assistance and a proper diet, perishes, because he cannot afford to obtain either. A delicate or an infirm woman requires repose and indulgence which she cannot command. The necessaries of life vary, not only with the climate and customs of a country but with the age, sex, and infirmities of the individuals who inhabit it; and wherever these necessaries are deficient mortality prevails. But if the increase of population occasionally outstrip the means of subsistence, it is no less owing to the ill-judged conduct of the upper classes, than to the imprudence of the lover orders of people.

CAROLINE

Do you allude to the encouragement of early marriages amongst the poor?

MRS. B.

Yes. We observed, that when a great population springs from ample means of subsistence, it is the highest blessing a country can enjoy; the children brought up in plenty, attain a healthy and vigorous man, hood, with strength to defend, and industry to enrich their country. Those who have not reflected on the subject have frequently confounded cause and effect, and have, with you, considered a great population, under all circumstances, as the cause of prosperity. Hence the most strenuous efforts have been made, not only by individuals but even by the legislature, to encourage early marriages and large families, conceiving that by so doing they were promoting the happiness and prosperity of their country.

CAROLINE

This is a most unfortunate error. But when population is again reduced, the evil corrects itself; for capital being thus rendered more adequate to the maintenance of this diminished population, the wages of labour will again rise.

MRS. B.

Certainly. But what misery attends this slow and dreadful remedy! And even when effected, it often happens, that as soon as the labouring classes find their condition improved, whether by a diminution of numbers, or an augmentation of capital which may spring up from some new source of industry, marriages again increase, a greater number of children are reared, and population once more outstrips the means of subsistence; so that the condition of the poor, after a temporary improvement, is again reduced to its former wretchedness.

CAROLINE

That is precisely what has occurred in the village near which we live. It was formerly, I have heard, but a small hamlet, the inhabitants of which gained a livelihood as farmers' labourers. Many years ago a cotton manufacture was set up in the neighbourhood, which afforded ample employment for the poor; and even the children, who were before idle, could now earn something towards their maintenance. This, during some years, had an admirable effect in raising the condition of the labouring classes. I have heard my grandfather say, that it was wonderful to see how rapidly the village improved, how many new cottages were built, and what numerous families they contained. But this prosperous state was not of very long duration. In the course of time the village became overstocked with labourers; and, though still populous, it is now sunk into a state of poverty and distress nearly as bad as that from which it had so recently emerged.

MRS. B.

You see, therefore, that this manufacture, which at first proved a blessing to the village, was, by the improvidence of the labourers, converted into an evil. Had the people been brought up with prudence and forethought, they would not have increased beyond the demand for labour, and the manufacture might still have afforded them the advantages it at first produced.

CAROLINE

This, then, must be the cause of the misery which so frequently prevails amongst the poor in manufacturing towns, where it would be so natural to expect that the facility of finding work would produce comfort and plenty.

MRS. B.

In large manufacturing districts, such as Birmingham and Manchester, I think that occasional distress proceeds from the fluctuations of trade; the demand for goods often varying, according to the caprice of fashion, or to the change of season. Were the workmen prudent, they would lay up a store for such occasions; for they but seldom occur, and their wages are high.

CAROLINE

It is true, I have heard, that skilful workmen, who could earn a livelihood by three or four days' labour in the week, would frequently spend the remainder of it in idleness and profligacy; so that high wages, in this case, seems productive of evil.

MRS. B.

I believe that it is much more common for great gains to act as a stimulus to industry. Like every other human quality, industry improves in proportion to the encouragement it receives, and it can have no greater encouragement and reward than high wages. It sometimes happens, it is true, that workmen act in the way you mention, but such conduct is far from being common; the greater number, when their wages are liberal, keep steadily to their work, and if they are paid by the piece, are even apt to overwork themselves.

CAROLINE

That I have observed. My father lately agreed to pay a certain sum for digging a sunk fence in our pleasure-grounds; and two of the under-gardeners engaged to do it after their day's work was over. I thought they would repent of their undertaking, when they came to such hard labour, after having performed their usual task; but I was astonished at their alacrity and perseverance: in the course of a week they completed the job, and received the price in addition to their usual wages.—I wonder that work is not always paid by the piece, it is such an encouragement to industry.

MRS. B.

All kinds of work do not admit of being so paid; for instance, the care of a garden could not be divided into jobs, and the gardener be paid so much for planting trees, so much for cleaning borders, so much for mowing grass, &c. Besides, I doubt whether it would be desirable that this mode of payment should be generally adopted, on account of the temptation it affords to labourers to over-work themselves; for notwithstanding all the advantages of industry, one would never wish it to be pushed to that extreme which would exhaust the strength of the labouring classes, and bring on disease and infirmity. The benefits resulting from industry are an increase of the comforts and conveniences of life; but it would be paying too dear for these to purchase them by a sickly and premature old age.

CAROLINE

No amelioration of the condition of the poor can then be permanent unless to industry they add prudence and foresight.

MRS. B.

Certainly. Were all men as considerate as your gardener, Thomas, and did they not marry till they had secured a provision for a family, or could earn a sufficiency to maintain it; in short, were children not brought into the world until there was bread to feed them, the distress which you have just been describing would be unknown, excepting in cases of unforeseen misfortunes, or unless produced by idleness or vice.

In order to be of permanent service to the labouring classes, we must not rest satisfied with encouraging industry; but endeavour by instruction to awaken their minds to a sense of remote consequences, as well as of immediate good, so that when they have succeeded in rendering their condition more comfortable, they may not rashly and inconsiderately increase their numbers beyond the means of subsistence.

CAROLINE

But if population be constantly kept within the limits of subsistence, would it not always remain stationary?

MRS. B.

Certainly not: where the people are industrious, capital will increase; then the increase of population will follow of course, and with advantage, so long as it is careful to follow the progressive steps of capital, and never to outstrip it.

CAROLINE

I now see evidently, that population should never be encouraged, but where there is great plenty of subsistence and employment.

MRS. B.

And *then* it requires no encouragement If men so often marry without having made any provision for a family, there is no danger of their not marrying when a subsistence is easily obtained; and their children will be healthy and long-lived in proportion as they are well fed, clothed, and taken care of. Population should therefore be left to regulate itself; and the only way in which the legislature can interfere with advantage, is to promote the education of the lower classes, in order to give them habits of industry and prudence. The natural tendency of population to increase will then be counterbalanced, by the tendency of man in civilised society to better his condition, and prosperity will result from these counteracting powers.

CAROLINE

Then, by the word tendency, you do not mean to infer that population actually does increase beyond the means of subsistence, but that it would, if it could do so.

MRS. B.

Certainly. In a well-constituted civilised country, population might constantly run a race with production, without ever outstripping it.

It is the natural tendency of population to increase beyond the means of subsistence; but it is the artificial tendency of man, in a civilised state, to counteract the *natural one;* and in proportion as civilisation or barbarism predominate, the natural or artificial tendency will prevail.

CAROLINE

I feel considerable satisfaction in having acquired correct ideas on this subject; but the knowledge I have gained is not without alloy. The miseries arising from an excess of population have left a very melancholy impression on my mind.

MRS. B.

Remember that you must consider the tendency of population to press upon the means of subsistence as a measure necessary to rouse our exertions; it is a law of nature, wisely calculated to call into activity the various powers of man. It is to this pressure that we owe the appropriation of land, and the consequent diversity of ranks and conditions which we have observed to be so essential to the progressive improvement of society; it is the foundation-stone of the great structure of civilisation, and the means by which scanty tribes of wandering savages have been transformed into populous nations of civilised beings. If then it produces want and wretchedness in ill-governed states, it feeds millions of industrious happy beings in a well-constituted society, and as civilisation and education, gain ground, the evil will always diminish and the good increase.

CAROLINE

Yet, as the world becomes more populous, the difficulty of procuring subsistence must surely increase?

MRS. B.

A period may, it is true, one day arrive when the earth will be so perfectly cultivated, and so fully peopled, that no further augmentation either of population or of subsistence can take place. How many generations will pass away before that epoch, it is impossible even to surmise; but, before that period arrives, we may fairly presume that the human character will be so far improved, both in virtue and knowledge, that population even then will not trespass upon the bounds of subsistence.

In the present state of the world, the inconvenience arising from this pressure on subsistence is so far from being confined to great nations and populous districts, that it is nowhere so severely felt as among the savage tribes, who are without resource when the supply of food afforded them by the chase, by fishing, or the spontaneous produce of the earth, proves deficient. In India, where the Hindoos subsist on rice alone, famines have repeatedly swept away thousands. The more improved the state of society, the less dreadful are these effects; but it is in newly-settled countries alone, and under free governments, such as the United States of America, that we can look for complete exemption from this evil.

We will conclude this subject by reading a passage in Mr. Malthus's Principles of Political Economy.

"From high wages, or the power of commanding a large portion of the necessaries of life, two very different results may follow; one, that of a rapid increase of population, in which case the high wages are chiefly spent in the maintenance of large and frequent families; and the other, that of a decided improvement in the modes of subsistence, and the conveniences and comforts enjoyed, without a proportionate acceleration in the rate of increase.

"In looking to these different results, the causes of them will evidently appear to be the different habits existing among the people of different countries, and at different times. In an inquiry into the causes of these different habits, we shall generally be able to trace those which produce the first result to all the circumstances which contribute to depress the lower classes of the people, which make them unable or unwilling to reason from the past to the future, and ready to acquiesce, for the sake of present gratification, in a very low standard of comfort and respectability; and those which produce the second result, to all the circumstances which tend to elevate the character of the lower classes of society, which make them approach the nearest to beings who 'look before and after, and who consequently cannot acquiesce patiently in the thought of depriving themselves and their children of the means of being respectable, virtuous, and happy.

"Among the circumstances which Contribute to the character first described, the most efficient will be found to be despotism, oppression, and ignorance: among those which contribute to the latter character, civil and political liberty, and education."

Do you understand now, why the rate of wages and the condition of the poor are better in countries which, like America, are rapidly growing rich, than in those which, like England, have long accumulated large capitals, but whose wealth is making but slower progress?

CAROLINE

Yes; it is because when capital augments very fast labour is in great demand and well rewarded. But when wealth, however great, increases less rapidly, population must proceed with the same retarded progress; or it will encroach on the means of subsistence, so that wages will fall, and distress come on.

MRS. B.

This is what I formerly alluded to, when I told you that you would find that the accession of wealth was more advantageous to a country, as well as to an individual, than the possession of any capital which did not increase.

I roust read you a passage of Paley on this subject, in which he expresses himself with remarkable perspicuity.

"The ease of subsistence and the encouragement of industry depend neither upon the price of labour nor upon the price of provisions, but upon the proportion which the one bears to the other. Now the "influx of wealth into a country naturally tends to advance this proportion; that is, every fresh accession of wealth raises the price of labour before it raises the price of provisions.

"It is not, therefore, the quantity of wealth collected into a country, but the continual increase of that quantity, from which the advantage arises to employment and population. It is only the accession of wealth which produces the effect; and it is only by wealth constantly flowing into or springing up in a country, that the effect can be constant."

You must not, however, imagine that the capital of this country remains stationary; on the contrary, we are making rapid advances in wealth, though we cannot pretend to equal the progress of a newly-settled country.

CONVERSATION X

ON THE CONDITION OF THE POOR

OF THE CULTIVATION OF COMMONS AND WASTE LANDS.—OF
EMIGRATION.—EDUCATION OP THE LOWER CLASSES.—
BENEFIT CLUBS—SAVING BANKS.—PAROCHIAL RELIEF.—
ALMS AND PRIVATE CHARITIES.—REWARDS.

CAROLINE

I HAVE been reflecting ever since our last interview, Mrs. B., whether there were no means of improving the condition of the poor, and it appears to me, that though we have not the same resource in extent of territory as they have in America, yet we have large tracts of waste land, which, by being brought into cultivation, would produce an additional stock of subsistence.

MRS. B.

You must remember that industry is limited by the extent of capital, and that no more labourers can be employed than we have the means of maintaining; they work for their daily bread, and without obtaining it, they neither could nor would work. All the labourers which the capital of the country can maintain being already employed, the only question is, whether it be better that they should work on land already in a state of cultivation, or in breaking up and bringing into culture new lands; and this point must be trusted to the decision of the landed proprietors, as it is no less their interest than that of the labouring classes that the greatest possible quantity of produce should be raised. To a certain extent it has been found more advantageous to lay out capital in improving the culture of old land, rather than to employ it in bringing new land into tillage; because all the best land having long been under cultivation, the soil of the waste land is extremely poor and ungrateful, and requires a great deal to be laid out on it before it brings in a return. But there is often capital sufficient for both these purposes; and of late years we have seen not only prodigious improvements in the processes of agriculture throughout the country, but a great number of commons inclosed and cultivated.

CAROLINE

I fear you will think me inconsistent, but I cannot help regretting the inclosure of commons; they are the only resource of the cottagers for the maintenance of a few lean cattle. Let me once more quote my favourite Goldsmith: —

> Where, then, ah! where shall poverty reside,
> To 'scape the pressure of contiguous pride?
> If to some common's fenceless limits stray'd,
> He drives his flock to pick the scanty blade,
> Those fenceless fields the sons of wealth divide,
> And e'en the bare-worn common is denied.

MRS. B.

You should recollect that we do not admit poets to be very good authority in political economy. If, instead of feeding a few lean cattle, a common, by being inclosed, will fatten a much greater number of fine cattle, you must allow that the quantity of subsistence will be increased, and the poor, though in a less direct manner, will fare the better for it. Labourers are required to inclose and cultivate those commons, the neighbouring cottagers are employed for that purpose, and this additional demand for labour turns to their immediate advantage. They not only receive an indemnity for their loss of right of common, but they find purchasers for the cattle they can no longer maintain in the proprietors of the new in-closures.

When Finchley Common was inclosed, it was divided amongst the inhabitants of that parish; and the cottagers and little shopkeepers sold the small slips of land which fell to their share to men of greater property, who thus became possessed of a sufficient quantity to make it answer to them to inclose and cultivate it; and the poorer classes were amply remunerated for their loss of commonage by the sale of their respective lots.

CAROLINE

But if we have it not in our power to provide for a redundant population by the cultivation of our waste lands, what objection is there to sending those who cannot find employment at home, to seek a maintenance in countries where it is more easily obtained, where there is a greater demand for labour? Or why should they not found new colonies in the yet unsettled parts of America?

MRS. B.

Emigration is undoubtedly a resource for an overstocked population; but one which is adopted in general, with great reluctance by individuals, and, till within these few years, has been discouraged by governments, from a mistaken apprehension of its diminishing the strength of the country.

CAROLINE

It might be wrong to encourage emigration to a very great extent; I meant only to provide abroad for those whom we cannot maintain at home.

MRS. B.

Under a free and equitable government there is little danger of emigration ever exceeding that point. The attachment to our native land is naturally so strong, and there are so many ties of kindred and association to break through before we can quit it, that no slight motive will induce a man to expatriate himself. An author deeply versed in the knowledge of the human mind says, *"La seule bonne loi contre les emigrations, est celle que la nature a gravé dans nos coeurs."* On this subject I am very willing to quote the Deserted Village: —

> Good Heaven! what sorrows gloom'd that parting day
> That call'd them from their native walks away!

Besides, the difficulties with which a colony of emigrants have to struggle before they can effect a settlement, and the hardships they must undergo until they have raised food for their subsistence, are so discouraging, that no motive less strong than that of necessity is likely to induce them to settle in an uncultivated land.

Some capital, too. is required for this as well as for all undertakings; the colonists must be provided with implements of husbandry and of art, and supplied with food and clothing, until they shall have succeeded in producing such necessaries for themselves; and though of late years governments have wisely decided on encouraging rather than checking emigration, few are tempted to abandon their country.

There are, it is true, some emigrations which are extremely detrimental to the wealth and prosperity of a country; these, however, are not occasioned by poverty, but result from the severity and hardships imposed by arbitrary governments on particular classes of men. Want of toleration in religion has caused the most considerable and numerous emigrations of this description. Such was that of the Huguenots from France at the revocation of the edict of Nantz. They were a skilful and industrious people, who carried their arts and manufactures into Germany, Prussia, Holland, and England, and deprived France of some of her most valuable subjects. Spain has never recovered the blow which her industry received by the expulsion of the Moors, under Ferdinand and Isabella. Not all the wealth of America has repaid her for this loss.

But to return to the population of England: the more we find ourselves in danger of over-population, the more desirous we should be to avail ourselves of those means which tend to prevent the evil; the most essential of which is a general diffusion of knowledge, which would excite greater attention in the lower classes to their future interests.

CAROLINE

You would teach them to acquire intellectual capital, in order that they might know how to obtain material capital?

MRS. B.

Yes. I would endeavour to give the rising generation such an education as would render them, not only moral and religious, but industrious, frugal, and provident. In proportion as the mind is informed we an able to calculate the consequences of our actions. It is the infant and the savage who live only for the present moment. Those whom instruction has taught to think, reflect upon the past, and look forward to the future. But, for this purpose, it is not enough to teach children to read and write. Education must be more liberally extended: it must give rise to prudence, not only by enlarging our understandings, but by softening our feelings, by humanising the heart, and promoting amiable affections. The rude and inconsiderate peasant marries without either foreseeing or caring for the miseries he may entail on his wife and children; but he who has been taught to value the comforts and decencies of life, will not heedlessly involve himself and all that is dear to him in poverty, and its long train of miseries.

CAROLINE

I am very happy to hear that you think instruction may produce this desirable end, since the zeal for the education of the poor that has been displayed of late years gives every prospect of success.

MRS. B.

The highest advantages, both religious, moral, and political, may be expected to result from this general ardour for the instruction of the poor. No great or decided improvement can be effected in the manners of the people but by the education of the rising generation. It is difficult, if not impossible to change the habits of men whose characters are formed and settled: the prejudices of ignorance, which have grown up with us, will not yield to new impressions; whilst youth and innocence may be moulded into any form you choose to give them. This has been remarkably well expressed in a foreign periodical work.* *"Tout est lié dans les dispositions morales et dans les habitudes de l'homme. Un travail qui met de l'ordre dans les ideés, prépare à l'ordre dans la conduite. L'exercice de l'attention la fortifie, et par elle le jugement et la memoire, les deux facultés les plus usuelles dans les affaires de la vie. L'instruction religieuse et morale infusées dans l'esprit et dans le coeur des enfans, à mesure que les notions élémentaires des lettres leur deviennent familières; la discipline et la règle qu'il est facile d'introduire dans les écoles, les façonnent aux devoirs dont l'accomplissement assure le maintien de l'ordre social, en même temps que le bonheur des individus qui s'y soumettent. Des hommes élevés de cette manière sont non-seulement plus intelligens, plus aptes à saisir et appliquer les idées utiles, plus économes, plus laborieux, que ceux qui sont demeurés ignorans; mais ils sont aussi plus modérés, plus patiens, plus sages, plus justes. Tous les rapports, dans l'intérieur des familles, en ont plus de douceur et de force; l'influence des parens est plus marquee et plus durable; le loisir n'est point accompagné des inconvéniens qu'il a pour les hommes illitérés; les relations de voisinage sont signaleés par plus d'égards, et celles de l'intérêt par plus d'équité."*

But, independently of schools, and the various insti-

* La Bibliothèque Universelle.

tutions for the education of youth, there are establishments among the lower classes which are peculiarly calculated to inculcate lessons of prudence and economy; I mean the various societies or clubs instituted by the poor themselves, the members of which, by the contribution of a small stipend, accumulate a fund. Among these, the most conspicuous and useful are, the Benefit Clubs or Friendly Societies, the fund of which is destined to afford relief and aid in times of sickness and distress. These associations have spread throughout the country, and their good effects are rendered evident, by comparing the condition of such of the labouring classes as belong to them with those of the same district who have no resource in times of distress but parochial relief or private charity; the former are comparatively cleanly, industrious, sober, frugal,—respecting themselves and respected by others. Depending, in times of casual sickness or accident, on funds created by their own industry, they maintain an honourable pride and independence of character; whilst the latter, in a season of distress, become a prey to dirt and wretchedness; and being dissatisfied with the scantiness of parish-relief, they are often driven to the commission of crimes. It is above a century since these clubs were first instituted; they received encouragement both from government and individuals, and have spread throughout the country. I dare say that your prudent gardener Thomas is a member of one of them.

CAROLINE

Yes; and he belongs to one which can boast of peculiar advantages, as most of the gentlemen in the neighbourhood subscribe to it; in order, by increasing the fund, and consequently the amount of the relief which the distressed members can receive, to encourage the poor to belong to it.

MRS. B.

That is an excellent mode of bestowing charity, for *you* are not only sure that you relieve the necessitous, but also the industrious poor. A similar plan has been adopted, within these few years, in a village in the neighbourhood of London, and has been attended with the greatest success. Various schemes had been devised by the charitable inhabitants of this village to relieve the necessities of their poor, and so much was done for them by the opulent, that they found little need to exert their own industry; whilst the poor in the neighbouring parishes, attracted by the munificence of the charitable donations, flocked to the place; so that, notwithstanding all their bounty, the rich still found themselves surrounded by objects of penury and distress. Convinced at length that they created as much poverty as they relieved, they came to a resolution of completely changing their system. They established benefit clubs; and the sums which they before gave away in alms were now subscribed to these societies, so as to afford very ample relief to its members in cases of distress. The consequence was, that the idle poor abandoned the place, and the industrious poor were so well provided for, that the village has assumed quite a new aspect, and penury and want are scarcely any more to be seen.

But the most admirable of all institutions, and one which has in a great measure superseded that of benefit clubs, and has most essentially contributed to the improvement of the condition of the poor, is that of the Savings Banks.

Scotland has the glory of having first established an institution, the merits of which are so universally acknowledged, that within a few years it has spread throughout the civilised world. "The object of this institution," says the *Edinburgh Review*, No. 4-9, "is to open to the lower orders a place of deposit for their small savings, with the allowance of a reasonable monthly interest, and with full liberty of withdrawing their money, at any tune, either is whole or in part,—an accommodation which it is impracticable for the ordinary banks to furnish."

These institutions, variously modified, according to the circumstances and localities of the different countries in which they are established, afford the greatest encouragement to industry, by securing the property of the labouring poor. How frequently it happens that an industrious man, after having toiled to accumulate a small sum, is inveigled by sharpers to a gambling table, or induced by adventurers to engage in some ill-judged and hazardous speculation, to lend it to a distressed or a treacherous friend,—not to mention the risk of its being lost or stolen. But now Savings Banks are established in every district in England, where the poor may without difficulty or trouble deposit the trifle they can spare from their earnings, and where, instead of being exposed to this variety of dangers, it accumulates; some interest being allowed them for their money. We may hope, therefore, that the influence of prudential habits will help to raise the poor above the degrading resource of parochial assistance, which, before the introduction of the new system of poor laws, fell so heavily on the middling classes of people as to ruin many of them; and with regard to the lowest classes, Is said to have given rise to more poverty than it relieved,

CAROLINE

Indeed! I cannot understand that.

MRS. B.

The certainty that the parish was bound to attend to their wants, rendered the poor less apprehensive of indigence than if they had been convinced that they most suffer all the wretchedness it entailed. When a young man married without having the means of supporting his family by his labour, and without having made some little provision against accidents or sickness, he depended upon the parish as a never-failing resource. He received from the parish relief proportioned to his wants, whether these arose from accident, from idleness, or other misconduct; often indeed when they had no real existence, but were falsely alleged in order to procure money which was afterwards spent at the alehouse. A profligate man knew that if he spent his wages at the public-house instead of providing for his family, his wife and children could at worst but go to the poor-house. Parish relief thus became the very cause of the mischief which it professed to remedy.

CAROLINE

True, and it appears to have encouraged the worst species of poverty, that arising from idleness and ill conduct

MRS. B.

The greatest evil that resulted from this provision for the poor was, that by encroaching on the funds destined for the maintenance of labourers it diminished Hie demand for labour, and consequently lowered wages. Whilst, therefore, on the one hand, the poor-rate raised up a population which required work to maintain it, on the other, it curtailed the means by which it was employed. The poor-rate bestowed in the form of alms, and but too frequently on the idle and profligate, that wealth which should have been the reward of active industry.

When it was once proposed to establish a poor's rate in France, the committee of mendicity, in rejecting it, thus expressed themselves on that of England:— *"Cet exemple est une grande et importante leçon pour nous, car, indépendamment des vices qu'elle nous presente et d'une depense monstreuse, et d'un encouragement necessaire à la fainéantise, elle nous découvre la plaie politique de l'Angleterre la plus dévorante, qu'il est également dangereux pour sa tranquillité, et son bonheur, de detruire ou de laisser subsister."*

CAROLINE

But what was to be done? The poor could not be allowed to starve, even when idle and vicious.

MRS. B.

Certainly not. A great deal has already been done by the new system of poor laws, and with the most favourable results. By the new regulations, the poor cannot receive any relief at their own houses, unless under very peculiar circumstances. Their only resource, therefore, is to take refuge in the workhouse; and their objection to this, from the restraint it imposes, has roused many a family to make exertions to maintain themselves, who, under the old system, would have gone on for years receiving parochial relief. Then it at once puts an end to the imposition of the-idle and profligate; who would rather go to work on their own account, than subject themselves to the confinement and strict regulations of the workhouse, where they would be compelled to labour for the benefit of the institution. A complete reform has been made in these workhouses, now called *Unions,* from several of them being united and forming one establishment. A system of judicious economy has been introduced, and in consequence of these measures, the expense of the poor rate is reduced nearly to one half, and instead of eight millions, now costs the nation only four millions. The remaining four millions is therefore saved to the public, and becomes so much additional capital, which goes to the payment of independent labourers, instead of being distributed by the parish officers to paupers.

CAROLINE

What an immense sum! Then the demand for labour must be increased by this increase of capital, and the wages of labour must rise?

MRS. B.

It certainly tends to such results, and in many places a rise of wages has already taken place.

Then it is not only the physical condition of the poor that is improved by this new system, but their moral character is raised; they have no longer any temptation to impose falsehoods on the parish officers to obtain relief; they know that they must rely on their own exertions for a livelihood; they become industrious, and in time acquire the self approbation of independence.

CAROLINE

Yet cases but too often occur when, from sickness or accident, such heavy distress falls upon a poor family that it is utterly out of their power to do without assistance.

MRS. B.

The workhouse, in such cases, opens wide its doors to receive the sufferers and provide them with food, lodging, raiment, medicine, or whatever else they may require. It is the idle and vicious who are alone losers by these new regulations.

CAROLINE

But I wonder that even they should not take refuge in so comfortable an asylum, since it is open to all.

MRS. B.

Care is taken that it should not be attractive to this description of paupers. The food and clothing, though sufficient to maintain the pauper in health, is of a coarse and homely kind. There would be a manifest injustice, and a discouragement to industry to allow those who subsist on charity to be as well provided for as the man who earns his bread by bard labour. Then every able-bodied inhabitant of the workhouse is compelled to labour, without receiving wages; it is therefore only unavoidable distress that can drive either the virtuous or the vicious to take refuge in the workhouse; and it is owing to the small number they have to provide for, that the extraordinary reduction of the poor rates is owing.

CAROLINE

But do not these new regulations drive many poor to beggary?

MRS. B.

The honest and industrious poor would sooner take

refuge in the workhouse than have recourse to such a degrading mode of obtaining a subsistence. It may enlarge the field for private charity to distressed families: but of all modes of bestowing charity that of indiscriminate alms is the most injudicious; it encourages both idleness and imposition, and gives the bread which should feed the industrious poor to the indolent and profligate. By affording a maintenance for beggars, it trains up people to that wretched means of subsistence as regularly as men are brought up to any respectable branch of industry. This is more especially notorious in Catholic countries, where alms-giving is universally considered as a religious duty; and particularly in those towns in which richly-endowed convents and religious establishments dispense large and indiscriminate donations.

Townsend, in his Travels in Spain, tells us, that "The Archbishop of Grenada once had the curiosity to count the number of beggars to whom he daily distributes bread at his doors. He found the men 2000, the women 3024, but at another time the *women* were 4000.

"Leon, destitute of commerce, is supported by the church. Beggars abound in every street, all fed by the convents and at the bishop's palace. Here they get their breakfast, there they dine. Beside food at St. Marca's, they receive every other day, the men a farthing, the women and children half as much. On this provision they live, they marry, and they perpetuate a miserable race. Were it possible to banish poverty and wretchedness by any other means than by industry and unremitted application, benevolence might safely be permitted to stretch forth the hand, and without distinction, to clothe

the naked, feed the hungry, give drink to the thirsty, " and furnish habitations to the desolate. But the misfortune is, that undistinguished benevolence offers a premium to indolence, prodigality, and "vice."

CAROLINE

All this is very true: but you must allow that it is extremely painful to pass, so frequently as we do, objects of distress in the streets, without affording them some trifling assistance.

MRS. B.

I cannot blame any one for indulging feelings of humanity: to pity and relieve the sufferings of our fellow-creatures is one of the first lessons which nature teaches us; but our actions should be regulated by good sense, not blindly directed by undistinguishing compassion. We should certainly consider it as a duty to ascertain whether the object whom we relieve is in real want, and we should proportion our charity, not only to his distress, but also to his merits. We ought to do much more for an industrious family, whom unforeseen or unavoidable accidents have reduced to poverty, than for one who has brought on distress through want of a well-regulated conduct. When we relieve objects of the latter description, it would be well at the same time to bestow a trifling reward on some individual among the labouring classes of the neighbourhood distinguished for his industry and good conduct. This would counteract the pernicious effect which cannot fail to be produced by assisting the indolent, whilst we suffer the industrious to remain without reward.

CAROLINE

But the advantages and comforts derived from industry constitute its natural recompense, and it seems to require no other reward.

Nor would it, if a similar result could not be obtained without effort; but when a hard-working labourer ob-serves that the family of his idle neighbour is as well provided for as his own—that the hand of charity supplies them with what he earns by the sweat of his brow—such reflections are apt to produce discontent, and tend to check his industry. While, therefore, we tacitly encourage idleness by relieving the distress it produces, we at the same time discourage that laborious industry which passes unnoticed. The value of pecuniary rewards is increased by their being bestowed as marks of approbation; so far from exciting a sense of humiliating dependence, they produce a feeling of a very opposite nature, which raises and improves the character—a consciousness of merit seen and approved by those to whom the poor look up. Such sentiments soften whilst they invigorate the labours of the industrious. Thus if help for the distressed and rewards for the meritorious poor were to go hand in hand, the one would do as much towards the prevention of poverty as the other towards relieving it.

CAROLINE

I had an opportunity last summer of witnessing a mode of improving the condition of the labouring poor, in which the system of rewards is introduced with the happiest effect. An extensive piece of ground has been laid out in gardens by a great landed proprietor in Hertfordshire, for such of his labourers as have none attached to their cottages. He lets the ground to them at the low rate of sixpence a year each. These gardens are sufficiently large to provide an ample supply of common vegetables for the labourer's family, and to employ his leisure hours in its cultivation; but not so extensive as to tempt him to withdraw his attention from his daily labour, and render the produce an article of sale. As a further means of exciting industry, the proprietor annually distributes three prizes as rewards to those whose gardens are found to be in the highest state of cultivation. This judicious mode of rewarding industry has been beneficial also in producing a spirit of emulation amongst the rival gardeners, whose grounds being separated only by paths, the comparative state of each is easily determined.

MRS. B.

This is indeed an excellent plan; the leisure hours which the labourers might probably have passed at the alehouse are occupied in raising an additional stock of wholesome food, and the money which would have been spent in drinking is saved for a better purpose—it may form perhaps the beginning of a capital, and in process of time secure a little independence for himself and his family.

CONVERSATION XI

ON VALUE AND PRICE

OF THE VALUE OF COMMODITIES.—OF THE DISTINCTION BE-
TWEEN EXCHANGEABLE VALUE AND PRICE.—OF THE
CAUSE OP VALUE.—OF VALUE IN USE, AND VALUE IN EX-
CHANGE.—OF THE COST OP PRODUCTION, OR NATURAL
VALUE OF COMMODITIES.—OF THE COMPONENT PARTS OF
THE COST OF PRODUCTION, RENT, PROFIT, AND WAGES.—OF
THEIR IMPERFECTION AS A MEASURE OF VALUE.—OF 8UP-
PLY AND DEMAND. —OF THE COMPONENT PARTS OF THE
EXCHANGEABLE VALUE OP COMMODITIES—HIGH PRICE
OF COMMODITIES ARISING PROM SCARCITY.—LOW PRICE
ARISING PROM EXCESSIVE SUPPLY.—LOW PRICE ARISING
PROM DIMINUTION OF COST OF PRODUCTION.

MRS. B.

Before we proceed to consider more specifically the several modes in which capital may be employed in order to produce an income, it is necessary that you should understand what is meant by the value of commodities.

CAROLINE

That cannot be very difficult; it is one of the first things we learn.

MRS. B.

What is learnt at an age when the understanding is not yet welt developed is not always well learnt. What do you understand by the value of commodities?

CAROLINE

We call things valuable which cost a great deal of money; a diamond necklace, for instance, is very valuable.

MRS. B.

But if, instead of money, you gave, in exchange for the necklace, silk or cotton goods, tea, sugar, or any other commodity, would you not still call the necklace valuable?

CAROLINE

Certainly I should; for, supposing the necklace to be worth £1,000, it is immaterial whether I give £1,000 in money, or £1,000 worth of any thing else in exchange for it.

MRS. B.

The value of a commodity is therefore estimated by the quantity of other things *generally* for which it will exchange, and hence it is frequently called exchangeable value.

CAROLINE

Or, in other words, the *price* of a commodity.

MRS. B.

No; *price* does not admit of so extensive a signification. The price of a commodity is its exchangeable value, estimated in *money only*. This is a distinction you should remember.

CAROLINE

But what is it that renders a commodity valuable? I always thought that its price was the cause of its value; but I begin to perceive that I was mistaken; for things are valuable independently of money; it is their real intrinsic value which induces people to give money for them.

MRS. B.

Certainly; money cannot impart value to commodities; it is merely the scale by which their value is measured; as a yard measures a piece of cloth.

CAROLINE

I think the value of things must consist in their utility, for we commonly value a commodity according to the use we can make of it. Food, clothing, houses, carriages, furniture, have all their several uses.

MRS. B.

That is true; yet there are some things of the most general and important utility, such, for instance, as light, air, and water, which, however indispensable to our welfare, have no exchangeable value; we give nothing for them, nor can any thing be obtained in exchange for them. Utility, therefore, though it constitutes one of the component parts of value in exchange, does not in all cases produce it.

CAROLINE

It is true, no one will give any thing for what is so plentiful, and so readily obtained that every one may hare as much as he requires, without making any sacrifice. I recollect now your saying that objects must be limited in supply in order to have value, and yet, Mrs. B., such things as light, air, and water, which are essential even to our existence, surely ought to be esteemed valuable.

MRS. B.

No doubt they are, but it is in a point of view different from that of exchangeable value. Dr. Adam Smith distinguishes two kinds of value; the one arising from utility, the other from what can be obtained in exchange. He says, "The word *value*, it is to be observed, has two different meanings; it sometimes expresses the utility of some particular object, and sometimes the power of purchasing other goods which the possession of that object conveys. The one may be called *value in use*, the other *value* in exchange. The things which have the greatest value in use have frequently little or no value in exchange; and, on the contrary, those that have the greatest value in exchange, have frequently little or no value in use. Nothing is more useful than water, but it will purchase scarce any thing; scarce any thing can be had in exchange for it. A diamond, on the contrary, has scarce any value in use, but a very great quantity of other goods may frequently be had in exchange for it."

Nature works for us gratuitously; and when the supplies us with articles in such abundance, that no labour is required to procure them, those articles, however useful they may be, have not exchangeable value; but when the labour of man becomes necessary to procure us the enjoyment of any commodity, he must be remunerated, and that commodity acquires a value; either a price is paid for it in money, or other things are given in exchange for it Light, air, and water are the free and bountiful gifts of nature, but if a man constructs a lamp, we must pay for the light it diffuses; if we are indebted to his labours for a ventilator, or even a fan, we pay for the air they procure us; and when water is conveyed through pipes into our houses, raised by pumps, or brought to us in any manner by the art of man, a price is paid for it

Utility may therefore be considered as the sole cause *of value in use*, whilst *value in exchange* may be produced by any circumstance which renders the possession of an object so difficult of attainment, and at the same time so desirable, that men are willing to give something in exchange for it. Thus not only utility, but beauty, curiosity, fashion, rarity, and many other qualities, may create exchangeable value; and it is to this value that, in political economy, we confine our attention.

CAROLINE

There are many articles of luxury which are perfectly devoid of utility; such, for instance, as pictures, jewels, artificial flowers, and other ornaments; these are valued either for their beauty, their curiosity, or their rarity.

But, Mrs. B., if an object is valuable in proportion as we are desirous to obtain it, its value will vary with respect to different persons to whom its possession may be more or less desirable. Thus, medicine to the sick, and food to the hungry, will be more valuable than to the healthy and well fed.

MRS. B.

The value of a commodity is not estimated by the sacrifice which those in the most urgent want would make rather than be deprived of it; but by what is requisite to be given in exchange, in order to obtain it. The apothecary knows that if he endeavoured to take advantage of the sick man's necessity to raise the price of his medicine, it would be procured at another shop; and that instead of making an exorbitant profit he would lose a customer; and if the hungry man were attempted to be imposed upon in a similar manner, he would purchase food elsewhere: thus competition (under ordinary circumstances) prevents undue advantage being taken of the wants of individuals.

CAROLINE

What is it, then, which regulates the exchangeable value of commodities? you have said that it was estimated by the quantity of things given in exchange for them, but I wish to know what it is that determines the specific quantity to be given?

MRS. B.

It is fundamentally regulated by the cost of production of the commodity; that is to say, the expense laid out upon it in order to bring it to a saleable state, A great deal of labour has been bestowed upon that book case; if the workmen who made it were not repaid, they would no longer make book-cases, but seek some more profitable employment. The price of a commodity, therefore, must be sufficient to defray the cost of production.

CAROLINE

But, Mrs. B., the money which this book-case cost does not all go to the workmen who made it; the materials of which it is made must be paid for; the upholsterer who sold it derives a profit from it

MRS. B.

It was his capital which purchased the raw materials, which furnished the tools, and set the journeymen to work; without this aid the book-case could not have been made. The price of commodities is the reward, not only of those who prepared or fabricated them but also of every productive labourer who has been employed in bringing them to a saleable state, for each of these concurred in giving value to the commodity.

We have formerly observed that no work can be undertaken without the use of capital, as well to maintain the labourer as to supply him with the implements to work with, and the materials to work upon. Subsisting upon this maintenance, and working with these implements, he is to transform the useless trunk of a tree into a useful or beautiful piece of furniture, which acquires value in proportion as it becomes an object of desire. The profit of capital is, therefore, a component part of the value of a commodity, as well as the wages of labour. There remains yet a third component part of the value of a commodity, which a little reflection will, I think enable you to discover.

CAROLINE

Agricultural produce must, besides the wages of labour, and profit of capital, pay the rent of the land on which it is raised. But this will not be the case with manufactured goods.

MRS. B.

The raw materials for manufactures are all, or almost all, the produce of land, and consequently must defray the expense of rent, the same as corn or hay.

Let us now observe how the value of a commodity resolves itself into these three component parts. Take, for instance, a load of hay; its price pays first, the wages of the labourer who cut down the grass and made it into hay; then the profits of the farmer who sells it; and, lastly, the rent of the field in which in grew. This, therefore, constitutes the whole cost of production of the load of hay, and may be called its *natural value.*

CAROLINE

Pray let me try whether I could trace the various payments made to the several persons concerned in the production of a loaf of bread.—Its price must first pay the wages of the journeyman baker who made it; then the profits of capital of the master-baker who sells it; next the wages of the miller who ground the corn, and the profits of the master who employs him; afterwards the wages of the several husbandmen who cultivated the field of corn; the profits of the farmer; and, lastly, a portion of the rent of his farm.

MRS. B.

Exactly so. All this may be summed up in *rent, profit,* and *wages,* the rent of the proprietor of the land, the profits of the several employers of capital, and the wages of the various labourers who give it qualities which render it an object of desire, and consequently a saleable commodity.

CAROLINE

And are these three component parts of the natural value of a commodity always essential to its production?

MRS. B.

No; for if corn or any other produce be raised on

hand of too poor a quality to afford rent, rent cannot form a component part of its value.

CAROLINE

Or if the owner of a field or garden cultivate it himself, he pays neither rent nor wages.

MRS. B.

True; but then his profits are proportionably greater, and one portion of them should be considered as rent, and another as wages; therefore, though the landlord cannot literally pay rent or wages to himself, both rent and wages must be considered as component parts of the value of the produce.

It sometimes happens that the proprietor of land, the farmer, and even the labourer, are united in one individual. We have already observed, that in many countries of Europe, and more especially in America, the cultivators of the land are frequently both proprietors and labourers, and reap the reward of rent, profit, and wages.

CAROLINE

And in this country a cottager who possesses a little garden cultivated by his own hands, and of which he brings the produce to market, likewise concentrates in himself all the advantages of proprietor, capitalist, and labourer; for he sells his vegetables for the same price as a market-gardener, who has to deduct from the price the rent of the garden and the wages of the labourer.

MRS. B.

But he is not, therefore, the greater gainer, for

if he has no rent to pay, it is because he has laid out a capital in the purchase of the land; and if he pays no wages, it is because he works himself, and employs that labour which might otherwise bring him wages; then some capital is used to purchase garden-tools, manure, or whatever may be requisite for the culture of his garden.

CAROLINE

I think I now understand perfectly well how rent, profit, and wages enter into the value of commodities. I may say, for instance, so much rent, profit, and wages has been expended in the production of this carpet, and therefore I must pay a sum of money for it, if I wish to purchase it; but how am I thence to infer what sum of money it is worth?

MRS. B.

By applying the same scale or measure to estimate the value of money that you have applied to estimate the value of the carpet. Examine what quantity of rent, profit, and wages was bestowed upon the production of the money, and you will be able to ascertain how much of it should be given in exchange for the carpet, or, in other words, what the carpet is worth in money. I paid 20 guineas for this carpet; I conclude therefore that the cost of production of the carpet is equal to the cost of production of 20 guineas.

CAROLINE

But it would be impossible to calculate with any degree of accuracy the quantity of rent, profit, and wages which a commodity cost, and still less that of the gold or silver for which, it is sold.

MRS. B.

Nor is it necessary to enter into this calculation; it is by long experience only that the world forms an estimation of the relative value of different commodities) sufficiently accurate for the purposes of exchange. The calculations to which we have been alluding, though true in principle, are by no means susceptible of being brought into practical use.

CAROLINE

Yet when barter was first introduced, one savage might say to another, " It is not just to offer me a hare, which is the produce of a day's hunting, in exchange for a bow which I have spent three days in making; I will not part with it unless you give me also the fruit which you gathered in the woods yesterday, and the fish you caught the day before; in short, I will not exchange the produce of my toil and trouble for less than the produce of an equal share of your toil and trouble." And surely this is much more clear and simple reasoning than to say that the bow is worth so much money?

MRS. B.

To a savage unacquainted with money it certainly is; but I believe that in the present times people understand better the value of a commodity estimated in money.

CAROLINE

But if it were practicable to calculate with precision the quantity of rent, profit, and wages which had been expended on the production of commodities, that, I suppose, would constitute an accurate measure of their value.

MRS. B.

No; because there are other circumstances, which, as we shall presently observe, affect the value of commodities. Besides, it would be impossible to calculate with any degree of accuracy the cost of production of a commodity, since rent, profit, and wages are all liable to vary in their own value; and we cannot adopt, as a *fixed* standard, a measure which is itself subject to change. If we were to measure a piece of cloth by a yard measure, which lengthened at one season of the year and shortened at another, it would not enable us to ascertain the length of the piece of cloth. Now, rent varies much according to the situation of the land, and the nature of the soil; profit, according to the abundance or scarcity of capital: but nothing fluctuates more than the wages of labour; it differs not only in different countries, but even in the same town, according to the demand for labour, the strength, the skill, and the ingenuity of the labourer. A skilful artisan may not only do more work, but may do it in a superior manner, and he will require payment in the articles of his workmanship not only for the labour he has bestowed on them, but also for the pains he has taken, and the time he has spent in acquiring his skill; the wages of a superior workman are for this reason much higher than those of a common labourer. Since, therefore, neither the quantity nor the quality of the labour bestowed on a commodity can be determined by the number of days or hours employed in producing it, time is not a measure of the value of labour; we must take into account the degrees of skill and attention which the work may require, as also the healthy, pleasant or unpleasant, easy or severe nature of the employment, all of which are to be paid accordingly.

CAROLINE

Thus the bow which employed the savage during three days might be worth twice the labour of the other savage during the same period of time; for much less skill is required to be a huntsman than to be a fabricator of bows and arrows.

MRS. B.

On the other hand, we find that eight hours of the labour of a coal-heaver will be paid much higher than the same number of hours of a weaver's labour, because, although the latter requires more skill, the first is much more severe and unpleasant labour. But the weaver will receive greater wages than a farmer's labourer, because the work of the latter is both more healthy and requires less skill.

Now, since it is impossible to enter into a calculation of all the shades of these various difficulties, rent, profit, and labour can never form an accurate standard of value.

CAROLINE

They have at least enabled me to acquire a much more clear and precise idea of value than I had before.

MRS. B.

It has given you a clear idea of the cost of production of a commodity; but that which you have conceived of value is yet far from being complete; for there are, as I have just observed, other circumstances to be considered which materially influence value of commodities. In a besieged town, for instance, provisions have frequently risen to twenty or thirty times their natural value, and have increased proportionally in price.

CAROLINE

Their increased price in this case is owing merely to the scarcity, not to any increase of value, for were they as plentiful as usual they would sell at the usual price.

MRS. B.

Their high price is the consequence of their increased value, for they would not only sell for a greater sum of money, but also exchange for a greater quan-tity of any commodities, except such as are convertible into food.

CAROLINE

Unless perhaps it were gunpowder, or any kind of am-munition, which in a besieged town might be as much in request as food.

MRS. B.

Very true; in that case ammunition would rise in value as well as provisions.

Plenty and scarcity are, then, circumstances which consid-erably affect the value of commodities. Tell me whether you understand the meaning of the words, plenty and scarcity.

CAROLINE

Yes, surely; when there is a great quantity of any thing, it is said to be plentiful;—when very little, it is scarce.

MRS. B.

It there was very little corn in a desert island, should you say there was a scarcity of corn there?

CAROLINE

No; because as there would be no one to eat it, none would be wanted; and scarcity implies an insufficiency.

MRS. B.

And when a few years ago there was a scarcity of corn in this country, do you think that the whole of the island produced only a small quantity?

CAROLINE.

No; not positively a small quantity, but a smaller quantity than was required to supply the whole of the population of the country with bread.

MRS. B.

Plenty and scarcity are therefore relative terms: a scarcity neither implies a small quantity, nor plenty a large one; but the first indicates an insufficiency, or less than is wanted; the last as much, or perhaps more than is required. When there is plenty, the supply of the commodity being at least equal to the demand, every one who can pay the cost of its production will be able to purchase it. If, on the contrary, the commodity be scarce, some of these must go without it, and the apprehension of this privation produces competition amongst those who are desirous of buying the commodity, and this raises its value above the cost of production.

CAROLINE

This, then, is the cause of the rise in the price of provisions in a besieged town?

MRS. B

Yes; or during a famine, or in any case of scarcity.

Whenever, on the contrary, the supply exceeds the demand, the price will fall below the natural value of the commodity.

You see, therefore, that the *natural value,* or cost of production, and *exchangeable value,* do not always coincide.

CAROLINE

The exchangeable value appears to me to consist of the natural value, subject either to augmentation or diminution, in proportion as the commodity is scarce or plentiful   .

MRS. B.

True; and when a commodity is once brought to market, it is not the cost of production but the degree of plenty or scarcity which settles its price; or, in other words, it is the proportion of the supply to the demand which regulates the *market price.*

CAROLINE

That is very clear; if there are fewer chickens brought to market than are wanted, the supply being inadequate to the demand, the market price will rise; if more than are wanted, the demand exceeds the supply, and the market price will fall.

MRS. B.

There is some little difficulty in forming a detr conception of the meaning of the word *demand;* what do you understand by it?

CAROLINE

I understand that those who go to market to buy chickens, by offering a price make a demand for them, that if there are more persons wanting to buy chickens than there are chickens to be sold, the demand is greater than the supply; if the contrary, the supply is greater than the demand.

MRS. B.

So far you are right; but when chickens, in consequence of scarcity, rise considerably in price, will those who intended to purchase chickens, but who are not willing to give the advanced price, still make a demand for them?

CAROLINE

Why, no—it would be absurd to say that they demanded a thing at market for which they would not pay the market price; yet as they would have bought chickens had they been at a reasonable price, the offer they had previously made must have tended to raise the market price.

MRS. B.

No doubt; they formed part of the competition of bidders; but when once the market price is fixed, the demand of all those, who either will not or cannot pay it, ceases.

CAROLINE

Certainly; I may either not be able to afford to pay the market price, in which case I want the means to purchase; or finding chickens too dear, I may prefer buying butcher's meat; if so, I want the will to purchase; but in either case my demand ceases.

MRS. B.

What demand then remains? That of those alone

who have both the power and the will to pay the market price.

This, which has been distinguished by the name of *effective demand,* will exactly coincide with the supply. It cannot exceed it, else you would have the will and the power to purchase more chickens than there are to be sold; and it cannot be inferior to it, otherwise the competition of buyers and sellers would have fixed the market price lower, in order to have disposed of all the supply.

CAROLINE

But should the supply prove so abundant as to reduce the market price below the natural value; if chickens, for instance, should sell for only sixpence each; surely the owners, rather than dispose of them to such a disadvantage, would take them back, and run the chance of selling them better another day, or at a another market; and if the whole were not sold, it appears to me that the supply would exceed the demand.

MRS. B.

If a seller is not distressed for ready money, and if he think the market price likely to improve, he will very naturally withdraw his goods, rather than sell them under the usual profits. But he who withdraws his goods from sale no longer furnishes a supply, any more than he who will not pay the market price offers a demand. The withdrawing a commodity which is in excess prevents the market price from falling so low as it would otherwise do; but the market price being once settled, the supply and demand, you see, will coincide.

CAROLINE.

But this is not the case with the demand and supply which regulates the market price; for if these coincided, commodities would always sell for their natural value, and there would never be any fluctuation in the market price.

MRS. B.

You must, however, recollect, that it is the cost of production of a commodity which essentially constitutes its exchangeable value; the proportion of supply and demand should be considered as only accidentally affecting it.

CAROLINE

Yet, when once the commodity is brought to market, it is the proportion of the supply to the demand which alone regulates the price. It is in vain that the owner of the chickens should declare that they cost him so much to rear and fatten; if the supply exceed the demand, he must sell them for less, or not sell them at all.

MRS. B.

True; but at a future period the market will suffer an alteration, for a commodity which will not fetch its natural value will cease to be produced.

To illustrate this, let us suppose that, by the breaking out of a continental war, our foreign trade should meet with such obstructions, that great part of the manufactured goods we had prepared for exportation will remain at home and overstock the market; the supply in this case exceeding the demand, the goods will fell in price below their natural value, in order to attract a greater number of purchasers; the consumption will thus be increased, but the manufacturers and dealers, having been obliged to sell the goods for less than they cost to produce, will be losers instead of gainers by their industry.

CAROLINE

I have heard that calicoes and English muslins were much cheaper during the last war than they were when peace was restored; and the shopkeepers said that the price at which they sold them during the war did not pay for the workmanship, independently of the materials.

MRS. B.

Therefore the cheapness of these goods, although it arose from plenty, so far from being a sign of prosperity, entailed ruin on the manufacturers and their labourers.

CAROLINE

But you observed that if the price of a commodity would not defray all the expenses of production, it would not be made.

MRS. B.

In the case we have alluded to, the fall in price did not take place till after the production of the commodities; and the expense of labour having been already bestowed on them, it is better to sell them at any price than to lose entirely their value. But the manufacturers would in future take care to fabricate a smaller quantity, in consequence of which many of their labourers would be deprived of work, and part of their capital be thrown out of employ.

Plenty and cheapness are really advantageous only when they arise from a diminution of the cost of production. Thus when the use of any new machinery or other improvement in the process of labour enables farmers or manufacturers to produce commodities at less expense, the reduction of price is beneficial both to the producer and the consumer; to the former, because cheapness increases the number of purchasers; to the latter, because he obtains the commodity at less expense.

CAROLINE

But when nature gives us a superabundant supply of corn, the fall in price it occasions is not, I suppose, attended with disadvantage?

MRS. B.

If the supply should be so great as to produce a glut in the market, and that the farmer should be under the necessity of selling his crops below the cost of production, the low price is not a benefit; for the evil arising from the check given to industry surpasses the immediate advantage of cheapness of corn. The farmers and their labourers would be the first sufferers; but it is probable that, in the end, the whole community would feel the effects the following season.

CAROLINE

True: for farmers would grow cautious, and cultivate less wheat, in order that it might not sell below its natural value; and, whilst they would be endeavouring more accurately to proportion the supply to the demand, the season might chance to be less productive than usual, so as to occasion a scarcity of corn, which would be followed by a rise in the price of bread above the expense of its production.

MRS. B.

Very well. Tell me now whether the demand for bread is greatest when wheat is scarce or when it is plentiful?

CAROLINE

The demand which regulates the market price it greatest when wheat is scarce. The utmost price that purchasers can afford will then be given for it But the effective demand is greatest when it is plentiful; because then bread is cheap, and more people have the power to purchase it.

MRS. B.

Thus, you see, when the supply equals the demand, the commodity is sold for its natural value, the producer making just the usual rate of profit. If the supply exceed the demand, it is sold below that value, the competition of producers or dealers to dispose of their goods, lowering the price. If the supply is lew than the demand, the competition of purchasers raises the price of the commodity above its natural value, and the dealers make extraordinary profits.

CAROLINE

It must, then, be the interest of the farmer that com should sell above its natural value; and the interest of the people that it should sell below it?

MRS. B.

If we extend our views beyond the present moment, it will appear that the interest of the producer and consumer of any commodity are the same; and that it is for the advantage of both that the price and natural value should coincide. If the consumers pay less for a commodity than its cost of production, the producers will take care to diminish the quantity in future, in order that competition may raise the price; for they *could not,* without exposing themselves to ruin; continue to supply the public with a commodity which did tot repay them. If, on the other hand, the consumers my more for an article than its natural value, the profiteers will be encouraged by their great profits to increase the supply, and the price will consequently fall until it is reduced to the natural value.

CAROLINE

I do not understand why the producers of a commodity should increase the supply, if the consequence is to lessen their profits?

MRS. B.

We are arguing under the supposition that competition is free and open, and in that case, you know, capital will immediately flow towards any branch of industry that affords extraordinary profits. If, therefore, the original producers of the profitable commodity did not increase the supply, they would soon meet with competitors, which would compel them to lower their price without increasing their sale.

"Price," Mr. Buchanan observes, with great happiness of expression, " is the nicely poised balance with which nature weighs and distributes to her children their respective shares of her gifts, to prevent waste, and make them last out till reproduced."

CAROLINE

But when I consider labour as a measure of value, I do not clearly understand whether I should estimate the quantity of labour bestowed on the production of a commodity, or the quantity of labour it will exchange for at market?

MRS. B.

The latter, certainly; the former constitutes hi natural value, but the latter its exchangeable value or market price, which is undoubtedly the only accurate measure of the value of a commodity when it is sold.

CAROLINE

Certainly. My earrings cost me five guineas last year, and that I suppose was their natural value; but now, though scarcely the worse for wear, I doubt whether I could sell them for a guinea, because they are out of fashion, and yet the price they would now fetch must be their real exchangeable value.

MRS. B.

That is true of all commodities; but jewels, and other articles whose price is influenced by the caprice of fashion, may be said to bear a fancy price, which does not come strictly under our rules.

We have dwelt a long time upon the subject of value, and we may now conclude that though a fluctuation in the exchangeable value of commodities may be occasioned by various circumstances, it will seldom deviate much from the natural value, or cost of production, which is a variable quality, to which (when the employment of capital is left open) the exchangeable value will always tend to approximate.

CAROLINE

Value and wealth, I perceive, are far from being synonymous terms; for the increased value of food, in times of scarcity, indicates a diminution of wealth?

MRS. B.

Certainly. Wealth depends upon the abundance of

commodities possessed, no matter what their production cost, whether the result of manual labour or machinery, whether obtained by fair or fraudulent means. The Romans were wealthy by conquest; the Carthaginians, by industry. But wealth is more equally distributed when it results from machinery, which, on the one hand, augments the wealth of a country by facilitating the production of commodities, whilst, on the other hand, it reduces the price of those commodities by reducing the cost of production.

CONVERSATION XII

ON INCOME

MODES OF EMPLOYING CAPITAL TO PRODUCE INCOME.—WHICH
OF THESE IS MOST ADVANTAGEOUS. —VARIES ACCORDING
TO THE STATE OF THE COUNTRY—GARNIER'S OBSERVA-
TIONS ON THE EMPLOYMENT OF CAPITAL.—EQUALITY
OF PROFITS AFFORDS A CRITERION OF THE DUB DISTRI-
BUTION OF CAPITAL.—NATURAL ARRANGEMENT OF THE
DISTRIBUTION OF CAPITAL.—EQUALITY OF PROFITS IN
AGRICULTURE, MANUFACTURES, AND TRADE.—WHY
THOSE PROFITS APPEAR UNEQUAL.

MRS. B.

IN our last conversation we have in some measure di-
gressed from our subject; but I trust that you have not
forgotten all we have said upon the accumulation of
capital. Let us now proceed to examine more specifically
the various ways in which it may be employed in order
to produce a revenue or income. Capital may be invested :—

In Agriculture, Mines,
Fisheries,
Manufactures, and Trade.

CAROLINE

Of all these ways of employing capital, agriculture, no doubt, must be the most advantageous to the country, as it produces the first necessaries of life.

MRS. B.

In these northern climates it is almost as essential to our existence to be clothed and lodged as to be fed, and manufactures are, you know, requisite for these purposes.

CAROLINE

True; but then agriculture has also the advantage of furnishing the raw materials for manufactures; it is the earth which supplies the produce with which our clothes are made and our houses built.

MRS. B.

Yet without manufactures these materials would not be produced; it is the demand of the manufacturer for such articles which causes them to be raised by the farmer; agriculture and manufactures thus react on each other to their mutual advantage.

CAROLINE

No doubt; but still it does not appear to me that they can be equally beneficial to the country. Manufactures do not, like agriculture, actually increase the produce of the earth; they create nothing new, but merely put together under another form the materials with which they are supplied by agriculture.

MRS. B.

True; but by such operations they frequently increase the value of these materials an hundred fold.

The powers of man in processes of art are unquestionably inferior to those of nature, in the production of vegetation; for its operations consist not merely in a new system of chemical or mechanical combinations, but in the formation of organized bodies, endowed with the principles of life and of reproduction. You are mistaken, however, if you suppose that, in agriculture, any more than in manufactures, a single new particle of matter is created; it is merely by a new system of arrangements performed in that great laboratory of nature, the bosom of the earth, in a manner which eludes our observation, that the wonders of vegetation are developed.

CAROLINE

But in agriculture nature facilitates the labours of man; she seems to work together with the husbandman; and, provided that he but ploughs the field and sows the seed, she performs all the remainder of the task. It is nature that unfolds the germ, and raises up the plant out of the ground; it is nature that nourishes it with genial showers, and ripens it with sunbeams, leaving the farmer little more to do than to gather in the fruits of her labours.

How different is the case in manufactures! *There* man must perform the whole of the work himself; and, notwithstanding the aid he derives from his mechanical or chemical inventions, it is all the result of his own toil; whether it be the labour of the head or the hands, it is all art.

MRS. B.

We are accustomed to speak of art in opposition to nature, without considering that art itself is natural to man. It is erroneous to suppose that a savage is in a state of nature because his faculties are not developed, and that he remains nearly as ignorant as at his birth. The continuance of such a state is unnatural to a rational being. A state of nature in the human species is a course of progressive improvement. Man is a rational animal, endowed with the faculties of invention and contrivance, which give him a considerable degree of command over the powers of nature, and render them in a great measure subservient to his use. He studies the peculiar properties of bodies in order to turn them to his advantage; he observes that light bodies float on the surface of the water, and he builds himself a boat; he feels the strength of the wind, and he raises sails; he discovers the powers of the magnet, and he directs his course by it to the most distant shores; but the water which supports the vessel, the wind which wafts it on, and the magnet which guides it, are all natural agents compelled by the art of man to serve his purposes.

We cannot, therefore, say that it is in agriculture alone that nature lends us her assistance. The miller is as much indebted to nature for grinding his corn as the fanner is for raising it. In manufactures, her share of the labour is sometimes even more considerable than in agriculture. You may recollect our observing, that the effect of machinery in facilitating labour consists chiefly in availing ourselves of the powers of nature to perform the principal part of the work; and there are some chemical processes of art for which we seem almost wholly indebted to nature. In bleaching, it is the air and light which perform the entire process; in the preparation of fermented liquors, we are ignorant even of the means which nature employs to accomplish this wonderful operation. In short, it would be difficult to point out any species of labour in which nature did not perform a share of the task.

CAROLINE

That is very true; and it requires only a little reflection to discover how much we owe to her assistance in every work of art. We could not make a watch without the property of elasticity natural to steel, which enables us to construct a spring; nor could the spring be fabricated without the natural agency of fire, rendered subservient to art

But, Mrs. B., in agriculture we avail ourselves of machinery as well as of those secret operations of nature which produce vegetation.

MRS. B.

Undoubtedly we do; for every tool which facilitates manual labour is a machine; the spade and hoe, which save us the trouble of scratching up the earth with our hands—the plough and harrow, which still more facilitate the process—the flail, which prevents the necessity of rubbing out the corn—and the threshing-machine, which again diminishes the labour. Machinery is, however, not susceptible of being applied to rural occupations with the same degree of perfection as to the arts, because the processes of agriculture are extremely diversified, carried on over an extensive space, and dependent to a very considerable degree on the vicissitudes of the seasons, over which we have no control.

Agriculture, manufactures, and commerce, are all essential to the well-being of a country; and the question is not whether an exclusive preference should be given to any one of these branches of industry, but what are the proportions which they should bear to each other, in order to conduce most to the prosperity of the community.

CAROLINE

That is all I ask. I never imagined that every other interest should be sacrificed to that of agriculture; but I feel persuaded that, in this country at least, trade and manufactures meet with greater encouragement than the cultivation of the land.

MRS. B.

That is a point on which I cannot pretend to decide; and when you are a little better acquainted with the subject, you will be more aware of its difficulties.

CAROLINE

But surely political economists ought to know in what proportions the capital of a country should be distributed among these different branches of industry?

MRS. B.

It is not easily ascertained; because these proportions vary exceedingly in different countries, according to their local situation or peculiar circumstances. In America, for instance, or any new country in which land is cheap, population but thinly scattered, and capital scarce, the prevailing branch of industry will be agriculture; for in such countries, when a labourer accumulates a little money, which (where wages are so high) he is soon enabled to do, he is immediately tempted, by the cheapness of land, to lay it out in a farm; and though the wealth of the Americans is so rapidly increasing, they have hitherto found it more advantageous to import the greater part of their manufactured goods than to establish manufactures at home, a circumstance not so much to be ascribed to a deficiency of capital as to their having a more profitable use for it.

CAROLINE

And in England, where the population is abundant and land comparatively scarce, we must find it advantageous to take their corn in exchange for our manufactures.

MRS. B.

No doubt; if old countries were not to purchase elsewhere some part of the agricultural produce they consume, new countries would not raise more than they required for their own consumption, for want of a foreign market to dispose of it.

In this country, where land is dear, if a labourer make a little money, he never thinks of purchasing land; he cannot even afford to rent a farm; but he may set up a shop, or invest his capital in a manufacture.

There are other circumstances which affect the destination of capital; such as the local situation of a country: if it abound with rivers and sea-ports, as is the case with England, so great a facility for the disposal of its manufactures in foreign parts will render that branch peculiarly advantageous.

CAROLINE

So then if agriculture suits one country best, manufactures are more profitable to another, and thus they mutually accommodate each other?

MRS. B.

Exactly. If in England the proportion of capital

employed in manufactures be more than is requisite for our own use, it is because we find our advantage in supplying other countries with manufactures in exchange for their produce, and that advantage arises from our being able to import it cheaper than we could produce it at home. Agriculture thus leads to manufactures and trade, as youth leads to manhood; the progress of the former is the most rapid, the latter adds the vigour and stability of mature growth. Gar-nier, in his Introduction to his French edition of Adam Smith's Essay, remarks on this subject, that,—

"It is almost in every instance an idle refinement to distinguish between the labour of those employed in agriculture, and those employed in manufactures and commerce; for wealth is necessarily the result of both descriptions of labour, and consumption can no more take place independently of the one than of the other. It is by their simultaneous concurrence that any thing becomes consumable, and of course that it comes to constitute wealth. The materials of all wealth originate in the bosom of the earth, but it is only by the aid of labour that they can ever truly constitute wealth; it is industry and labour which modify, divide, and combine the various productions of the soil, so as to render them fit for consumption."

CAROLINE

But, Mrs. B., though political economists cannot specify the proportion of capital which should be employed in these several branches of industry, have they no means of judging whether it is actually distributed in that proportion which is most conducive to the welfare of a country? Men follow their own taste and inclination in the employment of their capital, and I fear the public benefit has very little weight in the scale.

MRS. B.

Fortunately, there is a better guide than mere inclination to regulate our choice in the employment of capital, and that is *interest*. Men are induced to invest their capital in those branches of industry which yield the greatest profits; and the greatest profits are afforded by those employments of which the country is the most in need.

CAROLINE

I do not exactly understand why there should be such a perfect coincidence between the wants of the public and the interest of the capitalist?

MRS. B.

The public are willing to give the highest price for things of which they stand in greatest need. Let us suppose there to be a deficiency of clothing for the people; the competition to obtain a portion of it raises the price of clothing, and increases the profits of the manufacturer of clothes. What will follow? Men who are making smaller profits by the cultivation of land will transfer some of their capital to the more advantageous employment of manufacturing clothes; in consequence of this more clothes will be made, the deficiency will no longer exist, the eager competition to purchase them will subside, they will fall in price and reduce the profits of the manufacturer to those of the agriculturist; or, should these profits fall still lower, the farmer will take back the capital he had placed in manufactures to restore it to agriculture.

CAROLINE

That is an excellent contrivance in theory to place the profits of different employments of capital upon a level; but it appears to me to be very difficult to bring into practice; for the change from one species of industry to another must be attended with great difficulties and expense.

MRS. B.

Your observation is so just, that these difficulties are often insurmountable. Such transfers of capital and industry take place only when one mode of employing capital becomes permanently more profitable than another, and even then it is a work of time and of suffering; for a man will bear many losses before he will be induced to encounter the difficulties and disadvantages of a total change of occupation.

CAROLINE

A total change of business must be very difficult indeed: the skill and experience acquired in one branch of industry might be quite useless in another; then the machinery of manufactures can no more be converted into implements of husbandry than the latter could be rendered serviceable to the manufacturer. I should suppose that a farmer could not transfer his capital to manufactures or trade, nor a manufacturer or merchant to agriculture, but under disadvantages almost insuperable.

MRS. B.

Very true; and fortunately this is not requisite in

order to restore the level of profits when its variations are slight or temporary.

In all rich countries there are many persons who live on the income produced by lending their money at interest, and there are few merchants or manufacturers who limit their dealings to the employment of their own capital, without having recourse to the loans of these monied men. When the profits of any particular branch of industry are found to be rising above the common level, those engaged in it are induced to borrow more in order to enlarge their dealings, whilst some other branch of industry which experiences a diminution of profit contracts its dealings and discontinues borrowing. Mr. Ricardo observes*, that "When the demand for silks increases and that for cloth diminishes, the clothier does not remove with his capital to the silk trade, but he dismisses some of his workmen, he discontinues his demand for the loan from bankers and monied men; while the case of the silk manufacturer is the reverse: he wishes to employ more workmen, and thus his motive for borrowing is increased: he borrows more, and thus capital is transferred from one employment to another, without the necessity of a manufacturer discontinuing his usual occupation."

CAROLINE

Then the profits of agriculture and manufactures will always be, or at least tend to be, upon a footing of equality?

MRS. B.

Yes; tend to bet that is a very proper qualification,

* Principles of Political Economy, p. 84

for these changes are not produced on a sudden. The tendency to equalization of profits takes place not only in agriculture and manufactures, but in every other branch of industry. In a country where capital is allowed to follow its natural course, it will always flow into that channel which affords the highest profits till all employments of capital are nearly upon the same level

CAROLINE

You say nearly,—why not exactly the same?

MRS. B.

Because, generally speaking, agricultural pursuits are more congenial to the tastes of the majority of mankind than manfactures or commerce: and hence, in countries where fertile land is to be obtained at an easy rate, a man no sooner acquires a little capital than he is desirous of purchasing land, and retiring even to remote and almost unpeopled districts where he can live as the lord of his little domain; as is the case in America at present Yet this preference will not lead beyond a certain limit; therefore it may be stated that the profits of different employments of capital are nearly upon a level.

CAROLINE

How admirably this is arranged! The more I learn of political economy, the more it appears to me, that the laws which control the operations of nature are generally productive of greater evil than good.

MRS. B.

That would frequently be the case, but *generally* is too comprehensive a term. Every law that is enacted infringes more or less upon the natural order of things; and yet I should not hesitate to say, that the worst system of laws is preferable to no government at all. Art, we have observed, is natural to man; it is the result of reason, and leads him onwards in the progressive path of improvement. Instead of being chained down like the brute creation by instinct, he is free to follow where inclination leads. But as soon as he enters into a state of society, he feels the necessity of a control which nature has not imposed, and his reason enables him to devise one. He enacts laws which are more or less conducive to his good, in proportion as his rational faculties are developed and cultivated. Many of these laws, no doubt, are inimical to his welfare; yet the balance upon the whole is in their favour; the single law of the institution of property has conferred greater benefit on mankind than all the evils which spring from the worst system of government.

CAROLINE

But this level—this equality of profits to which you say every branch of industry naturally tends, cannot yet have taken place in England, since manufactures and trade are here allowed to yield greater profits than agriculture.

MRS. B.

You are mistaken in that opinion. It is true that it is more common to see merchants and manufacturers accumulate large and rapid fortunes than farmers. They are a class who generally employ capital upon a more extensive scale, hence their riches make a greater show. Yet, in the long run, trade and manufactures do not yield greater profits than agriculture.

CAROLINE

I cannot understand why the merchant and manufacturer should grow richer than the farmer, unless they make larger profits.

MRS. B.

You must observe, that though a farmer does not so frequently and rapidly amass wealth as a merchant, neither is he so often ruined. The risks a man encounters in trade are much greater than in farming. The merchant is liable to severe losses arising from contingencies in trade which scarcely affect the fanner, such as war, changes of fashion, and bad debts; he must therefore have a chance of making proportionally greater profits.

CAROLINE

That is to say that the chances of gain must balance the chances of loss?

MRS. B.

Yes; the merchant plays for a larger stake. If therefore he be so skilful or so fortunate as to make more than his average share of gains, he will accumulate wealth with greater rapidity than a farmer; but should either a deficiency of talents or of fortunate circumstances occasion an uncommon share of losses, be may become a bankrupt.

CAROLINE

But, Mrs. B., you should, on the other hand, consider that the farmer is exposed to the risk attending the uncertainty of the seasons; a cause which is continually operating, and over which he has no control.

MRS. B.

Yet, in these climates, the losses occasioned by such causes are seldom attended with ruinous consequences; for seasons which prove unfavourable to one kind of produce are often advantageous to another. And, besides, the produce of agriculture consisting chiefly of the necessaries of life, the demand for it cannot well be diminished, and the price rises, not only in proportion to the scarcity but even higher; so that tanners are said sometimes to make the greatest gains in a bad harvest.

We may then conclude that though agriculture, manufactures, and trade, do upon the whole afford similar profits, these profits are, amongst farmers, more equally shared than amongst merchants and manufacturers; some of whom amass immense wealth, whilst others become bankrupts.

The rate of profit, therefore, upon any employment of capital is, generally speaking, proportioned to the risks with which it is attended; but if calculated during a sufficient period of time, and upon a sufficient number of instances, to afford an average, all these different modes of employing capital will be found to yield similar profits.

It is thus that the distribution of capital amongst the several branches of agriculture, manufactures, and trade, preserves a due equilibrium; which, though it may be accidentally disturbed, cannot, whilst allowed to pursue its natural course, be permanently deranged.

CAROLINE

If this is the case one ought never to wish to interfere with the natural distribution of capital.

MRS. B.

You must not, however, consider this general equality of profits as being fixed and invariable, even in countries where government does not interfere with the direction of capital; it is frequently deranged by a variety of disturbing causes. The invention of any new branch of industry, or the improvement of an old one, will raise the profits of capital invested in it; but no sooner is this discovered, than others, who have capital that can be diverted to the new employment, engage in this advantageous concern, and competition reduces the profits to their due proportion. The opening of a trade with a new country, or the breaking out of a war which impedes foreign commerce, will affect the profits of the merchant: but these accidents disturb the equal rate of profits as the winds disturb the sea; and when they cease, it returns to its natural level.

CAROLINE

So then, though profits have always a tendency to equalization, it seems there are as many disturbing causes to prevent their attaining it as there is with the sea; and even if they should succeed, the level cannot be permanent.

MRS. B.

That is true. To-morrow we shall examine how an income is derived from land.

CONVERSATION XIII

ON INCOME DERIVED FROM PROPERTY IN LAND

RENT THE EFFECT, NOT THE CAUSE, OF THE HIGH PRICE OF AG-
RICULTURAL PRODUCE—CAUSES OF RENT: 1. THE FERTIL-
ITY OF THE EARTH; 2. DIVERSITY OF SOIL AND SITUATION
REQUIRING DIFFERENT DEGREES OF EXPENSE TO RAISE
SIMILAR PRODUCE.—ORIGIN OF RENT. —RENT INCREASES
POSITIVELY IN A PROGRESSIVE COUNTRY, AND DIMINISHES
RELATIVELY. — HIGH PRICE OF RAW PRO-DUCE NECESSARY
TO PROPORTION THE DEMAND TO THE SUPPLY.

CAROLINE

I HAVE been reflecting much upon the subject of income,
Mrs. B.; but I cannot comprehend how farmers can afford
to pay their rent if they do not make more than the usual
profits of capital. I had imagined that they began by raising
greater produce from the same capital than merchants or
manufacturers, but that the deduction of their rent eventually reduced their profits below those of other branches of
industry.

MRS. B.

You were right in the first part of your conjecture;
but how did you account for the folly of farmers in
choosing a mode of employing their, capital which,

after payment of their rent, yielded them less than the usual rate of profit?

CAROLINE

I believe that I did not consider that point. I had some vague idea of the superior security of landed property; and then I thought they might be influenced by the pleasures of a country life.

MRS. B.

Vague ideas will not enable us to trace inferences with accuracy, and to guard against them we should avoid the use of vague and indeterminate expressions. For instance—when you speak of the security of landed property being advantageous to a farmer, you do not consider that, in the capacity of farmer, a man possesses no landed property; he *rents* his farm; if he *purchases* it, he is a landed proprietor as well as a farmer. It did not therefore the security of landed property which is beneficial to a fanner, but the security or small risk in the raising and disposing of his crops.

A farmer, when be reckons his profits, takes his rent into consideration; he calculates upon making so much by the produce of his farm as will enable him to pay his rent besides the usual profits of his capital; he must expect therefore to sell his crops so as to afford that profit, otherwise he would not engage in the concern. Fanners then really produce more by the cultivation of land than the usual rate of profit; but they are not greater gainers by it, because the surplus is paid to the landlord in the form of rent.

CAROLINE

So then they are obliged to sell their produce at a higher price than they would otherwise do, in order to pay their rent; and every poor labourer who eats bread contributes towards the maintenance of an idle landlord.

MRS. B.

You may spare your censure, for rent does not increase the price of the produce of land. It is because agricultural produce sells for more than it cost to produce that the farmer pays a rent. Rent is therefore the *effect* and not the *cause* of the high price of agricultural produce.

CAROLINE

That is very extraordinary! If landed proprietors exact a rent for their farms, how can farmers afford to pay it, unless they sell their crops at a higher price for that purpose?

MRS. B.

A landlord cannot exact what a tenant is not willing to give; the contract between them is voluntary on both sides. If the produce of the farm can be sold for such a price as will repay the farmer the usual rate of profit on the capital employed, and yet leave a surplus, farmers will be found who will willingly pay that surplus to the landlord for the use of his land.

CAROLINE

But, Mrs. B., if rent does not raise the price of commodities, how can you consider it as forming a component part of their value?

CAROLINE

That part of the value of commodities which goes to the landlord in the form of rent would, were there no rent, go to the cultivator in the form of profits; it is, therefore, immaterial under which head it is considered.

CAROLINE

But if the profits of agriculture are not the effect of rent, why are they not reduced by competition, and brought down to the usual rate of profit? Why does not additional capital flow into that channel, and, by increasing the supply of agricultural produce, reduce its price?

MRS. B.

Agriculture is not, like manufactures, susceptible of an unlimited augmentation of supply. If hats and shoes are scarce, and sell at extraordinary high prices, a greater number of men will set up in the hat and shoemaking business, and, by increasing the quantity of those commodities, reduce their price; but land being limited in extent, farmers cannot with equal facility increase the quantity of corn and cattle.

CAROLINE

It might, however, be done to a very considerable extent by improvements in husbandry, and bringing new lands into cultivation.

MRS. B.

True; but to whatever extent this were accomplished, it would not have the effect of permanently diminishing the price of those commodities which constitute the necessaries of life, because population would increase in the same proportion, and the additional quantity of subsistence would be required to maintain the additional number of people; so that (after allowing a short period for the increase of population) there would remain the same relative proportion between the supply and the demand of the necessaries of life, and, consequently, no permanent reduction of price would take place. The necessaries of life therefore differ in this respect from all other commodities. If hats or shoes increase in plenty, they fall in price; but the necessaries of life have the peculiar property of creating a demand hi proportion to the augmentation of the supply.

CAROLINE

So that the country no sooner produces the bread than it produces the mouths to eat it. But what is it that makes agricultural produce sell at so high a price as to afford a rent besides the usual rate of profit? If it is not rent that occasions this high price, there must be some other cause for it.

MRS. B.

There are several circumstances which concur to raise and maintain the price of agricultural produce above its cost of production, and enable the farmer to pay rent Its first source is what upon a superficial view would seem to have the effect of diminishing price; it is that invaluable quality with which Providence has blessed the earth, of bringing forth food in abundance; an abundance more than sufficient to maintain the people who cultivate it.

CAROLINE

But if the produce is more than can be consumed, why are there so many poor?

MRS.B.

I was speaking only of the consumption of the cultivators of the land; but there are other people to be fed, those who manufacture our clothes as well as those who raise our food.

CAROLINE

Oh yes, and those who live at their ease and do nothing; every one must eat.

MRS. B.

You understand then, that if those who occupy the land and raise the crops consumed the whole of them, there would be no surplus to sell to others; and under such circumstances it would be impossible that the cultivator of the soil should pay rent. But the natural fertility of the earth is such as to render almost all soils capable of yielding some surplus produce which, remains after the farmer has defrayed all the expenses of cultivation, including the profits of his capital. It is this surplus that he pays as rent. The quantity of this surplus produce varies extremely, according to the degree of fertility of the soil, and enables a farmer to pay a higher or a lower rent.

CAROLINE

But, Mrs. B., in countries newly settled, where the greatest choice of fertile land is to be had, and where we are told that the harvests are so productive, as in many parts of America, no rent is paid.

MRS. B.

Wherever land is so plentiful that it may be cultivated by any one who takes possession of it, no man will pay a rent But the cultivator, nevertheless, makes

such a surplus produce as would enable him to pay rent
The only difference is, that, instead of transferring it to a
landlord, he keeps the whole himself. This is the reason
that such rapid fortunes are made by new settlers, in a fine
climate and a fertile soil.

It is the fertility of the soil, then, which *enables* the cultivator to pay a rent; but we must look for another cause
which *induces* him to do so.

CAROLINE

Yon speak as if it were left to his option, Mrs. B.; and,
if that were the case, I do not think that rent would ever
be paid.

MRS. B.

We shall see presently how far you are right.—When
a newly-settled country, such as the bland in which we
established a colony, augments its capital and population,
the demand for food will increase, its price will rise, and
more land will be taken into cultivation; and when all the
most fertile neighbouring districts are occupied, soil of an
inferior quality, or less advantageously situated, will be
brought under tillage. Now, corn, or any agricultural produce, raised upon less fertile soils, will stand the former
in a greater expense; more labour, more manure, and more
attention will be required to raise a less abundant crop, and
the cost of its production will, upon the whole, be greater.

CAROLINE

The original settlers, who had the first choice of
the land, have then an advantage over the others; they
will make the greatest profits, and accumulate fortunes soonest. For the several crops, when brought to

market, if of the same quality, will sell for the same price, whatever difference there may have been in the cost of their production; nay, it is even likely that the crops which cost the least to the farmer may fetch the highest price; for the most fertile soil will, in all probability, yield the finest produce.

MRS. B.

The first settlers have also another advantage; they will have selected the most favourable situations as well as the most fruitful soil; their fields will flourish on the borders of a navigable river, or surround the town which they have built, affording them a resource both for a home and a foreign market; whilst those who cultivate land in more remote parts must add all the charges of conveyance to the market where the produce is sold, or the port from whence it is exported. Let us suppose that the first settlers make 30 per cent, whilst the latter make only 25 per cent, of their capital. With the double advantage of the most fertile soil, and free from rent, it is no wonder if the first settlers should rapidly amass large capitals. Under such circumstances, it is not improbable that at an advanced age they may be desirous of retiring from the fatigues of an active life, yet without wishing to sell their property; under these circumstances, what then do you think they would do?

CAROLINE

Oh, I know; they would let their land to farmers, who would pay them for the use of it; and that payment would be rent.

MRS. B.

You are quite right. In a colony, the landed proprietor who wished to retire from an active life would readily find new settlers, who, rather than undertake to cultivate remote districts, of perhaps a still inferior soil, would pay an annual sum for the use of their land, and become their tenants.

CAROLINE

Certainly; it would answer to the new-comers to give the 5 per cent, which the first settlers make above the others, in consequence of having the most eligible land.

MRS. B.

This then is the origin of *Rent.* If the tenant pay a rent of 5 per cent., which is equal to one sixth of what the proprietor made by cultivation, his profits will be reduced to 25 per cent, and will consequently be upon a level with those of the second settlers, who remain both proprietors and farmers; and thus the profits of agriculture are reduced from 30 to 25 per cent

CAROLINE

That is still very great profits?

MRS. B.

Yes; at such a rate accumulation will still proceed with rapidity; and as the country grows rich and populous, the demand for corn will increase, and fresh land will be taken into cultivation. The new land being either more remote, or of an inferior quality, will be cultivated under still greater disadvantages, and will not yield, let us suppose, above 20 per cent profits. As soon as this happens, the second settlers will be able to obtain a rent for their land. For it will be as advantageous to a farmer to pay a rent of 5 percent, for land, by the cultivation of which he makes 25 per cent, as to give nothing for the use of the land when he makes only 20 per cent, of his capital.

The profits of agricultural capital are thus again reduced from 25 to 20 per cent.

CAROLINE

But do not the farmers who first rented laud continue making 25 per cent, by cultivating it?

MRS. B.

Only as long as their leases last; for as soon as their landlords find that the profits of capital are reduced to 20 per cent, they will not allow their tenants to make more, but require all the surplus profits above that sum to be paid them in the form of rent. Thus every fresh portion of land that is taken into cultivation, either of inferior quality or less favourably situated, produces the double effect of creating additional rents on the land before cultivated, and of reducing the profits of capital.

CAROLINE

Then is it not evident that every increase of the rent of land raises the price of the produce of land?

MRS. B.

No; rent is not the *cause,* but the *consequence* of the increased price of the produce: your mistake, therefore, is, "putting the cart before the horse."

CAROLINE

Well this is very difficult!

MRS. B.

In order to make it clearer let us retrace our steps. Tell me, why are inferior soils taken into cultivation?

CAROLINE

Because more bread is wanted for an increasing population.

MRS. B.

And how is it known that more bread is wanted?

CAROLINE

Because it rises in price.

MRS. B.

Then, what will be done to increase the supply?

CAROLINE

Landlords and farmers will be induced by the high price to raise more corn.

MRS. B.

But if the best soils are already under cultivation they will be compelled to have recourse to those of an inferior quality, and the corn will be produced at a greater expense.

CAROLINE

True; but the high price of corn will repay the cultivator for this additional expense.

MRS. B.

You see then that the rise of price of bread first takes place from the insufficiency of supply, and that inferior soils are afterwards brought into cultivation in consequence of the high price.

CAROLINE

But, Mrs. B., if the high price of bread were owing to a deficiency, when an adequate supply has been produced to satisfy the wants of the people the price should fall to what it was originally?

MRS. B.

Then the farmer would no longer be remunerated for the expense he had incurred in raising corn on inferior soils.

CAROLINE

That is true; there must therefore be some cause which keeps up the price of corn, independently of that which first raised it.

MRS. B.

And cannot you guess what it is?

CAROLINE

I think it must be the increased cost of production of the corn raised on inferior soils.

MRS. B.

You are quite right. If the high price did not continue after the additional supply was raised, the farmers would be losers, and would not continue the cultivation of soils which brought them loss instead of profit.

CAROLINE

But supposing, as might very probably happen, that the farmer, instead of raising precisely the additional supply of corn wanted, was to raise more; what effect would that have on its price?

MRS. B.

It would fall till it came to that point which would just pay the increased cost of production; beyond that it cannot fall without serious injury to the community, as it would induce the farmer to diminish the supply.

CAROLINE

Then I suppose that if, on the other hand, the additional supply raised was not enough to satisfy the wants of the population, the price would rise?

MRS. B.

Undoubtedly, and occasion more inferior soils to be cultivated. You see, therefore, that in proportion as recourse is had to land of an inferior quality, to provide food for an increasing population, the difficulty and consequently the expense of producing it is increased, and no produce will be cultivated which will not sell for so much as its cost of production. Every new tract of inferior soil, therefore, brought under tillage, which raises rents and diminishes profits, will also raise the price of raw produce; for every quartern of corn, and loaf of bread, whether grown on the finest soils at the least cost of production, or yielded by land the most unfavourably circumstanced, will fetch the same price in the market.

CAROLINE

Of course no one who buys it inquires or cares on what soil it has been grown; they look only to its quality; but it is curious enough to think that of two similar loaves of bread brought on the table, the cost of production of one of them may perhaps been three or four times as much as that of the other; and that one may have paid three-pence, whilst the other has only paid a halfpenny towards the rent of the land on which it was raised.

MRS. B.

The price of corn and of all raw produce is then regulated by the expense of producing it on soils of the worst quality or the most disadvantageously situated, which are incapable of paying a rent. And rent we may define to be the surplus produce of those superior soils which remains after all the expenses of cultivation arc deducted; in all cases the profits of the farmer are to be included in the expenses of cultivation.

CAROLINE

Under the double disadvantage of paying increasing rents to the farmer, and increasing expense of culture to the farmer, I wonder that corn is not dearer.

MRS. B.

The more rent the corn has to pay the less is its cost of production, so that the one counterbalances the other; and when you come to the land last cultivated, which pays no rent, the whole of the additional expense goes to defray the cost of production.

CAROLINE

Then, in all thriving countries, where population is increasing, corn must be constantly growing dearer?

MRS. B.

Yes; and not only corn, but all produce of the soil whatever. This effect is, however, modified and counterbalanced by a variety of circumstances. If the productive powers of nature diminish as we proceed in the cultivation of inferior soils, those of art increase with the progress of wealth. Every year improvements are made in agriculture, which augment the produce without proportionally increasing the expenses of cultivation, and enable corn to be brought cheaper to market. Besides, though land of an inferior quality is at first cultivated at an additional expense, it improves by tillage, so that the cost of production gradually diminishes; and by draining, manuring, and other ameliorating processes of agriculture, an ungrateful soil is in the course of time not unfrequently rendered fertile. Disadvantages of situation are also remedied with the progress of society,—the neighbourhood increases in population, new towns are built, and new markets opened; if therefore it were not indispensably necessary to continue bringing fresh land into cultivation to provide for an ever-growing population, corn would be produced at less expense, and would fall instead of rising in price.

CAROLINE

But if all the surplus produce which remains after the expenses of production are deducted goes to the landlord in the form of rent, improvements in agriculture will not lower the price of raw produce, but will increase the rent.

MRS. B.

I beg your pardon: you have just observed that the price of raw produce, in general, is regulated by the expense of producing it on soils of the poorest quality, and the most disadvantageously situated; therefore, the more we diminish the expense of raising it on such soils, and the more we can remedy the disadvantages of situation, the lower we shall fix the standard" price of raw produce. The cost of production of a loaf of bread raised on land of the lowest description is now ten-pence; if by improvements in agricultural labour we could reduce it to eight-pence, bread in general would sell at that price.

CAROLINE

Since the profits of farming naturally diminish as inferior soils are taken into culture, I wonder that more capital is not taken from land and placed in manufactures, where no such diminution of profits takes place.

MRS. B.

That would infallibly be the case were the profits of agriculture and of manufactures not very nearly equal; for you must observe that the bringing inferior soils into cultivation produces a general diminution of profits, not only in agricultural, but in all employments of capital whatever.

CAROLINE

In order to equalize profits it must be so; but I do not understand how it takes place?

MRS. B.

By producing a general rise of wages. The wages of labour, we have observed, are always kept by the capital-ist as low as the circumstances of the country will admit. If then agricultural produce, which constitutes the chief necessaries of life, rises in price, from an increased cost of production, how are the labouring classes to subsist unless their wages rise also?

If the price of corn were enhanced in consequence of a bad harvest, the poor must necessarily submit to the evil of scarcity; we have already observed that in this case there is no resource: but such a calamity would be only of a temporary nature; whilst a rise in the price of corn occasioned by increased cost of production would be permanent. The capitalist who intends keeping up the same stock of labourers must therefore consent to raise the general rate of wages: and not only farmers, but all persons employing labourers will be under the same necessity; since labourers, of whatever description, pay more for their food.

CAROLINE.

But this rise of wages is not analogous to that occasioned by accumulation of capital?

MRS. B.

Oh no; it is far from being attended with the same happy consequences; for it neither increases the demand for labour, nor does it improve the condition of the labouring classes. If the labourer receive more wages from his employer, it is not because capital abounds, but because his maintenance is dearer— dearer on account of the increased expense of pro-ducing it.

In order to impress this on your memory, and avoid confusion, I will enumerate the several causes which occasion a rise of wages.

1st. Wages rise in consequence of accumulation of capital; labour is then well rewarded, the profits of capital are low, population increases, and the country is in a state of prosperity.

2dly. Wages rise in consequence of the increased

cost of production of agricultural produce; then, though profits are diminished, labour is not better paid; it is the produce of the soil which is deficient, and there is less to divide between the labourer and his employer.

3dly. Wages sometimes rise in consequence of dear-ness of provisions occasioned by scarcity, the effect of which (unless it produces an importation of foreign corn), is merely to increase the price of the necessaries of life, so that the labourer suffers equally from the scarcity whether his wages rise or not.

CAROLINE

Then do not wages as well as the price of corn rise previously to the cultivation of inferior soils?

MRS. B.

They do; but this rise is owing to the first cause I have mentioned,—accumulation of capital,—and takes place some time previous to the cultivation of inferior soils.

CAROLINE

But since capital consists of food, of clothing, in a word, of all that can supply the wants of man, if it is increased before new land is brought into cultivation, it seems to supersede the necessity of that measure. Is it not rather inconsistent to say, that because the augmenting population is supplied by an increased capital, it requires a still further addition to it?

MRS. B.

Capital does not consist solely of the necessaries of life, but includes also conveniences, comforts, and luxuries; capital may increase, therefore, without an augmentation of food. Mr. Ricardo has so clearly explained this, in his Treatise on Political Economy, that I cannot do better than to read you the passage;

"When a high price of corn is the effect of an increasing demand, it is always preceded by an increase of wages; for demand cannot increase without an increase of means in the people to pay for that which they desire. An accumulation of capital naturally produces an increased competition among the employers of labour, and a consequent rise in its price."

CAROLINE

That is the first of the three causes which produces a rise of wages; and I recollect that such was the case in our colony.

MRS. B. *reading.*

"The increased wages are not immediately expended on food, but are first made to contribute to the other enjoyments of the labourer. His improved condition, however, induces and enables him to marry, and then the demand for food for the support of his family naturally supersedes that of those other enjoyments on which his wages were temporarily expended. Corn rises, then, because the demand for it increases; because there are those in the society who have improved means of paying for it; and the profits of the fanner will be raised above the general level of profits till the requisite quantity of capital has been employed on its production. Whether, after the supply has taken place, corn shall again fall to its former price, or shall continue permanently higher, will depend on the quality of the land from which the increased quantity of corn has been supplied. If it be obtained from land of the same fertility as that *which* was last in cultivation, and with no greater cost of labour, the price will fall to its former state; if from poorer land, it will continue permanently higher."

CAROLINE

Since my last observation has proved just, I will venture to make another. The rise of wages in consequence of accumulation of capital should be followed by a diminution of profits; this, therefore, would also precede the cultivation of inferior soils.

MRS. B.

And it does so. But the diminution of profits arising from abundance of capital and consequent increase of wages is, like its cause, but temporary. It is soon followed by an increasing population and demand for food. The enhanced price of raw produce then repays the farmer the expense of high wages, and his profits are for a time even greater than those of other employments of capital.

CAROLINE

Then, will not also the landlord come upon him for rent, previously to the cultivation of inferior soils?

MRS. B.

No, not any more than he would for having had a remarkably productive crop, his extraordinary profits being only temporary. If, as we have already observed, the increased demand for corn is supplied by land of as good quality as that previously cultivated, corn will fall to its former price, just as cloth or linen would first rise in price by an increasing demand, and fall again when that demand was supplied. But if the additional supply of cloth or linen could only be produced at a greater expense than before, those commodities could not then fall to their former price. An additional supply of corn is almost always produced under this disadvantage, being raised on land of inferior quality: corn therefore will remain permanently higher priced; and it is not till then that the landlord comes upon the cultivator of the better soil for rent.

Increase of capital could never produce a permanent fall of profits; for as soon as population increased to correspond with the capital, labour would fall, and profits be restored to their former rate. It is only when the cost of production of food is increased that the rise of wages and diminution of profits is permanent.

CAROLINE

But, Mrs. B., is there any cultivated land in this country which can afford no rent? I know that gentlemen frequently farm their own estates, but it is with a view either to amusement or advantage, not because they could not obtain a rent for them.

MRS. B.

It is only the soil of the worst quality under cultivation that affords no rent; and England is so far advanced in wealth and population, and has brought such numerous gradations of soil successively into cultivation, that I do not suppose there are now any considerable tracts of land under tillage which afford no rent; but in countries that have made less progress, such as Poland, Russia, and America, we know this to be the case; and in this country, as there is yet land which is suffered to lie waste, because at the present price of corn it is not worth cultivating independently of rent, it is not natural to suppose that from such very poor land we should suddenly rise to that of so good a quality that it will yield both rent and profit; there must undoubtedly be some of an intermediate nature, which will afford the usual rate of profit to the cultivator, but will produce no rent.

The inclosure of commons may afford us an example of land of this quality; they are, I believe, usually granted in lots to the parishioners, free of cost, who cultivate it on their own account; but I do not think they could obtain a rent for it, unless they previously laid out capital upon it in fencing, ditching, draining, manuring, &c., which are part of the necessary expenses of cultivation, and which, if the proprietor undergoes for the tenant, he naturally requires to be repaid. For it must be understood, that by the rent of land I do not mean the total rent of a farm, comprehending a dwelling-house, barns, stables, and farming-stock of various descriptions, but simply the use of the re-productive powers of the land.

CAROLINE

Commons newly cultivated, in the course of time, will in their turn, I suppose, afford a rent?

MRS. B.

No doubt they will, when their soil is improved, or that an increase of population shall have forced soils of still inferior quality into cultivation. But I conceive that a considerable quantity of land, for which rent is actually paid, may be incapable of affording it. A farm generally consists of a variety of soils; one field may yield double or quadruple the produce that another will. On farms of poor land there are probably some fields that yield no rent at all; that is to say, if taken separately, their produce would not more than repay the expenses of cultivation, and give the usual rate of profit, whilst other fields may be of so superior a quality, as to afford a greater proportion of rent than is paid per acre for the farm; an average is therefore taken, and the farmer pays more rent for the worst, and less for the best, than they would afford. The total rent of the farm includes also the rent of the various buildings and improvements made on the premises. But there is another case in which rent is not paid; it is this:—Supposing a farmer pays £200 rent for the use of the land, and lays out a capital of £500 in its cultivation, making the usual profits of ten per cent; if he is frugal and prudent he will probably lay by money; and, reflecting how he can best tarn these savings to advantage, it occurs to him that by laying it out in improving his farm he shall raise either more or better crops, and that all the gains he makes this way will be independent of rent, for he will increase his profits without increasing his rent.

CAROLINE

That is very true; for the rent must be deducted from the £500 capital which he first employed on his farm, and no rent will be deducted from the sum last employed.

MRS. B.

Therefore every time a farmer is enabled to lay out more money on his farm, the profits arising from this sum are clear of rent; just as if it were employed in raising produce on land which paid no rent.

CAROLINE

It comes to the same, no doubt. But at the end of

the lease will not the landlord, seeing how well the farmer is off, increase his rent?

MRS. B.

That will depend on the amount of the profits the farmer derives from the employment of his additional capital. If it does not yield more than the usual rate of profit the farmer could not afford to pay rent upon it; and the landlord would not venture to demand it, lest the farmer should be induced to withdraw that portion of his capital from the land, and employ it more profitably elsewhere; for capital which yields only the usual rate of profit cannot afford to pay rent.

CAROLINE

No, certainly; for after deducting the rent he would make less than the usual rate of profit; and he would employ his spare capital in some other branch of industry.

MRS. B.

Very true; but should the fanner's profits on this additional capital exceed the usual rate of profit, the landlord will certainly call upon him for additional rent, because he can afford to pay it.

CAROLINE.

Yet that seems to me a hard case.

MRS. B.

You cannot expect that the landlord should supply the farmer with land, on which he employs his additional capital, without remuneration.

CAROLINE

He gives him no more land than he had before the employment of his savings.

MRS. B.

True; but the more he makes from that land the more he must pay for it.

CAROLINE

It must, however, discourage farmers from laying out their savings on the land.

MRS. B.

The landlord refrains from demanding additional rent so long as the lease lasts. During that period the farmer employs the money rent free, and that affords him sufficient encouragement to lay out his savings on the land.

CAROLINE

All this is perfectly clear; but I am not at all pleased to learn that as a country advances in the accumulation of wealth, *rent,* the portion of the idle landlord, augments, while *profits,* the portion of the industrious farmer, diminish.

MRS. B.

These idle landlords, of whom you complain, neither lower the profits of capital nor raise the price of agricultural produce. Both these effects result from the diversity of soils successively brought into cultivation. Were rents, therefore, to be abolished, the only effect produced would be to enable farmers to live like gentlemen, as they would be enriched by that share of the produce of their farms which before fell to the lot of the landlord.

CAROLINE

And would not that be a very desirable change? Is it not better that those who labour should grow rich, rather than those who live upon the fruits of the labours of others?

MRS. B.

The yeomanry are a class of men who cultivate their own property; and if you wish to encourage their industry, you must allow them to reap the full reward of their labours,—to accumulate wealth, and, when wealthy, to indulge in ease and repose, and to let their land to others, if they prefer this plan to that of cultivating it themselves. Were landed proprietors prohibited from letting their land when rich, they would nevertheless become idle, and would neglect the farming business; which being left to the care of servants, the cultivation would suffer, and the country, as well as the proprietor, be injured by the diminution of the produce. In civilised countries, landed property has been obtained by industry, or by wealth, the fruits of industry, and should be secured in its full value, not only to the individual who has earned it, but to his heirs for ever.

CAROLINE

But these wealthy men, who indulge in ease and repose, are no better members of society than the indolent savage.

MRS. B.

The love of ease, so commonly found among the rich and great, so far from being adverse to production or consumption, is quite the reverse; they are indolent, not like the savage, from a want of taste for enjoyment, but because their wealth enables them to obtain these enjoyments through the agency of others.

Besides, though it is true that rents rise as a country advances in prosperity, this rise is not in proportion to the increasing produce of the soil, owing to additional capital laid upon it Rent formerly used to bring in to the landlord one-third of the produce of his land; it has since fallen to one-fourth, and has lately been estimated as low as one-fifth; so that the landlord, whilst he receives a higher rent, has a smaller share of the whole produce.

CAROLINE

That is some consolation. But could no means be devised to abolish rents, and compel farmers to reduce in consequence the price of their produce, so that neither the landlord nor the farmer, but the public, should enjoy the benefit of the surplus produce which constitutes rent? Surely this would reduce the price of provisions, and of all agricultural produce.

MRS. B.

Since the price of raw produce is regulated by the expense of producing it on the poorest soils under cultivation, which can afford no rent, it could not fall in consequence of the abolition of rents. But supposing that it did so, what advantages would you expect to result from the reduction of prices so produced?

CAROLINE

If food were cheaper, people would be able to consume more, and the poor would have plenty.

MRS. B.

How so? would the land be more productive in consequence of the abolition of rent; and if more should not be produced, how could the people consume more? An increased consumption without an increased supply will, as we have remarked on a former occasion, lead to a famine. The price of a quartern loaf is now ten-pence; I conclude, therefore, that at that price the consumption of bread will be so proportioned to the quantity wanted that the stock of wheat will last till the next harvest. The adoption of your compulsory measures might reduce the price of a quartern loaf to seven-pence; and every poor family being thus enabled to increase their consumption of bread, the stock of wheat would not last out till the ensuing harvest. Then the following year, instead of raising more corn to make up the deficiency, the poorest land, which yields no rent, and but just affords the profits of capital at the present price of raw produce, would, by such a diminution of price, be thrown out of cultivation; and the produce of the country would thus be considerably diminished.

CAROLINE

Very true. I did not foresee that consequence. And a scarcity would perhaps raise the price of bread higher than it was before.

MRS. B.

How much would it be necessary for bread to rise in price in order to make the corn last till the next crops came in?

CAROLINE

To the price at which it now sells, ten-pence.

MRS. B.

We return then to the rent-price, though no rent is paid: you see, therefore, the fallacy of your proposed measures. The high price, of which you so bitterly complain, is the price necessary to proportion the consumption to the supply, so as to make it last till the ensuing harvest.

CAROLINE

So far from being mortified, Mrs. B., I am pleased with my disappointment, as it has been the means of convincing me that if the poor are obliged to pay a high price for the necessaries of life, it is for their own benefit as well as that of the mighty lords of the land; since it ensures them a uniform supply throughout the year.

MRS. B.

The labouring classes are besides in a great measure relieved from the burthen of high prices, as their wages rise in proportion; but observe, that this is the case only when high prices are occasioned by increased cost of production, not by scarcity.

CAROLINE

I the more willingly acquit rent of the accusation of creating high prices, since I see that there are two other sources from whence that evil may flow; the diversity of soil, and the necessity of proportioning the consumption to the supply.

MRS. B.

Since you acknowledge that high prices are necessary to prevent scarcity, you should, I think, no longer consider them as an evil.

An inquiry into the effects of human laws and institutions often discovers error; but whatever flows in the course of nature springs from a pure source, and the more accurately we examine it the more admiration we feel for its Author.

Thus, though rent cannot in itself be considered as

an evil, since we have traced its cause to the natural fertility of the earth and the diversity of soil, and have ascertained its effect to be to regulate the consumption of food to the supply, yet every artificial measure which tends to raise the price of agricultural produce, so as to enable the farmer to pay a higher rent, is certainly injurious; therefore restrictions on the free importation of corn, or any other species of raw produce, which raises the price of those articles at home, is taking an additional sum out of the pocket of the consumer to put into that of the landlord.

CAROLINE.

And have such restrictions immediately the effect of raising rents?

MRS. B.

No; not until the leases expire. During their continuance the farmer enjoys all the adventitious gains, or suffers all the losses that may occur; but when his lease is renewed, it must correspond with the rate of profit, and rise or fall in proportion to the gains which the farmer expects to make, so as to give the whole of the surplus produce to the landlord, and leave only the usual profits of capital to the farmer. It may happen, indeed, either from ignorance or carelessness, and sometimes from motives of humanity, that the landlord does not exact all that the farmer can afford to pay; but these are accidental circumstances, and the whole of the surplus produce constitutes the fair and usual rent. Rent may therefore be considered as a necessary tax which the consumer pays to the landlord; the farmer being merely the vehicle of conveyance from the one to the other.

This theory of the origin and progress of rent,

which I hope I have now explained to your satisfaction, was first developed by Mr. Malthus, and its consequences have since been more fully traced, and some important inferences deduced from it, by Mr. Ricardo, some passages of which I have read to you.

CAROLINE

I hope I have understood all you have said oo the subject; but I beg that you will allow me to recapitulate the principal heads, in order to see if I am not mistaken. In proportion as capital accumulates, the demand for labour increases, which raises wages, improves the condition of the poor, and enables them to rear a greater number of children; this increases the demand for subsistence, raises the price of corn temporarily, and induces the farmer to take more land into cultivation: if the new land be of inferior quality, the crops are produced at an increased expense, which raises the price of raw produce generally, and creates rent on superior soils. Corn, now become permanently dearer, causes a permanent rise of wages, and a corresponding fall of profits.

MRS. B.

Your recapitulation is very correct, and I am glad to find you have understood me so well; for the subject of rent having been more recently investigated than most other branches of political economy, it is neither so thoroughly developed nor so well understood.

CONVERSATION XIV

ON INCOME DERIVED FROM THE CULTIVATION OF LAND

TWO CAPITALS EMPLOYED ON LAND.—TWO REVENUES DE-
RIVED FROM IT.—OF THE CAPITAL AND PROFITS OF THE
FARMER.—OF THE DURATION AND TERMS OF LEASES.—OF
TITHES.—EXTRACT FROM PALEY.—OF PROPRIETORS
FARMING THEIR OWN ESTATES.—EXTRACT FROM TOWNS
END'S TRAVELS.—FARMS HELD IN ADMINISTRATION.—
ADVANTAGE OF AN OPULENT TENANTRY.—METAYER
SYSTEM OF FARMING.—SMALL LANDED PROPERTIES.—
EXTRACT FROM ARTHUR YOUNG'S TRAVELS.—DAIRY
ESTABLISHMENTS IN SWITZERLAND.—SMALL FARMS.—
SIZE OF FARMS IN BELGIUM AND TUSCANY.—OF MINES.—OF
FISHERIES.

CAROLINE

FROM the subject of our last conversation I have learnt that agriculture yields two distinct incomes: one to the proprietor, the other to the cultivator of the land.

MRS. B.

And it employs also two capitals to produce those incomes; the one to purchase, the other to culti-vate the land. A man who lays out money in the purchase of land becomes a landed proprietor, and obtains a revenue in the form of rent. He who lays out capital in the cultivation of land becomes a farmer, and obtains a revenue in the form of produce.

CAROLINE

I thought that the land was the capital from which the farmer derived his profits.

MRS. B.

You mistake: the land is the capital of its proprietor, and as such yields him an income; whatever the farmer obtains from it, is derived from cultivation; that is to say, from the labour and expense he bestows on the soil.

CAROLINE

But if he sells his crops for more than they cost him to produce, the profits he thus makes mil enable him to defray the expenses of cultivation.

MRS. B.

These profits, after paying the rent, will do little more than enable him to maintain his family; and how could he set to work the first year without some capital to carry on the expenses of the farm. A farmer requires capital to pay his labourers, and to purchase his farming-stock, such as cattle, wagons, ploughs, &c. In a word, the cultivation of land is to the farmer what the operation of machinery is to the manufacturer; it is the bare land and the farming build-ings which he rents. The crops which are upon the ground when the agreement is made are paid for independently, and become the property of the farmer. Unless therefore he has a capital to defray these expenses, he cannot take the lease of a farm.

CAROLINE

I always supposed that the produce of a farm was sufficient to defray its expenses; nor can I understand how profits are to be derived from a farm, if the cultivation and rent cost more than its produce will repay.

MRS. B.

It is not so. The capital of the farmer is employed as the means of cultivating his farm; and when at the end of the year, after paying his rent, his labourers, and keeping his stock in repair, he finds himself in possession, not only of his original capital but also of a surplus or profit, it is a proof that the farm produces more than the cost of its rent and cultivation. The case is similar in all employment of capital. The manufacturer who lays it out in the purchase of raw materials, and in paying the labour which is afterwards expended on them, or the merchant whose capital is employed in the purchase of goods for sale, could not carry on their respective occupations without first laying out their capital: but it is returned to them, together with the profits which have accrued by its employment. Each of these occupations bring in more than is laid out, but none of them could be carried on without a capital.

CAROLINE

Oh yes; I recollect the labourer produces for his employer more than he receives from him as wages, and this surplus is the source of bis master's profit; but if the farmer had not wherewithal to pay his labourer's wages, he could not set them to work.

MRS. B.

And you may recollect still more recently of our

talking of the profits which a former made on the capital he employed on his farm.

It is then upon this capital that he calculates his profits. Let us suppose that a farmer employs a capital of the value of £3000 on his farm: he may, possibly, after deducting the rent and the expenses of cultivation, make ten per cent or £300 profit.

CAROLINE

That is to say, that at the end of the year he would find himself £300 richer than he was before?

MRS. B.

Provided that he had spent none of his gains during the course of the year. But as his family are commonly maintained by the produce of the farm, he will at the end of the year be actually richer or poorer according to the proportion which his domestic expenses have borne to his gains. But these cannot be considered as a deduction from his profits, as the expense of the maintenance of his family must fall upon his revenue in whatever way it is obtained.

CAROLINE

And what is the usual rent paid for such a farm?

MRS. B.

It depends in a great measure upon the extent and condition of the land. A considerable farm, in a good state of cultivation, and possessing the advantage of a fertile soil, may not require a capital of more than £3000 to carry it on; whilst a farm of only half that extent, if in a bad condition, and with an ungrateful *toil, may* require as large a capital to be laid out on it. But a very different rent would be paid for these two farms.

CAROLINE

The large productive farm will naturally pay a higher rent than the smaller ill-conditioned one?

MRS. B.

And the difference of rent will equalize the profits which a farmer would derive from employing the same quantity of capital on each of these farms. Taking an average of the state of culture, a farm which requires £4000 capital may pay a rent of about £200, the share of the farmer being nearly double that of the landlord.

CAROLINE

You said, in our last conversation, that the rent of land had lately been estimated as low as one fifth of the produce. A farm such as you have described would therefore yield produce worth £1000, in which case the profits of the farmer would be above three times as great as those of the landlord.

MRS. B.

You forget that from the total or gross produce must be deducted, not only the rent but also the expenses of cultivation; these are generally estimated at one half of the produce, after deducting the rent; there will remain, therefore, £400, which is 10 per cent profit on the £4000 capital employed on the farm. If from this sum the farmer saves £50, he may lay it out in the improvement of his land, which will render the produce more plentiful the following year; an advantage of which be will derive the full benefit, as his rent will remain the same to the end of the lease.

CAROLINE

But, on granting a new lease, the proprietor, I suppose, would expect a higher rent for a farm which had been thus improved?

MRS. B.

No doubt; it is therefore desirable that land should not be let on short leases, because farmers would have no inducement to improve the condition of their land without the prospect of reaping the benefit of it for some years to come.

CAROLINE

But, towards the end of the lease, this objection would remain in force?

MRS. B.

True; and to prevent this, farmers generally obtain a renewal of their leases some time before they are elapsed. Besides, it would be contrary to the interest of the landlord to deal hardly with his tenants on such occasions, as it would discourage them from improving their farms; an advantage in which the landlord must eventually partake.

In Staffordshire, Nottinghamshire, and some other parts of the country, it is not customary to grant leases; the tenants hold their farms at the will of the landlord. There is, however, a sort of conventional agreement between the parties, that, except in cases of misconduct, the farmer shall not be removed, nor have his rent raised during a certain period. Some people are of opinion that this mode of letting land is preferable to granting a lease; because, they say, the industry of the farmer is stimulated both by hope and fear; the hope of profit from his labours, and the fear of being turned out should he neglect the improvement of his farm: but, in arguing thus, they do not consider that this fear must operate in two ways; for in proportion to the improvement which the farmer makes so is the temptation to the landlord, if he be needy or illiberal, to turn him out, or to exact an increase of rent. In short, there can be no greater check to industry than the insecurity of the profits it produces; and how can a farmer feel his interests secure whilst he is dependent on the will of his landlord?

CAROLINE

Besides, though a farmer may repose great confidence in the character of the individual whose land he holds, the uncertainty of life renders him dependent also upon his heir, and this may perhaps be some wild extravagant youth, who, without regard to his ultimate interest, will exact the highest rents from his tenants.

MRS. B.

Security is, no doubt, the most important point for the encouragement of industry; and the greatest, indeed the only encouragement which government can give to agriculture, is to secure to the farmer all the power over the soil that is necessary for its perfect cultivation, and to ensure to him the profits of every improvement he may make. I will read you a passage from Paley on this subject:—

"The principal expedient by which laws can promote the encouragement of agriculture, is to adjust the laws of property as nearly as possible by the following rules: 1st, To give to the occupier all the power over the soil which is necessary for its perfect cultivation: 2dly, To assign the whole profit of every improvement to the persons by whom it is carried on. Now it is indifferent to the public in whose hand this power of the land resides, if it be rightly used; it matters not to whom the land be longs if it be well cultivated.

"Agriculture is discouraged by every constitution of landed property which lets in those who have no concern in the improvement to a participation of the profit This objection is applicable to all such customs of manors as subject the proprietor, upon the death of the lord or tenant, or the alienation of the estate, to a fine apportioned to the improved value of the land. But of all institutions which are in this way adverse to cultivation and improvement, none is so noxious as that of tithes. When years perhaps of care and toil have matured an improvement, when the husbandman sees his new crops ripen to his industry, the moment he is ready to put his sickle to the grain, he finds himself compelled to divide his harvest with a stranger. Tithes are a tax not only upon industry, which feeds mankind, but upon that species of exertion which it is "the aim of all wise laws to cherish and promote."

CAROLINE

It is indeed much to be regretted that a provision for the clergy should not be raised in some other manner.

MRS. B.

Since all right of property is derived from legal institutions, the clergy have an equal right to their tithes as the landed proprietors to their estates; yet I believe that few of the clergy venture to levy tithes to the extent of their rights, for they cannot do it

without incurring the ill-will and opposition of their parishioners. The system must therefore certainly be defective
which appears to dispossess one man of the fruits of his
industry, whilst it will not allow another to take, without
exciting vexation and disturbance, that which the law has
assigned to him as his property.

CAROLINE

And this opposition of interests must be prejudicial both
to religion and morals, by creating an endless source of
contention between the clergy and their parishioners. But,
Mrs. B., since the price of raw produce is regulated by
the expense of producing it in soils of the worst quality
under cultivation, should not tithes be considered as a
part of that expense? The occupier is bound by the law
of the land to pay a tenth of the produce to the clergy, as
much as he is bound by the law of nature to sow the seed
for raising that produce: it appears to me, therefore, that
both should enter equally into the expenses of production; and if so, it is the purchaser or consumer, who, by
paying a higher price for agricultural produce, defrays the
expense of tithes.

MRS. B.

This point has been ably discussed by Mr. Ricardo; and
he proves, that if all the lands of a country were subject to
this tax, it would, as you observe, increase the price of raw
produce, and consequently be paid by the consumer; but in
a country like this, where a considerable part of the land is
tithe-free, and Scotland wholly so, the price of raw produce
is in a great degree regulated by the expense at which that
portion of it which is raised on tithe-free lands can be brought

to market: for the cultivators of these lands can afford to sell their produce cheaper than those whose lands are burdened with it.

CAROLINE

Then the price of raw produce in this country is regulated by the expenses of production on the worst soil free of tithe.

MRS. B.

Not altogether so. It is in some measure a question of proportion between the quantity of land which pays tithe and the quantity which is tithe-free.

CAROLINE

But so far as the price of raw produce is regulated by the expense of raising it on the worst soils under cultivation that are tithe-free, the burden of tithe falls on the cultivator of the other lands.

MRS. B.

If he is at the same time the proprietor it does; but if he only farms the land, he will give a higher rent for that which is free of tithe than for that which is charged with this tax. So far, therefore, as the price of raw produce is regulated by the expense of raising it on tithe-free lands, the burden of tithe on lands which are subjected to this tax falls on the landlord.

CAROLINE

Since it is so desirable for the cultivator to have unlimited power over the soil, I should have thought that it would have been particularly advantageous for landed proprietors to cultivate their own estates, instead of letting them to farmers; and yet it is a common observation that gentlemen make the least profits by agriculture. This is the more unaccountable, because being both landlord and farmer, the proprietor must receive the two incomes comprised in the produce of the land,—rent and profit.

MRS. B.

But recollect that he also employs two capitals, in order to make the two incomes; the one to purchase the land, the other to cultivate it. The reason why gentlemen who cultivate their own estates do not usually make profits equal to those of a common farmer, is either because they do not understand the business so well, or that they do not bestow the same care and attention upon it. The common farmer usually devotes the whole of his time to his farm, either in the capacity of bailiff or that of labourer; while the gentleman farmer never earns the wages of labour, and generally leaves the important office of bailiff to be performed by a substitute; therefore, were the gentleman to raise as plentiful crops as the farmer they would be produced at a more considerable expense, and his gains would be proportionally diminished. As to the value of the rent, it must be reckoned independently, as he receives it in his quality of landlord.

CAROLINE

It would then probably increase the agricultural produce of the country if gentlemen were always to let their land instead of farming it themselves.

MRS. B.

On the contrary, I believe it to be very desirable that some few gentlemen, in different parts of the

country, should cultivate their own estates. Being generally men of greater information than common farmers,
they are more willing to make experiments, and adopt
any new mode in the various agricultural processes which
may appear eligible. Besides, the land is frequently better
improved in the hands of the proprietor than in those of a
labouring farmer; as the proprietor has usually the advantage of a larger capital to lay out on his land, and then he
is not restrained by the apprehension that his rent will be
ultimately raised in proportion to the additional value which
be gives to the land.

Townsend, in his Travels in Spain, has made some
very judicious observations on English gentlemen
farmers.

"By residing," he says, "on their own estates, they not
only spend money among their tenants, which by its
circulation sets every thing in motion, and becomes productive of new wealth, but their amusement is to make
improvements. By planting, draining, and breaking up
lands which would have remained unprofitable, they
try new experiments, which their tenants could not afford, and which, if successful, are soon adopted by their
neighbours. They introduce the best breed of cattle, the
best implements of husbandry, and the best mode of agriculture; they excite emulation, they promote the mend-
ing of the roads, and secure good police in the villages
around them. Being present, they prevent their tenants
from being plundered by their stewards: they encourage
those who are sober, diligent, and skilful; and they get rid
of those who would impoverish their estates. Their farmers, too, finding a ready market for the produce of the soil,

become rich, increase their stock, and by their growing wealth make the land more productive than it was before."

CAROLINE

You have enumerated so many advantages on the opposite side of the question, that I begin to think that it would be more beneficial to the country that all landed proprietors should cultivate their own estates; for though they might not be great gainers by it themselves, yet the country would derive all the advantage from the improvement of the soil, and the introduction of scientific agriculture.

MRS. B.

A few gentlemen farmers in each county will be sufficient for the latter purpose. Were it common for proprietors to farm their own estates, I am convinced that it would be extremely injurious to agricultural produce; for no command of capital, no scientific knowledge, can, in a general point of view, compensate for the keen and vigilant eye of the industrious farmer, who sees that every thing is turned to the best account.

CAROLINE

I should suggest as a medium between these two modes, that a landed proprietor should neither farm his estate nor let it, but employ an agent to cultivate it for him, whose salary should be proportioned to the produce which he raises on the land.

MRS. B.

Such, I believe, was the species of tenure by which farms were held by the vassals of the nobles when they were first emancipated from slavery, and that military services were no longer, as in feudal times, considered as a sufficient remuneration for the occupancy of land. To give the cultivator any interest in the produce lie raises acts certainly as a spur to his industry; but it is one much less powerful than the security and independence of the leasehold-farmer, who, after paying a stipulated rent, enjoys the whole advantage of the efforts of his industry.

Townsend informs us, that most of the great estates in Spain are held in administration, that is, cultivated by agents or stewards for the account of the proprietor; and it is principally to this cause that he attributes the low state of agriculture. "No country," he observes, "can suffer more than Spain for want of a rich tenantry, and perhaps none in this respect can rival England. We find universally that wealth produces wealth; but then to produce it from the earth a due proportion of it must be in the pocket of the farmer. Many gentlemen among us, either for amusement, or with a view to gain, have given attention to agriculture, and have occupied much land; they have produced luxuriant crops, and have introduced good husbandry; but I apprehend few can boast of having made much profit, and most are ready to confess that they have suffered some loss. If, then, residing on their own estates, with all their attention, they are losers, how great would be the loss if in distant provinces they employed only stewards to plough, to sow, to sell, and to eat up the produce of their lands?"

There are, however, in warmer climates, some species of produce, which from their peculiar nature farmers would not venture to undertake to cultivate on their own account, and proprietors would be unwilling to trust entirely to their management. Such is the culture of the vine and the olive, plants which require the utmost care and attention during a number of years before they begin to yield any fruit; and farmers are seldom sufficiently opulent to engage in a species of husbandry the profits of which are so long protracted. On the other hand, as these plants may be very materially injured by being allowed to bear fruit either prematurely or too luxuriantly, and as the interest of the farmer looks rather to immediate than remote profits, it is not considered safe to trust such plantations entirely to his care. Vineyards and olive-grounds are therefore, I am informed, cultivated by the farmer in half account with the proprietor, who shares with him equally the expenses and the profits. This is called the *Métayer system* of cultivation: it was formerly very common on the continent for all kinds of produce, and still prevails in Italy, where the land is so extremely subdivided, that the Métayer farmers, frequently subsisting upon half the produce of not more than five or six acres of land, are seldom superior in condition to our peasantry. In France and Switzerland this system of farming is confined almost exclusively to the culture of the vine and the olive. But how requisite soever the system may be for particular plantations, the usual mode in this country of granting leases, I conceive to be, not only most advantageous to the farmer, but ultimately so to the landed proprietor, who can procure the highest rent for the land best cultivated; and it is also most beneficial to the country by yielding the greatest produce. But in Spain this mode could not be adopted for want of an affluent tenantry. The wealth of the country is chiefly engrossed by the nobles and clergy; there is a total deficiency of yeomen who cultivate their own land; and the middling classes are few in number, and so destitute of capital that they are incapable of taking a lease of land.

CAROLINE

I often wish that the property of land was more subdivided in this country. How delightful it would be to see every cottage surrounded by a few acres belonging to the cottager, which would enable him to keep a cow, a few pigs, and partly at least to support his family on the produce of his little farm. Do you recollect Goldsmith's lines?—

"A time there was, ere England's griefs began, When every rood of ground maintained its man:
But now, alas!
Along the lawn where scatter'd hamlets rose, Unwieldy wealth and cumb'rous pomp repose,
And every want to luxury allied."

MRS. B.

I shall point out to you a passage in Arthur Young's Travels in France, in which this question is discussed.

CAROLINE *reads.*

"I saw nothing respectable in small properties, except most unremitting industry. Indeed it is necessary to impress on the reader's mind that though the husbandry I met with in a great variety of instances was as bad as can well be conceived, yet the industry of the possessors was so conspicuous and meritorious that no commendations would be too great for it. It was sufficient to prove that property in land is the most active instigator to severe and incessant labour. And this truth, is of such force and extent that I know no way so sure of carrying tillage to a mountain-top as by permitting the adjoining villagers to acquire it in property; in fact we see that in the mountains of Languedoc they have conveyed earth in baskets on their backs to form a soil where nature has denied it."

MRS. B.

Land that is too poor to afford a rent, you will recollect, may still yield sufficiently to pay the proprietor for its cultivation; it is therefore the property of such soils alone which will ensure their being cultivated.—But go on.

CAROLINE *reads.*

"But great inconveniency arises in small properties from the universal division which takes place after the death of the proprietor. Thus I have seen some farms which originally consisted of 40 or 50 acres reduced to half an acre, with a family as much attached to it as if it were an hundred acres. The population flowing from this extreme division is often but the multiplication of wretchedness. Men increase beyond the demand of towns and manufactures, and the consequence is distress, and numbers dying of diseases arising from insufficient nourishment. Hence small properties much divided form the greatest source of misery that can be conceived.

"In England small properties are exceedingly rare; our labouring poor are justly emulous of being the proprietors of their cottages, and that scrap of land which forms the garden; but they seldom think of buying land enough to employ themselves. A man that has two or three hundred pounds with us does not buy a field, but stocks a farm. In every part of England in which I have been, there is no comparison between the case of a day-labourer and of a very little farmer: we have no people that fare so ill and work so hard as the latter. No labour is so wretchedly performed and so dear as that of hired hands accustomed to work for themselves; there is a disgust and listlessness that cannot escape an intelligent observer, and nothing but real distress will drive such little proprietors to work at all for others. Can any thing be apparently so absurd as a strong hearty man walking some miles and losing a day's work in order to sell a dozen of eggs or a chicken, the value of which would not be equal to the labour of conveying it, were the people usefully employed?"

CAROLINE

This reminds me of a poor woman in Savoy, who kept a few cows among the mountains two or three leagues distant from Geneva. Having no other market for her milk, she carried it regularly every day to that town for sale; thus the greater part of her time was spent on the road, whilst it might certainly have been much more profitably employed had she been dairy-maid to some considerable farmer, who, having milk enough to turn it to butter and cheese, could in that state send it wholesale to market.

MRS. B.

The inconvenience you allude to has been obviated in many of the villages of Switzerland, especially in the neighbourhood of Geneva, by the introduction of a peculiar species of public dairy establishments, which, I understand, originated in the plains of Lombardy. To these dairies, called *Fruiteries,* the farmers in the vicinity bring their daily stock of milk, which is converted into butter and cheese, and returned to them in that form, the establishment retaining only such a portion as is necessary to defray its expenses.

There are also considerable dairy establishments in the Swiss mountains, but these are commonly private property; the proprietor of the mountain-pasture usually hiring cows of the neighbouring farmers, who are commonly repaid in the manufactured produce of the dairy.

Small landed properties are extremely common in Switzerland; and I confess that the observations I have made during a long residence in that country have not led me to form the same conclusions as Arthur Young.

When a farm is insufficient for the maintenance of more than a single family, the law which enjoins an equal division of the property after the death of the father, among his children, is easily evaded; the children, instead of waiting for that event to parcel out the land into portions, which would be nearly without value from their minuteness, agree that one of the brothers shall succeed to the landed property, and pay to the other children an equivalent for their share; this is done either immediately on their coming to the inheritance, or by installments, as circumstances will admit In the mean time, those who have thus sold their birth-right learn some trade, or other mode of gaining a livelihood.

In the Canton of Berne it is usually the youngest son who remains at home with his father, and succeeds to the estate when it is too small to be divided.

There are also many districts in France, particularly in Burgundy, where farms of about ten acres are known to have existed to the same extent for above a century and a half;—the theorist, according to an apparently unanswerable calculation, would have reduced these farms to a few square yards during such a period of time; but human nature is very ingenious in devising methods for eluding or softening the effects of a law which has an unfavourable tendency.

CAROLINE

I heard a gentleman who is recently returned from France say, that three servants, whom he had hired at Marseilles, had all been men of landed property; but that the portion of inheritance to each had been so small that they had disposed of it to other members of their families, in order to gain a livelihood as servants.

MRS. B.

When this or any other cause prevents the extreme partition of landed property, the principal objections to small properties are removed; and the disadvantage arising from deficiency of capital may be in a great measure compensated by the stimulus given to the industry of a man who cultivates his own land. It appears to me that no means can be better calculated to develop the faculties of the peasantry, to inspire them with that foresight, and inculcate those prudential habits which we have observed to be so eminently essential to their welfare, than by their becoming possessors of a little landed property. This system is especially adapted to mountainous countries, where the strongest motives to industry are required to induce men to climb the steep rock in order to cultivate a small patch of earth favourably situated on its acclivity.

Neither can I agree with Arthur Young as to the disinclination of small proprietors to work for hire. In the Canton de Vaud, it is usual for the French-border peasantry, after having got in their own harvests, to descend the mountains of the Jura and assist in the labours of the Vaudois: there they meet the Savoyards, whose crops, situated in the elevated valleys of the Alps, are not yet ripe; all parties unite their labours, apparently in a most joyous manner, and I am inclined to think that the prospect of receiving a pecuniary reward gives them an additional stimulus. Those who usually work without pay feel a particular gratification in acquiring a little ready cash, and what they gain in this way goes to their clothing and a few little luxuries: —the shops at Geneva are thronged after harvest time, both with French and Savoyard peasants, who are laying out their earnings.

CAROLINE

I have heard that the condition of the lower agricultural classes in France has been very much improved by the sale of the national domains, at the commencement of the Revolution in that country; that it has enabled the small farmers and many of the peasantry to become landed proprietors, and thus to cultivate their own land; and that this subdivision of property has proved so beneficial, that, notwithstanding all the evils they have since had to contend with, they are yet in a very thriving condition.

MRS. B.

By the sale of the national domains very small proprietors, whose land was scarcely equal to the maintenance of their families, were enabled to enlarge their farms. The ill consequences arising from an extreme subdivision of land would thus be remedied. But we must recollect, that at the commencement of the French Revolution the restrictive and oppressive laws which checked the progress of every branch of industry were abolished; this gave vigour to agricultural pursuits. Then the sale of confiscated lands, at a period when its tenure was considered as extremely insecure, rendered them so cheap, that it was almost as easy to purchase an estate in France as in America, with the additional advantage of its being already in a state of cultivation. These circumstances all concurred to improve the condition of the small landed proprietors. With a view of amassing little capitals to lay out upon their new domains, they have acquired habits of industry and economy, and such habits are of themselves a treasure to a country. At the same time it must be admitted, that very serious disadvantages result from a great division of landed property, even though the extreme division we have alluded to should be avoided. The small landed proprietor is deficient both in capital and in education: he has not the means of laying out money in the improvement of his land; and his ignorance generally renders him averse to any new process of agriculture, even though it should not be attended with additional expense. His land is therefore cultivated in a very inferior manner; he is frequently obliged to sell his crops at an unprofitable period, and in seasons of distress he is nearly without resource.

CAROLINE

And are there the same objections to small leasehold farms?

MRS. B.

In a great measure. It is poverty alone which induces a man to take a very small farm; and a poor farmer cannot make those exertions which are requisite for good husbandry. The profits of a considerable farmer enable him to improve his land; those of a small one are entirely consumed in the maintenance of his family; his land is therefore badly cultivated, and he has little or no surplus produce to send to market.

CAROLINE

What sized farms do you suppose to be most beneficial to a country?

MRS. B.

That must vary extremely, according to the local situation, the nature of the climate and soil, and the capital of the farmer. In Belgium, which is esteemed one of the best cultivated countries in Europe, I am informed that the farms are upon an average about 40 acres; and in Tuscany, another spot remarkable for the excellence of its agriculture, the farms seldom exceed 10 or 15 acres, all cultivated upon the Métayer system; but in this favoured climate the fields yield such abundant crops that the produce approaches more nearly to that of a Belgic farm than you would imagine from the difference of their extent.

In this country there is, I think, a strong predilection in favour of considerable farms. Were I to give an opinion, I should say that a farm should never be so large that the farmer cannot superintend the whole of the cultivation himself; nor so small as not to enable him to keep up that farming stock establishment necessary for the best system of husbandry. But this is a point which may be safely left to regulate itself I do not apprehend that the country can suffer by the different size of farms; for there are very *few* small landed properties; and as it is the interest of the landlord to draw the greatest possible income from his estate, he will let his farms of such dimensions as he conceives his tenant will be able to turn to the best account. To a very opulent farmer he may be induced to grant a lease of a large farm; whilst he will refuse that of a single field to a cottager who would exhaust instead of improving the rent.

The advantages of considerable farms have been so ably delineated in one of the numbers of the Edinburgh Review that I shall read you the passage:—

"It is quite evident that some of the most valuable mechanical inventions could never have come into general use if there had been no farms of more than 100 or 150 acres; that no great improvement could have been made in our live stock; that there would have been still less room than there is at present for the division of labour, and for its accumulation for the purpose of dispatch at particular seasons; that there would not have been that systematic arrangement by which every different quality of soil is made to produce those crops, and to feed those sorts of animals for which it is best calculated; that it would have been almost impracticable to practise convertible husbandry at all, which, by combining tillage and pasturage on the same farm, contributes so powerfully to sustain and augment the fertility of the soil; that the surplus produce for the supply of towns would have been inconsiderable at all times, and from the general poverty of small tenants brought to market in too great abundance in the early part of the season, instead of apportioning it over the whole year; and in bad seasons there would have been no surplus at all:—and that, in short, as no person of capital or enterprise would ever have entered into the profession, our extensive moors and morasses, and indeed all our inferior soils, must have remained in their natural state, or been partially and most unprofitably improved under the delegated management of great proprietors."

It is now, I think, high time to conclude the subject of agriculture; and it is necessary to say only a few words on Mining, a branch of industry which I have placed next to agriculture, on account of its analogy to it in affording a rent.

Mines, like the surface of the earth, yielding different quantities of produce according to their respective degrees of richness, all those which are not of the poorest quality must afford a rent.

CAROLINE

The price of the metals, then, like that of corn, must be regulated by the expense of producing it from the last mines opened?

MRS. B.

Your observation applies with more correctness to the produce of the surface of the earth; the land last cultivated is generally the poorest, or labours under other disadvantages, which have prevented its being sooner brought under the plough; but mines being less open to observation, new mines are not unfrequently discovered which yield more metal than others previously worked. You should rather say, therefore, that the price of metal is regulated by the expense of extracting it from the poorest mines now worked.

The same laws apply to coal-pits, which, notwithstanding the great assistance derived from machinery, give work to several hundred thousand labourers who earn their maintenance, besides the profits of their employer and the rent of the proprietor; and this rent is in general more considerable than that of agricultural land, as the produce of coal-pits is more valuable than that of the soil.

CAROLINE

The mines containing metals are, I suppose, of still greater value?

MRS. B.

Yes, and their rent proportionally higher; but the profits of the capitalist who rents them, and of the labourers who work them, are not greater. As the value of a mine, however, depends upon the quantity as well as on the quality of the metal it affords, it frequently happens that a lead-mine will fetch a higher rent than a silver-mine. The expense of working coalpits is less than that of metallic mines. The coal requires nothing more than to be extracted from the earth; but with the metals the labour is much more complicated; they must be separated from the ore in the furnace, and undergo a variety of processes before they are fit for the purposes of art.

The risk and uncertainty attending mining is greater than that of any other employment of capital; and accordingly we find both larger fortunes made and more people ruined in that than in any other branch of industry.

CAROLINE

The chance of gain, then, compensates for the risk of loss; but upon the whole I suppose the profits are similar to those derived from other modes of employing capital?

MRS. B.

I am inclined to believe the profits of mining to be rather below the common standard. In all hazardous enterprises men are prone to trust to their good fortune, and generally consider the chances more in their favour than an accurate calculation would warrant. This is evinced by the readiness with which men venture to stake their money in lotteries, though it is well known that the chances of gain are decidedly against them. Mining speculations are more advantageous lotteries no doubt, but they contain a prodigious number of blanks, and only a few great prizes. Sanguine hopes and expectations in some measure supply the place of actual gains; yet if the average profits of mining should at any time fall so low as to discourage the spirit of enterprise, and diminish the requisite supply of metals, their price would rise until it had brought back a sufficient capital to that branch of industry.

I have mentioned fisheries as a source of employment for capital, and a means of affording an income. Very large capitals are engaged in the whale, the cod, and the herring fisheries, besides those smaller ones which supply the country with fresh fish. But as the sea in which these fisheries are carried on is not susceptible of becoming private property, they yield no rent. There are, however, some considerable inland river fisheries which belong to individuals, and bring in a rent. No fewer than forty-one different salmon fisheries upon the river Tweed are rented for several thousands a-year; and I am informed that the Duke of Gordon lets a salmon fishery on the Spey for

£7,000 a year. In the Scotch fisheries it is very common to take four or five score of salmon at a draught. In England there are also considerable salmon fisheries in the Tyne, the Trent, the Severn, and the Thames.

CAROLINE

The rent of fisheries depends, I suppose, upon some rivers abounding more with fish than others.

MRS. B.

Yes; all rent is derived from the same principle, the lesser quantity of labour required to produce the commodity in some situations than in others.

We have already noticed the manner in which an income is obtained from manufactures; what further observations we have to make on this branch of industry we shall defer till we enter on the subject of trade, with which it is so naturally connected.

CAROLINE

And will that be the subject of our next conversation?

MRS. B.

No; we have yet many general remarks to make upon income. And it will be necessary also, before we turn our attention to trade or commerce, that you should understand the nature and use of money, without a knowledge of which it would be extremely difficult to render the subject per-spicuous.

CONVERSATION XV

ON THE INCOME OF THOSE WHO DO NOT EMPLOY THEIR CAPITAL THEMSELVES

RENT, OR INCOME DERIVED FROM LETTING LAND.—INTEREST OF MONEY, OR INCOME DERIVED FROM LOANS.—CAUSES OF THE DIFFERENT RATE OF INTEREST YIELDED BY LAND OR BY MONEY.—CAUSES OF THE FLUCTUATIONS OF INTEREST.—RATE OF INTEREST IN INDIA, IN CHINA, AND IN AMERICA.—OF USURY.—GOVERNMENT LOANS, OR INCOME DERIVED FROM THE FUNDS.—OF UNPRODUCTIVE LABOURERS, OR THOSE WHO DERIVE AN INCOME FROM THE EXPENDITURE OF OTHERS.

CAROLINE

I THINK I now understand very well how an income is derived from agriculture and manufactures; and also how it is produced by trade; but there are many men of property who follow none of these occupations; how, therefore, can their capital yield an income?

MRS. B.

When a man possesses a very large property, he frequently will not be at the trouble of employing it himself; but will engage some other person to do it for him. You have seen that a landed proprietor who does not farm his own estate derives an income from the farmer in the form of rent.

CAROLINE

But I allude to men of fortune without landed property, who live upon their income, although their capital is not employed.

MRS. B.

Reflect a moment, and you will be convinced that no capital can yield an income without being employed. If, therefore, the owner does not invest it in some branch of industry himself, another person must do it for him. A capitalist under such circumstances may be supposed to say, " I am possessed of an ample stock of subsistence for labourers, and of materials for workmanship, but I will engage some other person to take charge of so troublesome an undertaking as that of setting the people to work, and collecting the profits derived from their labours."

CAROLINE

This person must be handsomely remunerated for the time and pains he bestows on the management of a capital which is not his own.

MRS. B.

No doubt; a considerable share of the profits derived from the use of capital must go to him who takes charge of it; but when a man's property is very large, he would rather lose that share than be at the trouble of managing it himself. Thus you see that the employer and the proprietor of capital are frequently different persons.

CAROLINE

Yet I do not recollect ever to have heard of a man of fortune making use of an agent to employ his capital.

MRS. B.

He does not engage an agent on his own account, but he lends his capital to some person who employs it on his own account by investing it either in agriculture, manufactures, or trade, and who pays him so much per cent, for the use of it. This is called lending money at interest.

CAROLINE

Is it then simply *money* that is lent; or *capital* consisting of produce?

MRS. B.

It is eventually the same; for money gives the borrower a command over a proportional share of the produce of the country. If the money would not purchase the things which the borrower wanted, it would not answer his purpose; but it will procure him either materials or implements for work, maintenance for labourers, stock for farming, or merchandise for trade; in a word, it will enable him to exert his industry in whatever way he chooses.

CAROLINE

I should have imagined that it would have been more advantageous to the capitalist to have engaged an agent at a stipulated salary, for the purpose of undertaking the use of his capital

MRS. B.

Your plan would probably not answer so well; for if, instead of lending his capital at interest, a, man of property paid an agent to employ it for him, the agent would be less cautious what risks he engaged in as he would not be a sufferer by losses.

CAROLINE

But is not the loan of capital at interest liable to the same objection? If the employer of capital be ruined, the proprietor of it must share the same fate.

MRS. B.

This is a misfortune that not unfrequently happens; yet there is less risk incurred in this mode than if the employer of capital could injure the proprietor without being himself involved in the same fate; and it would be so if he acted as clerk or agent, as he would lose only his salary, although the proprietor might be utterly ruined.

Prudent men seldom lend capital without good security. If the loan be made to a merchant, it is not unfrequent to require other merchants, or men of property, to become responsible for the payment. If to a man of landed property, the capital is lent upon the security of his estate; that is to say, if the loan be not repaid according to agreement, the lender has the right to seize that particular property, upon the security of which the capital was advanced. This is called lending money upon the security of mortgage.

CAROLINE

That must be the best kind of security, for the land cannot be made away with. It is making fixed capital responsible for circulating capital.

The man who borrows capital with a view to employ it, must necessarily expect to make greater profits than will pay the interest of the loan, otherwise he would be no gainer by it.

MRS. B.

Certainly. The average profits of the use of

capital may be estimated at about double the interest of money. Legal interest, that is to say, the highest rate which the law allows to be given, is five per cent and the usual profits of trade are about ten per cent.

CAROLINE

Therefore the lender and the borrower, or in other words the proprietor and employer of capital, commonly divide the profits arising from it equally between them: the one making as much by his property as the other by his industry.

The landed proprietor who lets his land to a farmer, I conceive to be situated in the same manner as the man who lends his capital at interest, neither of them choosing to undertake the employment of their capitals themselves, but procuring some other person to do it for them; and the rent the farmer pays for the use of the land is similar to the interest paid for the use of capital.

MRS. B.

It is so; and the advantages derived from letting land are analogous to those which result from the loan of capital. We have observed that if the farmer, instead of paying a rent, received a certain stipend for his labour, and reserved the whole of the produce for the landlord, he would certainly be less attentive to the cultivation of the land than if his gains resulted from the value of the produce raised.

There is, however, one essential difference between borrowing capital and renting land. The man who borrows capital to be employed in trade or manufactures, requires nothing more to enable him to prosecute his business; whilst the farmer who borrows land cannot undertake the cultivation of it without the assistance of another capital, which he must either possess or borrow for that purpose.

CAROLINE

Then there is another difference. The landed proprietor and the farmer do not divide the profits arising from the cultivation of the land equally between them, as is usually, you say, the case with the lender and borrower of capital; for the former makes greater profits by the use of the land than the proprietor by the rent.

MRS. B.

There are several reasons for this difference. In the first place, you must recollect that the profits of capital vary with the degrees of risk to which it is exposed; and then consider that an income derived from the rent of land is much more secure than any other kind of income. For if the farmer ruin himself, he cannot make away with the land: he may be obliged to quit his farm, but then his stock is liable to seizure for the payment of rent.

Another considerable advantage attached to landed property is, that in proportion as agriculture improves, the produce of the land increases; this augments the profits of the farmer, and enables the landlord to raise his rent. And lastly, we must call to mind the obser-vations we made on the origin of rent; and we shall find that in proportion as agriculture extends, and new and inferior lands are taken into cultivation, the rent of land rises. If you weigh all these advantages, you will no longer be surprised that a landed proprietor should be satisfied with making between three and four per cent, of his capital, instead of lending it at five per cent, interest with more or less risk of loss, and a certainty that the capital will not improve.

CAROLINE

The real profit, therefore, to be derived from the loan of capital perfectly secure, is between three and four per cent, and whatever is received above that sum may be considered as an indemnification for the risk to which it is exposed?

MRS. B.

If you take the improveable nature of rent, as well as its perfect security into the calculation, some deduction may be allowed in consideration of the certain prospect of future increase; the profit to be derived from the loan of capital, even when the security is perfect, may therefore be estimated somewhat higher than that which is afforded by the rent of land.

We must now make a few observations upon the interest of money.

The interest of money, or price paid for the loan of capital, was formerly much higher than it is at present. It has gradually diminished for some centuries past.

CAROLINE

And why should that be the case?

MRS. B.

Whenever great profits can be made by the employment of capital great interest will be given for the loan of it; when, on the contrary, but small profits can be made, the interest will be low.

Thus, as I have already pointed out to you, when a

nation advances in opulence and population, so as to render it requisite to take inferior soils into cultivation, the necessaries of life become dearer, the wages of labour rise, the profits on capital are low, and the interest of money will generally correspond with the rate of such profits, for the borrower can afford to pay only in proportion to the profits he expects to make by the use of it.

A great and sudden accession of capital, by increasing the demand for labour, will raise wages and diminish profits; but this effect will last only till population increases in the same ratio,—it is then that it win be necessary to turn up new and inferior land, and the effect becomes permanent. Thus the greater or lesser demand for labour makes profits and interest fluctuate; but the only steady and permanent cause of the diminution of profits and of interest is the cultivation of inferior soils.

During the reign of the Emperor Augustus, the interest of money at Rome fell from ten to four per cent, owing to the great influx of wealth from the conquered provinces. In India, where the proportion of capital to the number of labourers is comparatively small, wages are extremely low, and the profits of capital and interest of money exorbitantly high. The common rate of interest was for a long time twelve per cent., and I have heard that it is not unusual to make as much as twenty, or even thirty per cent, interest In China, interest is six per cent, per month.

CAROLINE

And is interest low in America, where labourers are scarce and wages high?

MRS. B.

No, it is not; on account of the great profits made by agriculture. In a country not yet fully peopled, where there is so great a choice of fertile land, that scarcely any of an inferior quality is brought into cultivation, and consequently where little or no rent is paid, the cultivator can afford to give high wages, and yet make great profits; and wherever great gains can be made by the use of capital, high interest will be given for the loan of it: therefore, though capital has been increasing in America more rapidly than in any other country, yet as immediate and advantageous employment is found for every accession of capital by the cultivation of new and fruitful lands, the interest of money does not fail

In all old-established fully peopled countries the low interest of money is sign of great accumulation of capital, abundant population, extensive cultivation of a variety of soils, high price of raw produce, high wages of labour, and small profits.

CAROLINE

If I understand you right, you mean to say that a borrower will give but little for the loan of capital when he can make but small profits by the use of it; that he can make but small profits when he must pay high wages; that wages will be high whenever subsistence is dear; that subsistence will be dear when inferior soils are taken into cultivation; that inferior soils are taken into cultivation when population multiplies, and that population multiplies when wages are high, in consequence of accumulation of capital.

MRS. B.

Thus we trace low interest to a source which is the origin of national prosperity—accumulation of capital.

CAROLINE

But I thought that the interest of money was fixed by law, and incapable of fluctuation?

MRS. B.

The legal interest in this country is 5 per cent; it may fall below that rate, though it cannot rise above it without becoming usury. In former times, to receive any remuneration for the loan of money was regarded much in the same light as usury is at present; that is to say, as taking an unfair advantage of the borrower.

CAROLINE

Such an opinion could have been entertained by those only who understood nothing of the reproductive nature of capital; for had they been aware of the profits to be made by the employment of money, they could not have considered it as unfair to pay for the use of it.

MRS. B.

Our forefathers had no pretensions to a knowledge of political economy; it is a science of much later date. The prejudice against lending money at interest appears not to have prevailed in very ancient times, but to have originated in the darkness of the middle ages: for the interest of money was legally instituted both amongst the Grecians and the Romans. It must have been an established practice in the time of Solon, since it is upon record that he reduced the legal interest to 12 per cent. The Bramins, in India, are said to have taken 2½ per cent, monthly, so far back as 3000 years, and yet legal interest was not established in modern Europe until the year 1546.

Macpherson, in his History of Commerce, makes the

following observations on the unpopularity of receiving interest for the loan of money: "In the year 1251," he observes, "the consequence of the clamour and persecution raised against those who took interest for the use of money was so violent, that they were obliged to charge it much higher than the natural price, (which if it had been let alone would have found its level,) in order to compensate for the opprobrium, and frequently the plunder, which they suffered; and thence the usual rate of interest was, what we should now call, most exorbitant and scandalous usury." And what we now call exorbitant, and scandalous usury proceeds in a great measure from a similar prejudice, which prevents the interest of money, like all other pecuniary interests, from finding its natural level, and stamps with criminality and the odium of usury any bargain in which money is lent at a higher interest than 5 per cent, however great the risk incurred by the lender. Why should there be a limit to the terms on which money may be borrowed any more than to the borrowing, or, I should rather say, to the hiring any other commodity?

CAROLINE

Would not such unlimited freedom of interest afford too great encouragement to capitalists to supply prodigals and thoughtless youths with money, and thus facilitate their means of squandering it?

MRS. B.

Men of this description find no difficulty in borrowing of usurers, provided they are able to give security for the payment, and without such security they would not obtain the loan of money either from men of respectability or from crafty usurers. The only difference now is, that they must pay a higher price for the loan, because the lender requires to be remunerated, not only for the use of the money, and the risk he incurs, but also for the ignominy and criminality attached to the proceeding; this necessarily takes it out of the hands of men of honourable character, and throws it into those of people who, having no value for reputation, are much more likely to take undue advantage of the distress of men who are in urgent want of money, and of the unguarded thoughtlessness of prodigal youth.

There is yet another means by which a man of property may derive an income from his capital without employing it himself: it is by lending it to a borrower who is distinguished from all others by the singularity of his dealings—who borrows not only without any intention of making profits by the use of the capital; but also, in general, without any prospect of repaying the principal of the debt.

CAROLINE

Without any prospect of repaying the debt! And where can he find people who will agree to lend capital on such terms?

MRS. B.

This extraordinary borrower is no other than the government of the country. When government makes a loan, that is to say, borrows capital, it is for the purpose of spending it as soon as procured; and the proprietors of this capital, or as they are usually denominated, the public creditors or stockholders, scarcely ever expect that the debt should be repaid. Yet notwithstanding this circumstance men are willing to lend their money to government even upon lower terms than to other borrowers. This arises from two causes; the first that the security of government for the punctual payment of the interest is better than that of any individual; and the second, that the public creditor has an indirect means of getting back his capital whenever he pleases, without being repaid by government.

CAROLINE

In what way?

MRS. B.

By selling his right to receive the interest, to any individual who wishes to invest his capital in the funds, and who will then stand in the place of the original creditor.

CAROLINE

And can he always sell that right for the sum he originally lent to government?

MRS. B.

Not always exactly; he will sometimes get more and sometimes less, according to the state of the market. If there are many creditors or stockholders desirous to sell, and but few capitalists wishing to buy, he will get less; if many buyers and few sellers, he will obtain more: in the latter case the stocks are said to be high, or rising; in the former, to be low, or falling.

CAROLINE

But since government spends the capital borrowed instead of deriving any profit from it, by what means is the interest paid?

MRS. B.

It is paid by taxes levied expressly for that purpose.

CAROLINE

If, then, government spends what is borrowed, the capital no longer exists, and the stockholder remains possessed of only an imaginary or fictitious capital.

MRS. B.

True; but he remains possessed of the right to receive an annual payment, or annuity, equal to the stipulated interest, till the government pays him back the principal. And this annuity (where the government can be depended upon) will always sell for its value to such persons as have capital which they wish to lend at interest It is thus that the stockholder is enabled to realise this fictitious capital, whenever he chooses, by selling his stock. The capital is, therefore, not lost to the individual; but it is entirely lost to the country. The stock may be sold, but the sale does not re-create the capital that has been spent; it merely transfers to the seller capital already existing in the hands of the buyer, and which would equally have existed whether the stock were sold or not. So long, however, as it can be exchanged for real capital, and in the mean time produces a substantial income to the possessor, it affords him all the enjoyments that can be derived from wealth.

CAROLINE

And is it not very injurious to the prosperity of a country that the government should spend its capital?

MRS. B.

No doubt; but under some circumstances it is an un-avoidable evil. In cases of urgent danger during a war, it is often necessary to raise larger sums of money, and with more expedition, than can be obtained by taxes; recourse is then had to loans, which, if not paid off, accumulate by repetitions, and become at length a heavy national debt, and a great burden to the country, owing to the taxes that must be raised in order to pay the interest to the stockholder.

CAROLINE

But as it is quite optional whether you buy stock or not, why should it be considered as a burden.

MRS. B.

The burden is not to the stockholder, but to the country at large; not to those who buy the stock, but to those who pay the taxes out of which dividends or interest are paid.

We may return to this subject at some future time; let me now ask you whether you fully understand how those who do not employ their capital themselves derive an income from it,

CAROLINE.

Through the agency of others, who, if the capital consists in land, pay them rent; if in money, pay them interest.

MRS. B.

Very well; take care, however, not to be misled by the term *money,* for no man's capital consists wholly in money. It must consist chiefly either in lands or saleable produce, rude or manufactured; all of which is *estimated* in money. And you cannot, at I said before, have clear ideas on this subject until the nature and use of money have been explained to you.

We have now examined all the modes by which men derive an income from their capital; there yet remains to be noticed a class of men who are maintained by the income of others.

CAROLINE

Do you mean labourers, who are maintained by wages, and bring a profit to their employers.

MRS. B.

No; these, whom we have distinguished by the name of *productive labourers,* are maintained by the *capital* of others; whilst the class of men to whom I now allude are maintained by the *income* of others. They are labourers, it is true; but of this peculiar description, that their labour is unproductive; they consume without re-producing: their labour, therefore, can add nothing to the future wealth of the country, and hence they are called *unproductive labourer.*

CAROLINE

I think I guess what description of people you mean; are not menial servants unproductive labourers?

MRS. B.

Yes, they form one of the classes of that description; for their labour, however useful, does not augment the riches of the country. A productive labourer is paid out of the value of the work he produces: this work remains with his employer, and may be either accumulated or exchanged for other commodities; but the labour of the menial servant is of a different nature; he renders services to his master, but produces nothing which can add to his wealth, and so far from increasing his income he is an expense to him, his wages being necessarily paid with the produce of some other labour.

CAROLINE

There iS no doubt an essential difference between these two kinds of labourers: keeping a number of workmen is a source of wealth, from the products of their labour; whilst keeping a number of menial servants is a source of expense, for their services yield no products. Thus the more workmen a tailor or a shoemaker employs the richer he becomes, while the more servants he keeps the poorer he grows.

MRS. B.

Because these different classes of labourers are paid, the one by the employment of his capital, the other by the expenditure of his income. Franklin, in his correspondence, expresses this difference with his usual perspicuity and neatness: —"The first elements of wealth are obtained by labour from the earth and waters. I have land and I raise corn: with this I feed a family that does nothing; my corn will be consumed, and at the end of the year I shall be no richer than I was at the beginning. But if, while I feed them, I employ them, some in spinning, others in hewing timber and sawing boards, others in making bricks for building, the value of my corn will be arrested, and remain with me, and at the end of the year we may all be better clothed and better lodged. And if, instead of employing a man I feed in making bricks, I employ him in fiddling for me, the corn he eats is gone, and no part of his manufacture remains to augment the wealth and conveniences of the family: I shall therefore be the poorer for this fiddling man, unless the rest of my family work more or eat less to make up the deficiency he occasions."

CAROLINE

But the fiddler might perhaps be a hired musician, cot a servant.

MRS. B.

The class of unproductive labourers is far from being confined to menial servants; it extends to all who are employed in services, whether by individuals or by the public: actors, singers, dancers, in a word all those who are maintained by the productive labour of others, are of this description.

CAROLINE

Is it not to be regretted that these people cannot be compelled to adopt a more useful mode of employment.

MRS. B.

Far from it, for their services, though of an unproductive nature, are generally useful. Menial servants, for instance, by relieving the productive labourer of much necessary work, enable him to do more than he could otherwise accomplish. Thus a man engaged in the employment of a considerable capital can spend his time to greater advantage, both to himself and to the community, than in cleaning his own shoes and cooking his own dinner.

CAROLINE

The use of servants is evidently attended with some of the benefits of the division of labour.

MRS. B.

You will probably be surprised to hear that many of the most valuable ranks of society are included in the class of unproductive labourers. The divine, the physician, the soldier, ministers of state, and magistrates, all render services to the community of this description.

CAROLINE.

Indeed! I little imagined that the class of unproductive labourers had been so respectable. And although their services are of an unproductive nature, they are, I think, in many instances, more valuable members of society than some of the productive labourers. A magistrate, who faithfully administers justice; a physician, who restores health; a clergyman, who teaches religion and morals; are certainly of more essential benefit to the community, than the confectioner or the perfumer, or indeed of any of the productive labourers whatever.

MRS. B.

No doubt they are. There is no greater stimulus to industry than security of property; justice is therefore essentially necessary to encourage productive labour; and the legislator and magistrate, though they do not immediately produce commodities, are as necessary to their production as the labours of the husbandman or artisan; and these different species of labour constitute one of the most useful branches of the division of labour.

CONVERSATION XVI

ON MONEY

MRS. B.

In our last conversation on capital lent, we talked of the interest of money; let us now proceed to examine the use of money itself.

Without this general medium of exchange, civilisation could never have made any considerable progress; for as the subdivisions of labour increased, insuperable difficulties would be experienced in carrying on traffic by exchange. The butcher might want bread, at a time that the baker did not want meat; or they might each be desirous of exchanging their respective commodities, but these might not be of equal value.

CAROLINE

It would be very difficult, I believe, at any time to make such reckonings exactly balance each other.

MRS. B.

In order to avoid this inconvenience, it became necessary for every man to be provided with something which would be willingly taken at all times in exchange for goods. Hence arose that useful substitute of commodities, *money,* which, being exclusively appropriated to exchanges, every one was ready either to receive or to part with for that purpose.

CAROLINE

When the baker did not want meat he would take the butcher's money in exchange for his bread, because that money would enable him to obtain from others what he did want.

MRS. B.

Various commodities have been employed to answer the purpose of money. Mr. Salt, in his Travels in Abyssinia, informs us, that wedges of salt are used in that country for small currency, coined money being extremely scarce. A wedge of rock-salt, weighing between two and three pounds, was estimated at 1-30th of a dollar.

CAROLINE

How extremely inconvenient such a bulky article must be as a substitute for money coined; the carriage of it to any distance would cost almost as much as the salt was worth.

MRS. B.

A commodity of this nature could be used for the purpose of money in those countries only where very few mercantile transactions take place, and where labour is very cheap. Tobacco, shells, and a great variety of other articles, have been used at different times, and in different countries, as mediums of exchange; but nothing has ever been found to answer this end so well as the metals. They are the least perishable of all commodities; they are susceptible, by the process of fusion, of being divided into any number of parts without loss, and being the heaviest, they are the least bulky of all bodies. These properties render them peculiarly appropriate for the purposes of commerce and circulation.

CAROLINE

The use of metals as money must be very ancient, for mention is made in history of the iron coin of the Greeks, and the copper coin of the Romans.

MRS. B.

Nor are gold and silver coins of modern date; but they were scarce before the discovery of the American mines. The first gold coins were struck at Rome, about 200 years before Christ; those of silver about 65 years earlier. Previous to that period the *as*, which was of copper, was the only coin in common use.

CAROLINE

It is said in the Bible that Abraham gave 400 shekels of silver for the purchase of the field of Machpelah, to bury Sarah in; was that coined money?

MRS. B.

No; I believe there was no coined money of so ancient a date. The metals were originally used for the purpose of money in bars; and it is mentioned that Abraham weighed the silver for the purpose; which would have been unnecessary had it been coined. Before the invention of coining, the use of the metals as a medium of exchange was attended with great inconvenience; it being necessary not only to weigh, but also to assay the metal, to ascertain both its quantity and its degree of purity.

The invention of coining superseded this inconvenience; for coining money is affixing to a piece of metal a particular stamp or impression, which declares that it is of a certain weight and quality. Thus, the impression on a guinea signifies that it is a piece of gold of certain fineness, weighing 107 grains nearly.

CAROLINE

Money must also be of great use in fixing the value of commodities; before its introduction the butcher and the baker might dispute which was worth most, the joint of meat or the loaf of bread which they wished to exchange.

MRS. B.

Yes; money became useful, not only as a medium of exchange but also as a common measure of value. You will learn hereafter that it is not, any more than labour, a very accurate measure, when the values of one period are compared with the values of another distant period; but for the common purposes of traffic it answers sufficiently well.

Previous to the invention of money, men were much at a loss how to estimate the value of their property. In order to express that value they were necessarily obliged to compare it to something else, and having no settled standard, they would naturally choose objects of known and established value. Accordingly we read both in Scripture and in the ancient poets, of a man's property being worth so many oxen and so many flocks and herds. Dr. Clarke informs us, that even at the present day, the Calmuc Tartan reckon the value of a coat of mail from six to eight, and up to the value of fifty hones. In civilised countries every one estimates his capital by the quantity of money it is worth; — he does not really possess the sum in money, but his property, whatever be its nature or kind, is equivalent to such a sum of money. For instance, a man who is worth a capital of £20,000 may perhaps not be possessed of £20, in money; but his property, whether land or commodities, if sold, would bring him £20,000.

CAROLINE

When gold is brought into this country, pray how is it paid for? Something must be given in exchange for it; and yet that something cannot be money.

MRS.B.

Certainly not. A bullion merchant would derive no advantage from a trade in which he would be employed in exchanging a certain weight of gold and silver in one country, for a similar weight of gold and silver in another country: he would lose not only all the profits of trade, but the expenses of the freight, &c.; so that in fact he would be exchanging £100 for £90, or £95.

We pay for gold and silver in commodities; woollen cloths, hardware, calicoes, linens, and a variety of others.

CAROLINE

Then we purchase gold with goods, just as we purchase goods with gold.

MRS. B.

Exactly; those who take our goods in exchange for gold bullion buy goods with gold; only, as the gold is not coined, it may rather be called an exchange of commodities than a purchase.

CAROLINE

And if the mines should prove less productive than usual, or any circumstance should render gold scarce, and thus raise its exchangeable value, we must export a greater quantity of goods to exchange for the same quantity of gold.

MRS. B.

Undoubtedly. The natural value of gold bullion, like that of any other commodity, may be estimated by its cost of production; that is to say, the labour bestowed upon it, both to extract it from the mines, and bring it to the place where it is to be sold; and its exchangeable value fluctuates according to the proportion of the supply to the demand. This fluctuation, however, can be discovered only by the greater or smaller quantity of goods for which the same quantity of gold will exchange. For as gold and silver may be bought with any kind of goods, they are not susceptible of a standard of value like that of other commodities which is estimated in one particular article—money.

CAROLINE

As gold and silver are the standard of value of all other commodities, all other commodities, I conceive, must be affected by an alteration in the exchangeable value of gold and silver.

MRS. B.

And this is the reason why money is not an accurate standard of the value of commodities: for if money by its plenty diminish in value, less goods will be given in exchange for it; it therefore enhances the price of commodities, that is to say their *exchangeable value estimated in money,* and renders them dearer. Whilst if money by its scarcity increase in value, more goods will be given in exchange for it: it then lowers the price of commodities, and renders them cheaper.

CAROLINE

A deficiency of any article raises its exchangeable value, and consequently its price, above its natural value; thus a deficiency of gold or silver would make a smaller quantity exchange for the same quantity of goods as before; and therefore a loaf of bread would sell for less money, or, in other words, would be cheaper.

MRS. B.

Yes; and not only bread, but meat, clothes, furniture, houses; in short, every thing would be cheaper, in consequence of the scarcity of the precious metals.

CAROLINE

Then would a scarcity of money be advantageous to a country by rendering things cheap?

MRS. B.

You forget that cheapness is advantageous only when it arises from that plenty which results from a reduction of the cost of production, not when it proceeds from a scarcity of money. In the latter case, the supply remaining stationary, commodities are lower in price, without any alteration in their general exchangeable value. They may, therefore, be considered rather as nominally than really cheaper. If, for instance, a loaf of bread should sell for a penny, though there should not be a single loaf more in the country than when it sold for a shilling, the cheapness would not make bread more plentiful.

CAROLINE

But if the price of bread were so low as a penny, though the supply should not be increased, the labouring classes would increase their consumption of it so considerably as to produce a scarcity, if not a famine, before the next harvest. This *nominal,* or I would call it *false,* cheapness, must, therefore, be prejudicial, instead of beneficial, to a country.

MRS. B.

The consequence you have drawn from it is erroneous; for the labouring classes would not be able to purchase a greater quantity of bread than usual, owing to the scarcity of money. The wages of labour would not be exempted from the general fall in price which this scarcity would produce: the labourers, as well as the bread they eat, would be paid in pence instead of shillings, and their power oi purchasing bread would neither be increased nor diminished.

CAROLINE

True; I did not consider that consequence. I suppose, then, that if the contrary case, occurred,—that is, if the quantity of money were considerably augmented, either by the discovery of a mine in the country, or by any other means,—a general rise in the price of commodities would take place?

MRS. B.

Undoubtedly; but without producing any scarcity. Therefore, though commodities would rise in price, their value would not be increased, and the commodities being the same in quantity, the public would be equally well supplied; but as money fell or became depreciated in value from its excess, fewer commodities would be given in exchange for the same sum; or more money must be paid for the same commodity. A loaf of bread might cost two shillings instead of one, but as the wages of labour would at the same time be doubled, the labourer would suffer no privation from the increase of price. You now see the propriety of making the distinction between the value and the *price* of a commodity.

It is very possible for the price of a commodity to rise, whilst its value falls. A loaf of bread may rise in price from one to two shillings; but money may be so depreciated by excess that *two* shillings may not procure so much meat, butter, and cheese, as one shilling did before; therefore a loaf of bread would no longer exchange for so much of those commodities, and its exchangeable value, compared with other things generally, would have fallen; while its *price,* or exchangeable value estimated in *money only,* would have risen.

CAROLINE

And when the price alters, how can we distinguish

whether it is the goods or the money which change in value?

MRS. B.

There is no point so difficult to ascertain as a variation of value, because we have no fixed standard measure of value; neither nature nor art furnishes us with a commodity whose value is incapable of change; and such alone would afford us an accurate standard of value.

CAROLINE

How useful such a commodity would be; for we cannot estimate the value of any thing without comparing it with the value of something else; and if that something else is liable to variation, it is but of little assistance to us: it is supporting the earth by the elephant, and the elephant by the tortoise; but we still remain in the same dilemma. When a man says he is worth 500 acres of land, we can form scarcely any judgment of his wealth, unless he tells us what the acres are worth: his land may be situated m the most fruitful parts of England, or it may be in the wilds of America, or the deserts of Arabia; and if he values his land in money, and says my acres are worth, or would sell for, £1,000, we can form some notion of their real value, but still not an accurate one; for we do not know what is the real value of the money, whether it is plentiful or scarce, cheap or dear; nor can we ever learn it unless we had some invariable standard by which to measure it.

MRS. B.

Now supposing money to be depreciated in value 25 per cent, and that the expense of manufacturing a piece of muslin, from some improvement in the process, fell from four to three shillings a yard, at what price would the muslin sell?

CAROLINE

It would retain its original price of four shillings, though it would really be cheaper; for the diminution of the value of money would exactly counterbalance the diminution of the cost of production of the muslin.

MRS. B.

Very well; and if, on the contrary, money should become scarce at the same time as the cost of product tion of a commodity diminished, then these two causes, acting in conjunction instead of opposition, the commodity would be both nominally and realty cheaper.

CAROLINE

The muslin in that case would fall from four to two shillings a yard.*

MRS. B.

In order still further to reduce the price of the muslin, we may suppose the supply to exceed the demand, so as to oblige the manufacturer to sell it below its cost of production; and thus the price might fall so low as one shilling, or even sixpence a yard.

But of all these reductions of price, that which proceeds from a diminished cost of production is the only one from which general advantage is derived; that arising from the depreciation of money producing

---

* Accurately calculated the muslin would sell for two shillings and three pence a yard, because the rise in the value of money would be reckoned upon the reduced cost of production.

merely a nominal cheapness; and that which results from an excess of supply being decidedly an evil, inasmuch as it creates distress and discourages industry.

CAROLINE

It appears, then, from what you have said, that an increase or diminution of money in a country does not really affect the pecuniary circumstances of any one.

MRS. B.

I beg your pardon; all classes of men are temporarily affected when the change is abrupt; because the due level is not immediately ascertained, and until that takes place, the pressure falls unequally. But, independently of this, there are many classes of people who would be very sensibly and permanently injured by an alteration in the exchangeable value of money.

Let us suppose, for instance, that the proprietor of a field lets it for a long lease at a rent of £20 a year; and that some years afterwards, money having risen in value, and he being in want of hay for his horses, purchases the crop of hay for £15. In this case the landlord will continue to receive £20 a year for the rent, and yet pay but £15 for the produce, so that the farmer will lose £5, besides the profits of his capital. Is not this a very serious injury?

CAROLINE

No doubt; and this would be the case with all leases; for it is immaterial to whom the fanner sells his crops; if the market-price has fallen, he must be a loser.

MRS. B.

Yes. Were money raised to double its former value, the rent would purchase double the quantity of commodities that it did before; for £100 in money would exchange for a quantity of goods which was reckoned worth £200 previous to the alteration; so that rent, though nominally the same, would in reality-be doubled, and it would be so much unjustly taken out of the pocket of the tenant to put into that of the landlord.

CAROLINE

This evil, however, admits of a remedy when a new lease is made?

MRS. B.

True; but should the old one have several yean to run, the farmer may be ruined first; and though it is true that it does not violate any law, it is a manifest infraction of the security of property, which is the foundation of all wealth, and the strongest motive for its accumulation. There is not a more active and steady stimulus to industry than the certainty of reaping the fruits of our labour.

CAROLINE

Then I suppose that when money is depreciated in value, in consequence of being more plentiful, the case would be reversed; the farmer would be benefited and the landlord would be the loser; for the rent would not be really worth so much as it was before?

MRS. B.

Undoubtedly. Another class of people who are materially affected by an alteration in the value of money, are the unproductive labourers. Their pay is generally a regular stipend, not liable to the same variation as the wages of productive labourers. The pay of the army and navy, of all the officers under government, and of the learned professions, is fixed; those persons must therefore suffer all the evil, or enjoy all the benefit arising from an alteration in the value of money.

CAROLINE

The higher classes of the unproductive labourers might be able to support the hardship resulting from a depreciation of the value of money; but how can the common sailor or soldier do so? It is absolutely necessary that their pay should enable them to procure a suitable subsistence.

MRS. B.

They are usually paid, partly in money and partly in provisions and clothing, and are not therefore such sufferers by a depreciation of money as they would be if paid entirely in currency. It has nevertheless been found necessary of late to augment the pay of both army and navy.

CAROLINE

The value of money has then fallen?

MRS. B.

Yes, it has; but I must defer explaining the reason of this fall till our next interview. A third class of people who are considerably injured by a depreciation of the value of money, are those who have lent money at interest for a long period of time, persons who live on annuities, and particularly the stockholders in the public funds. Not only is the interest they receive depreciated, but also the value of their capital The interest they receive for their stock remains nominally the same, whatever diminution may have taken place in the value of money; and their income being thus apparently stationary, they partake in the general disadvantage of the rise of prices, without being enabled to avail themselves of the compensation arising from the greater abundance of money. Professional men, and all those who receive salaries, have ultimately the remedy of an increase of pay; but the stockholder has no resource: his income wastes away, and he perceives his means of procuring his accustomed enjoyments gradually diminish, without being able to trace the source from whence the evil springs; for as his income remains nominally the same, he is not aware of any diminution of wealth.

CAROLINE

How very much I have been mistaken in my idea of money I Instead of being the only, or at least the principal article which (as I thought) constituted wealth; it seems, on the contrary, to be the only one which is unworthy of that title, since it does not con-tribute to the riches of a country. An excess of money renders other things dear; a deficiency of it makes them cheap; but it appears to me that a country is not one atom the richer for all the money it possesses. Money, therefore, I think, cannot be called wealth, but merely its representative, like the counters at cards; and its chief use seems to consist in its affording us a convenient medium of exchange, and a useful, though imperfect standard of value.

MRS. B.

No; money cannot with justice be compared to counters, for it is not, like them, a sign or representative of value, but really possesses (or ought to possess) the value for which it exchanges. A bank-note, which can hardly be said to have any intrinsic value, is, like counters at cards, simply a sign of value; but when you purchase goods for a guinea, you give a piece of gold of equivalent value in exchange.

In order to judge whether money forms any part of the wealth of a nation, let us refer to our definition of wealth. I believe we said that every article, either of utility or luxury, provided it were limited in supply, constituted wealth. Now I leave you to judge whether money, considered either as a medium of exchange, or as a standard of value, is not eminently useful; since by facilitating the circulation of commodities it indirectly contributes to their multiplication.

CAROLINE

That is true, certainly, with regard to the money actually required for circulation; but should it exceed that sum, the surplus would be of no value to us.

MRS. B.

The same might be said of a superfluous quantity of any kind of wealth; more tables and chairs, or a greater quantity of gowns and coats than are wanted, would be equally useless, and would equally be depreciated in value.

CAROLINE

But then we could export such commodities, and exchange them for goods which we did want.

MRS. B.

And why not do the same with money? When we have more money than is required for the purpose of circulation, we export it, by purchasing foreign goods; without this resource, a superfluity of money is perfectly useless, and will no more contribute to the production of wealth, than a superfluous number of mills would contribute to the production of flour.

CAROLINE

I had always imagined that the more money a country possessed, the more affluent was its condition.

MRS. B.

And that usually is the case. The error lies in mistaking the cause for the effect A great quantity of money is necessary to circulate a great quantity of commodities. Rich flourishing countries require abundance of money, and possess the means of obtaining it; but this abundance is the consequence, not the cause of their wealth, which consists in the commodities circulated, rather than in the circulating medium. Specie, we have just said, constitutes wealth so far as it is required for circulation; but if a country possess one guinea more than is necessary for that purpose, the wealth which purchased that guinea has been thrown away.

CAROLINE

Yet what a common observation it is, that plenty of money animates the industry of a country, and encourages commerce; and this seems to be proved by the miserable and barbarous state of Europe previous to the discovery of the American mines.

MRS. B.

The discovery of America was certainly a very efficient cause in rousing the industry of Europe from the state of stagnation into which it was sunk by ignorance and barbarism. But had America possessed no mines, I doubt whether the advantage we have derived from our connection with that country would not have been almost equally great: we could easily find a substitute for the specie with which she supplies us, but never for the abundance and variety of wealth which she is incessantly pouring in upon us. The increase of European comforts, of affluence, of luxury, is attributed to the influx of the treasures of the new world—and with reason; but those treasures are the sugar, the coffee, the indigo, the tobacco, the drugs, &c. which America exports, to obtain which we must send her commodities that have been produced by the employment of our poor. Gold and silver, though they have greatly excited our avarice and ambition, have eventually contributed but little to stimulate our industry.

It is not to the multiplication of the precious metals that we are indebted for our improved agriculture, our prosperous commerce, and the variety and excellence of our manufactures; nor do I believe that it was their scarcity which deprived our ancestors of these advantages. It was because they were ignorant and barbarous, and that we are comparatively enlightened and civilized; comparatively, I may indeed say, for error is still active in retarding the progress of improvement, and it is but since the year 1819 that oar government has allowed of the exportation of specie, although it is now fifty years since Adam Smith fully proved the impolicy of this prohibition.

CAROLINE

When the exportation of specie was prohibited, the only use that could be made of a superfluous quantity of it, would be to melt it down and re-convert it into bullion.

MRS. B.

But melting the coin was, at the same time, equally illegal. A superfluous quantity of money, therefore, (were these laws never infringed) was necessarily added to the circulation, and depreciated the value of the whole.

How different is the situation of the country now that such prohibitory laws no longer exist! No sooner does money accumulate so as to occasion a depreciation of its value, or, in other words, an advance in the price of commodities, than our merchants export specie, to purchase foreign goods; while at the same time foreign merchants send their goods to this country where prices have risen, and exchange them, not for other goods, which are dear, but for money, which is cheap.

CAROLINE

That is to say, they will sell, but not purchase?

MRS. B.

Precisely:—it is thus that a country is drained of its superfluous specie; as this traffic goes on, money rises in value, commodities fall in price, and foreign; merchants again exchange their goods for commodities of the country, instead of receiving payment for it in specie.

No apprehension need therefore be entertained of ill consequences arising either from the melting down or exporting the coin of the country. This exportation will take place secretly whenever there is a superfluity, however severe the law may be against it; the only difference is, that instead of being carried on in an open and regular manner by merchants of respectability, it is thrown into the hands of men of despicable character, who are tempted by extraordinary profits to engage in this illicit traffic.

Could Spain and Portugal, countries which receive all the precious metals imported from America to Europe, have carried into effect the absurd restrictive laws by which they attempted to keep their gold and silver at home, those metals would eventually have become of little more value to them than lead and copper.

If you have understood what I have said, you will now be able to tell me what effect will be produced in the mercantile transactions of a country, which is not shackled by restrictive laws, when a scarcity of money produces a fall in the price of commodities.

CAROLINE

In that case the very reverse will happen of what we before observed. Foreign merchants will come and buy goods, and instead of offering merchandise in exchange, will bring money in payment; for they will be willing to make purchases, but not sales at a cheap market

MRS. B.

It is thus that gold and silver are diffused throughout all parts of the civilised world; wherever there is a deficiency, it flows in from every quarter; and wherever there is a redundancy, the tide sets in an opposite direction. It is the regular diffusion of the precious metals, and their constant tendency to an equality of value, which renders them so peculiarly calculated for a general standard. Were money as liable to variation of value as the commodities for which it serves as a medium of exchange, it would be totally unfit for a standard.

CONVERSATION XVII

Subject of MONEY continued

OF THE DEPRECIATION OF GOLD AND SILVER.—OF THE ADUL-
TERATION AND DEPRECIATION OF COINED MONEY.—OF
BANKS.—OF PAPER MONEY.—EFFECTS OF PAPER MONEY
WHEN NOT PAYABLE IN SPECIE ON DEMAND.—OF THE
PROPORTION OF CURRENCY TO THE COMMODITIES TO BE
CIRCULATED BY IT.

CAROLINE

I HAVE been reflecting much upon the subject of our last conversation, Mrs. B.; and it has occurred to me, that though there may be no permanent excess and deprecia- tion of specie in any particular country, yet it must gradu- ally decrease in value throughout the world: for money is very little liable to wear; a great quantity of the precious metals is annually extracted from the mines, and though a considerable portion of it may be converted into plate and jewellery, yet the greater part, I suppose, goes to the mint to be coined, and this additional quantity must produce a depreciation of value?

MRS. B.

An increase of supply will not occasion deprecia- tion of value, if there should at the same time be a proportional increase of demand, and we most recollect that the consumable produce of the earth increases as well as that of the mines—the commodities to be circulated as well as the medium of circulation; and it is not the actual quantity of money, but the proportion which it bears to the quantity of commodities for which it is to serve as a medium of exchange, that regulates the price of those commodities.

Let us suppose the price of a loaf of bread to be one shilling; and say, if 1000 more loaves of bread be produced every year by agriculture, and such an additional number of shillings be obtained from the mines as will be necessary to circulate them, the price of a loaf will then remain the same, and the value of money will not, by this additional quantity of specie, be depreciated.

CAROLINE
But, Mrs. B., you do not consider that when the thousand additional loaves are eaten, the additional shillings will remain.

MRS. B.
The greater part of these loaves will be eaten by those who will not only reproduce them, but probably increase the number the following year.

CAROLINE
In that case it would be very possible that the progress of agriculture and manufactures should not only keep pace with, but even precede that of the mines.

MRS. B.
If the quantity of the precious metals annually extracted from the mines be exactly what is required

for the arts, and for the additional specie necessary to circulate the increasing produce of the land, there will be no change in the value of money, and commodities will continue to be bought and sold at their former prices. If less gold and silver be extracted than is requisite for these purposes, goods will fall in price; and if, on the contrary, a greater quantity be produced, goods will rise in price, the fluctuations in the price of commodities gradually and constantly conforming to the variations of the scale by which their value is measured.

Dr. Adam Smith was of opinion that for many years past the supply of gold and silver did not exceed the demand; but several later writers conceive that he was mistaken on this point. I am very far from being a competent judge of such a question, but I confess that I feel inclined to favour the opinion of a general depreciation.

Previous to the discovery of America the exchangeable value of money was certainly much greater than it has been since that period. Some notion may be formed of the difference of the value of money in ancient and in modern times from the amount of the income which Xerxes, King of Persia, derived from his wealthy and extensive empire, and which enabled him to maintain his mighty fleets and armies; it is said in history to have amounted to only three millions sterling.

CAROLINE

The prodigality and extravagance of the Romans was then, in fact, still greater than it appears, since the immense sums they expended upon luxuries were then more valuable than they would be at the present times.

MRS. B.

As the wealth of the Romans arose in a great measure from the spoliation of the countries they conquered, gold and silver formed an essential part of their plunder; specie, therefore, might possibly be of lest value there than in other parts of the world at the same period.

Independently, however, of the increase of quantity which produces a depreciation in the value of the precious metals themselves, there are causes quite foreign to this, which have considerable effect on the value of the money into which they have been coined. One of these is the adulteration of the coin. A pound sterling, or twenty shillings, originally weighed a pound of silver; hence its denomination. But sovereigns, in making new coinages, frequently found it convenient to adulterate the metal by mixing it with alloy. It was a means of increasing the value of their treasures, by paying their debts with a much less quantity of the precious metals, and thus defrauding their creditor-subjects, who in the first instance were not aware of the change.

In the year 1351, Edward the Third, distressed by the debts he had incurred in his chimerical attempts to conquer France, adopted this mode of paying his creditors with less money than he borrowed of them. He ordered a pound of silver to be coined into 266, instead of 240 pennies. Having experienced the beneficial effects of this expedient, he soon after coined 270 pennies out of the same pound. By this imposition, not only the creditors of the crown, but all other creditors were defrauded of about a tenth of their property; being compelled to receive in payment money of less value than that they had lent. Considerable inconvenience was also experienced from the alteration in the standard of value; as soon as it was discovered, it produced a general rise in the price of commodities, and the poor were greatly distressed by the enhancement of prices of the necessaries of life.

CAROLINE

But did not wages rise in the same proportion?

MRS. B.

Eventually they did, no doubt; but after such a revolution in prices as an event of this nature produces, a length of time is required to restore the due level; and the rich always resist the rise of wages as long as it is in their power. In the instance I have mentioned it does not appear that the labouring class made any effort to obtain a compensation by a rise of wages, until a dreadful pestilence, which originated in the east, extended its ravages to England, and carried off the greater part of the lower classes. The survivors then took advantage of the scarcity of hands to raise their terms; but the king, instead of allowing the remedy to pursue its natural course, considered this attempt of the labourers to raise their wages as an unwarrantable exaction; and in order to prevent it, enacted the *statute of labourers*. This statute ordained that labourers should receive no more than the wages which were paid previous to the adulteration of the coin.

It would be difficult to conceive a law more calculated to repress the efforts of industry or create more distress. But Edward, urged by the weight of his accumulated debts, continued to depreciate the value of the coin; endeavouring to conceal the fraud by the introduction of a new silver coin called a *groat,* but in value only 3¼ pence; and in 1358 he made 75 groats, or 800 pennies, out of a pound of silver.

CAROLINE

What a prodigious depreciation in the course of so short a period of time! And have similar expedients been resorted to by successive sovereigns?

MRS. B.

Ycs; so repeatedly that 20 shillings, or a pound sterling, instead of containing, as formerly, a pound of silver, now weighs rather less than four ounces of that metal.

CAROLINE

But this is a partial depreciation, which affects only the coin of Great Britain. Have other countries adopted so unjust and pernicious a measure?

MRS. B.

It is so tempting an expedient for sovereigns, that it has been resorted to in almost all countries where money is used. In the time of Charlemagne the French livre weighed a pound, of 12 ounces. Philip the First adulterated it with one-third of alloy. Philip of Valois practised the same fraud on gold coin, and it has been repeated by successive sovereigns till the depreciation of the French livre is even greater than that of our pound sterling, it being now worth not more than ten-pence.

As far back as the time of the Romans this surreptitious mode of obtaining wealth had been discovered, and was practised. The Roman *as,* which originally contained a pound of brass, was in the course of time diminished to half an ounce.

CAROLINE

But now that the world must be fully aware of the imposition, I should think that governments would not venture to have recourse to such expedients.

MRS. B.

This country has increased so much in wealth, that in the present times less difficulty is experienced in raising taxes; and the facility of making loans has induced government to give the preference to that mode of obtaining money during a time of war, or whenever any extraordinary expenses are incurred.

Of late years a new mode of augmenting the currency of the country has been invented, by substituting for the precious metals a more convenient and more economical medium of exchange, under the form of *paper-money.*

CAROLINE

Paper-money! There can be no real value in money made of paper?

MRS. B.

Little or none intrinsically, as I said before; yet it has been found to answer most of the purposes of specie.—You remember that money was first invented to avoid the inconvenience of baiter. When a commodity is sold for money it is under a confidence, on the part of the seller, that he will be able with the money to purchase any other commodity of equal value that he may want. It is of no consequence to him of what material the money be made, provided it have this quality.

CAROLINE

True; but paper can never have that quality: who would part with any thing of value for a bit of paper?

MRS. B.

Suppose I were to give you a paper containing my promise to pay you £100 in money whenever you demanded it; would you not consider the promise so formally given nearly of the same value as the money itself?

CAROLINE

Yes; because I have perfect confidence in you: but a stranger would not.

MRS. B.

Suppose that, instead of my promise to pay you £100, I should give you a piece of paper containing a promise to the same effect of some of the wealthiest and best known merchants in London?

CAROLINE

My confidence in the value of such paper would be in proportion to the reliance I could place on the promise of such merchants.

MRS. B.

Exactly so. Such confidence is the foundation of all banking establishments, which are in general a partner-ship of wealthy and respectable merchants, in whom the public repose so great a confidence that they are willing to take their promissory note, commonly called a *bank-note,* instead of money.

CAROLINE

A bank-note then is a written engagement or promise

to pay the sum, whatever it be, that is specified in the note?

MRS. B.

It is; and these notes become current as a medium of exchange; having no intrinsic value, they are merely the sign or representative of wealth; but are received by the public under the persuasion that they will be paid in money by the bank which issues them, whenever it may be required.

CAROLINE

This is indeed an excellent invention; what a saving of expense! The establishment of a bank of paper-money appears to me very similar to the discovery of a mine of gold in the country: or indeed the bank has even some advantages over the mine, for it is certain of being productive, and yet it is attended with much less expense.

MRS. B.

The saving of capital to a country by the substitution of paper to a metallic currency, is perhaps still greater than you imagine. If, for example, the currency of Great Britain be estimated at twenty millions of sovereigns, and the ordinary rate of profit at 8 per cent, it is evident that this currency costs the country above a million and a half a year; for had not the twenty millions been employed as coin, they would have been invested in different branches of industry, and yielded above a million and a half profit Besides, the loss of coin occasioned by fires, shipwrecks, and other accidents, is very considerable, and requires an annual addition to be made to the stock of currency in order to fill up the void. Thus, you see that it is an expensive luxury for a country to maintain twenty millions of gold in circulation.

CAROLINE

I am only surprised that facts like these should not have given rise to paper-money long before the present period. Pray, is the invention of paper-money quite of modern date?

MRS. B.

There is, I believe, no vestige of any thing of the kind in ancient history; unless we should consider as such a species of stamped leather used as money by the Carthaginians; and as they had also coined money, it is possible that their stamped leather might be considered merely as a sign or representative of real value, analogous to our paper-money.

CAROLINE

The leather was probably a species of parchment, the substance commonly used for writing on before the invention of paper, and the impression stamped on it might signify the sum of money which the piece of leather was to represent, or pass for.

MRS. B.

These are points upon which, in the imperfect state of our knowledge of Carthaginian currency, it would be difficult to determine; it is fortunate, therefore, that they are questions more of curiosity than of utility.

The first bank we are distinctly acquainted with was established at Amsterdam in the year 1609*;

---

* It is said, however, that a bank was established at Venice *at* least two centuries before.

but this institution was of a different kind from what I have been describing. It issued no paper, but received the deposit of coined money, an account of which was taken in the books of the bank; and through the medium of these books, transfers of property were made from one individual to another, as occasion required, without the money being once removed from the strong chests in which it was originally deposited.

CAROLINE

There does not seem to be any economy in this species of bank; whilst those which issue bank notes, by the substitution of a cheap circulating medium, render that of gold and silver superfluous, and enable it to be sent abroad to purchase foreign commodities.

MRS. B.

And, should foreign countries adopt the same economical expedient, and send us their superfluous specie...?

CAROLINE

True, I did not consider that. If paper-money were generally adopted, every country would be overstocked with specie; for though the establishment of a bank in any one country may force the superfluous money into others, this cannot happen if banks are set up in every country. They are far, therefore, from being attended with the advantages I at first imagined.

MRS. B.

By issuing paper-money, so much is, in fact, added

to the circulation throughout the civilised world; and inasmuch as it supersedes the use of the precious metals, and therefore lessens the demand, it must to a certain degree lessen their value. The immediate effect of opening a new bank is certainly to drive some portion of the specie out of the country in which the bank is established. It does not, however, force out the whole quantity which the paper represents; for, independently of the general excess to which we have alluded, a bank must keep a certain quantity of specie in reserve, to be enabled to fulfill the promise of paying its notes on demand.

CAROLINE

But it is not necessary that a bank should keep a fund of specie, like that of Amsterdam, equal to the value of its notes; for if so, no saving would result from the use of paper-money.

MRS. B.

Certainly not. The profits of the bank arise from the employment of the capital thus saved, which consists of the difference between the amount of notes issued and the specie reserved in the bank. It is so improbable that every person possessed of notes should apply at once for payment, that there is no necessity for providing a fund equal to the amount of the notes in circulation in order to fulfill the engagement. Banks discover from experience what is the proportion of specie requisite to enable them to answer the average demand made upon them; and they regulate the quantity of notes they issue accordingly: for if they failed in their engagement to pay them in cash on demand, they would become bankrupt.

CAROLINE

Yet I have heard that many years ago the Bank of England did not pay its notes in specie.

MRS. B.

That is true; but it was in consequence of an act of parliament having been passed purposely to grant it this privilege for a specified time.

CAROLINE

And when a Bank of England note could no longer be exchanged at pleasure for specie, in what did its value consist?

MRS. B.

In the expectation that it would one day be paid in specie: this opinion rendered bank-notes still current: had such confidence been destroyed, their value would have been reduced to that of the paper of which they are made.

CAROLINE

But when the Bank of England was not obliged to pay its notes in cash, it was at liberty to issue any quantity however great. In short, it seems to have discovered the philosopher's stone; for, though it may not have found the means of making gold, it possessed a substitute which answered the purpose equally well.

MRS. B.

Excepting that, having no intrinsic value, it cannot be exported in case of excess; and you may recollect our observing that no use could be made of any super-fluous quantity of money but to exchange it for foreign goods. An excess of currency produced by an over-issue of bank-notes must therefore remain in the country, and cause a depreciation in the value of money, which would be discovered by a general rue in the prices of commodities, and would be attended with all the evils enumerated in our last conversation.

CAROLINE

And is there not great danger of a bank issuing an excess of notes when it is not restricted by the obligation of paying them in specie?

MRS. B.

A very considerable risk is certainly incurred by such an exemption.

When a bank issues more notes than are required for the purpose of circulation, its effect in depreciating the value of the currency, and raising the price of commodities, is at first very trifling, because as soon as that effect is perceived, the coined money begins to disappear. Notwithstanding the prohibition of law, it never fails to make its escape out of the country. It is either clandestinely sent abroad, or privately melted and exported in bullion. As long, therefore, as an over-issue of notes serves to replace the coin which it forces out of the country, there is but little augmentation of the circulating medium; but if, after the specie has disappeared, the bank still continue to force an additional quantity of notes into circulation, the excess will be absorbed in it, the value of the currency will be proportionally depreciated, and a corresponding rise will take place in the price of commodities.

CAROLINE

But is it known whether the Bank of England

materially increased its issue of notes when it was exonerated from the obligation of paying them in cash?

MRS. B.

Of that there is no doubt; though it was the opinion of some people that the supply of notes did not exceed the demand;—that the paper-mine (as you call it) increased its produce only in proportion to the increase of the produce of the country, and the peculiar exigencies of the times, political circumstances having deranged the natural order of things, and rendered, during the late revolutions of Europe, a more than usual quantity of currency necessary.

CAROLINE

But was it not during the last war that all our gold coin disappeared, and was supposed to be melted down or exported? And was there not a general rise in the price of provisions and commodities at the same period?

MRS. B.

That is certainly true; still the question was disputed whether these circumstances might not be owing to the war, and the taxes it entailed upon us, rather than to an over-issue of bank-notes. England was under the necessity of paying her troops on the Continent, and of subsidising foreign sovereigns; and the opinion was maintained by ignorant people, that this was a sufficient reason to account for the disappearance of our specie, and to render an additional issue of bank-notes necessary.

But the strongest argument in favour of a depreciation of the currency is, that guineas no longer passed for the same value as gold bullion, which is the natural standard of the value of coined money.

CAROLINE.

Has the gold then been adulterated, and an ounce of gold coined into more than £3, 17 shillings, and 10½ pence?

MRS. B.

No; but gold bullion partook of the general rise of commodities, and, instead of selling for £3, 17 shillings, and 10½ pence, it sold for above £, and even once was as high as £5 an ounce.

CAROLINE

But why did not guineas rise in the same proportion? I cannot conceive how they can be less valuable than a similar weight of the gold of which they are made?

MRS. B.

The coined and the uncoined gold, it is true, remained in reality of the same value, but as it is not lawful to pass a guinea for more than a pound-note and a shilling, the guineas were compelled to share the fate of the paper-currency; and if that was depreciated all the coined money of the country, whether gold or silver, must have been so likewise.

CAROLINE

Then, if it had not been illegal, every one would have melted his depreciated guineas and shillings, and converted them into gold and silver bullion?

MRS. B.

Certainly. It is this which caused our specie to disappear, and transported it to foreign countries, where it was freed from the shackles of a depreciated paper-currency, and enabled to fetch its real value in exchange for goods; it is this also which, as we before observed, brought foreign goods to be sold at our market, because it was dear; and sent our money to purchase goods at foreign markets, because they were cheap.

CAROLINE

But if an ounce of gold rises in price from £3, 17 shillings, and 10½ pence to £5 is it not rather the value of the bullion that has risen than the currency that has fallen?

MRS. B.

Gold bullion, like every other commodity, rises in *price* only, not in *value;* and that rise is owing to the depreciation of the currency in which its price is estimated: were there no depreciation, bullion and guineas would both be worth £3, 17 shillings, and 10½ pence an ounce.

Let us now conclude our observations on currency, which we may henceforth consider as consisting not merely of specie, but of coined and of paper-money.

CAROLINE

It is not, I suppose, necessary that the value of the currency of a country should be equal to the value of the commodities to be circulated by it?

MRS. B.

By no means. The same guinea or bank-note will serve the purpose of transferring from one individual to another several hundred pounds' worth of goods in the course of a short time. There are besides many expedients for economizing money, the most remarkable of which is an arrangement made amongst bankers. Their clerks meet every day after the heart of business to exchange the draughts made on each other for the preceding day. If, for instance, the banking-house A. has draughts to the amount of £20,000 on the banking-house B., the latter has also, in all probability, draughts upon the former, though they may not be to the same amount; the two houses exchange these draughts as far as they will balance each other, and the necessity of providing money for the payment of the whole is thus obviated. By this economical expedient, which is carried on amongst all the bankers in London east of St. Paul's, I understand that about £200,000 performs the function of four or five millions.

CAROLINE

And what do you suppose to be the proportion of the money to the value of the commodities to be circulated by it?

MRS. B.

That, I believe, it would be impossible to ascertain. Mr. Sismondi, in his valuable Treatise on Commercial Wealth, compares these respective quantities to mechanical powers, which, though of different weights, balance each other from the equality of their momentum; and, to follow up the comparison, he observes, that though commodities are by far the most considerable in quantity, yet that the velocity with which currency circulates compensates for its deficiency.

CAROLINE

This is an extremely ingenious comparison, and I should suppose the analogy to be perfectly correct; for the less money there is in circulation, the more frequently it will be transferred from one to another in exchange for goods.

MRS. B.

The analogy will, however, bear only to a certain extent; otherwise, whatever were the proportions of currency and of commodities, they would always balance each other, and the price of commodities would never be affected by the increase or diminution of the quantity of currency.

CONVERSATION XVIII

ON INCOME FROM COMMERCE

DIFFERENCE OF WHOLESALE AND RETAIL TRADE.—GENERAL ADVANTAGES OF TRADE.—HOW IT ENRICHES A COUNTRY.—ADVANTAGES OF RETAIL TRADE.—GREAT PROFITS OF SMALL CAPITALS EXPLAINED.—ADVANTAGES OF QUICK RETURN OF CAPITAL TO FARMERS AND MANUFACTURERS.—ADVANTAGES OF ROADS, CANALS, ETC.—DIFFERENCES OF THE HOME TRADE, FOREIGN TRADE, AND CARRYING TRADE.—OF THE HOME TRADE: IT RETURNS CAPITAL QUICKER.

MRS. B.

WE mentioned commerce as one of the modes of employing capital to produce an income; but deferred investigating its effects until you had acquired some knowledge of the nature and use of money. We may now, therefore, proceed to examine in what manner commerce enriches individuals, and augments the wealth of a country.

Those who engage their capitals in commerce or trade act as agents or middle-men between the producers and the consumers of the fruits of the earth; they purchase them of the former, and sell them to the latter; and it is by the profits on the sale that capital so employed yields an income.

There are two distinct sets of men engaged in trade:—merchants, who purchase commodities (either in a rude or a manufactured state) of those who produce them,—this is called wholesale trade; and shopkeepers, who purchase goods in smaller quantities of the merchants, and distribute them to the public according to the demand,—this constitutes the retail trade.

CAROLINE

Trade will no doubt bring an income to those who employ their capital in it; but I do not conceive how it contributes to the wealth of the country manufacturers, for neither merchants nor shopkeepers produce any thing new; they add nothing to the general stock of wealth, but merely distribute that which is produced by others. It is true, that mercantile men form a considerable part of the community; but if their profits are taken out of the pockets of their countrymen, they may make fortunes without enriching their country.

MRS. B.

Trade increases the wealth of a nation, not immediately by raising produce, like agriculture, nor by working up raw materials, like manufactures; but it gives an additional value to commodities by bringing them from places where they are plentiful to those where they are scarce; it enables us to procure what we want more, in exchange for what we want less; and, by providing the means of a more extended distribution of commodities, it gives a spur to the industry both of the agricultural and manufacturing classes. It would be impossible, you know, for every town or district to produce the several kinds of commodities required for its consumption; different soils and climates, and various species of skill and industry, are requisite for that purpose. Some lands are best calculated for corn, others for pasture; some towns are celebrated for their cotton manufactures, others for their woollen cloths. Every place has, therefore, an excess of some kind of commodities, and a deficiency of others; which renders a system of exchanges necessary, not only between individuals (as we observed in treating of the origin of barter), but between towns and countries to the most distant regions of the earth.

Now merchants exchange the surplus produce of one place for that of another. A man who deals in any particular commodity makes it his business to find out in what parts that commodity is most abundant, and will be sold at the lowest price; and in what parts it is most scarce, and will fetch the highest price, and then to ascertain the least expensive mode of conveying it from the one to the other market.

CAROLINE

In this they consult their own interest; since to purchase at the cheapest and sell at the dearest market will give them the greatest profits.

MRS. B.

No doubt; but it is wisely and beneficially ordained by Providence, that in consulting their own interest they are at the same time favouring that of the community. When merchants hasten to send their goods to a market where they will sell at a high price, they supply those who are in want of such goods: the higher the price the more urgent is the demand: it *is* a deficiency that has rendered them dear, and by furnishing the market with an ample supply, merchants not only satisfy the wants of the purchasers, but ultimately lower the price of the commodity.

Do you think that manufacturers would be able to dispose of an equal quantity of goods without the intervention of mercantile men? In such a case, Manchester would be reduced to distribute its cottons merely within its own precincts and environs, instead of supplying, as it now does, not only the demand of all England, but even that of the most remote provinces of America,

Trade encourages industry, in the second place, by rendering commodities cheaper. The merchant, by dealing in large quantities, is enabled to bring goods to market at a less expense of conveyance, and can therefore afford to sell them on lower terms than if the consumer were obliged to send for them to the places where they are produced.

CAROLINE

Yet things may generally be bought at the lowest price where they are produced or manufactured?

MRS. B.

True; but if you add the charges of a private conveyance, they will cost you much dearer. Had we no means of procuring coals than by sending a wagon to Newcastle, though we should pay less for them there than in London, they would, from the expense of carriage, cost us more. Merchants who deal in large quantities have a regular system of conveyance for their goods, which considerably diminishes the charges. The coals are by them transported in ships to the different sea-ports, and thence conveyed in barges to the inland parts of the country wherever water-carriage is practicable.

CAROLINE

It would, to be sure, not only be very expensive, but extremely inconvenient, were we obliged to send to distant parts for the commodities they produce. If, for instance, it were necessary to send to Sheffield to purchase a set of knives and forks; to Leeds for a coat, and to Norwich for a shawl;—or, without going so far, were it requisite to send into the country for corn, meat, hay, in short, every thing which the country produces, these things would cost us much more than if we bought them of shopkeepers.

But admitting that trade, by facilitating the distribution of commodities, and rendering them cheaper, promotes their consumption, I cannot understand how that can conduce to the wealth of a country: it increases its comforts and enjoyments, but it seems to me to encourage expenditure rather than production.

MRS. B.

It would be rather difficult to encourage the one independently of the other, unless you could purchase what has not been produced. To increase the comforts and enjoyments of a country is the ultimate aim of national wealth, and it is only by augmenting these productions that we can increase the enjoyment of them. Now whilst trade promotes consumption, by rendering commodities cheaper, it encourages industry in the producer, to augment the supply. A reduction of price brings a commodity within the reach of a greater number of persons, which increases the demand for it; the man who could afford to wear only a linen frock, will, when commodities are cheaper, be able to wear a coat He who could allow himself but one coat in the year, can now without extravagance wear two.

This increasing demand for commodities stimulates the industry of the farmer and manufacturer, and they enrich themselves by furnishing the requisite supplies. With their wealth their consumption also augments; for the wants of men increase with their means of satisfying them; and when they add to their income, they usually add also to their expenditure. The farmer has more to satisfy the desires of the manufacturer; and the manufacturer produces more to supply the demands of the farmer: so that each is enabled to give and receive a greater quantity of things in exchange. These exchanges, it is true, are made through the agency of merchants, and by the means of money, but they are effectually exchanges of commodities, as really as if the manufacturer supplied the farmer with clothing in exchange for provisions. The increase of saleable commodities affects in a similar manner all classes of people. The proprietor of land improves his fortune by the increasing value of his rents, which the prosperous state of agriculture enables the farmer to pay; and the labourer betters his condition by the rise in the rate of wages resulting from the increased demand for labour. The whole may be summed up by saying, that the quantity of commodities being increased, a larger portion will fall to the lot of every consumer who has any share in their production.

CAROLINE

I now begin to understand the general advantages resulting from commerce. The retail trade carried on by shopkeepers must be attended with the same happy effects. It would be extremely inconvenient to the rich, and impracticable for the poor, to purchase the commodities they wanted in such large quantities as are disposed of by merchants and wholesale dealers. Were there no such trade as a butcher, for instance, every family would be obliged to purchase a whole sheep or a whole ox of the farmer.

MRS. B.

Retail trade is one of the most useful subdivisions of labour. Nothing can be more desirable than that the poor, who are maintained, by daily or weekly wages, should be able to purchase their provisions in as small quantities as possible.

CAROLINE

Yet I have often regretted the high price which the lower orders of people are obliged to pay for fuel, candles, grocery, and various little articles with which they are supplied by the chandlers' shops; whilst the higher ranks, who can afford to purchase the same goods in larger quantities, obtain them of more extensive dealers at a cheaper rate.

MRS. B.

You must consider that were there no small shopkeepers, the lower classes would be reduced to the utmost distress; and these petty dealers cannot afford to sell their penny-worths, without being paid for the additional labour and trouble such kind of traffic requires. Their profits cannot be exorbitant; otherwise competition would in time reduce them to their natural standard.

CAROLINE

But by selling very small quantities at a higher price, they must make more than the usual rate of profit; and how do you reconcile this to the common level of profit in all employment of capital?

MRS. B.

By reckoning whatever gains they make above the usual profits of capital, as *wages,* that is to say, the reward of their personal labour. The smaller is the capital which a man employs, the greater is the proportion which his wages will bear to the profits of his capital. A man who sells oranges in the streets has laid out perhaps a capital of 20 or 30 shillings on the goods in which he deals; the usual profits of trade on such a sum is two or three shillings a year; but if he did not carry about oranges for sale, he would work as a labourer, and get perhaps two shillings a day wages; these two shillings a day, or 626 shillings a year, the man must make by the sale of his oranges, in addition to the usual profits of trade; the whole of his gains go, however, under the name of profits, because the distinction can be made only in theory.

CAROLINE

But all tradesmen and mercantile men devote their time and attention to their business: should not, therefore, a portion of their gains be considered as the reward of their personal labour, which must be valuable in proportion to the extent and importance of the concern in which they are engaged?

MRS. B.

No doubt; yet it will bear but a small proportion

to their profits, compared with that of petty dealers. A merchant who makes in trade an income of £5000 a year, were he to engage himself as clerk, would probably not obtain a salary of above £500; his wages would therefore be equal to only one tenth of his profits, whilst those of the man who sold oranges would be above 200 times the amount of the profits of his capital.

Another advantage resulting to the fanner and manufacturer, from the disposal of their goods to merchants, is the quick return of the capital they have employed in their production; for they receive the price of their goods from the merchant much sooner than they would, were they obliged to collect it gradually from the consumers.

Let us suppose a cotton manufacturer who devotes a capital of a thousand pounds to the employment of as many labourers as it will maintain, and sells their work to a wholesale dealer for £1,100. With this money he immediately sets his men and his mills to work again; whilst, if he retailed the goods himself, though instead of £1,100 he might perhaps get £1,200 or even £1,300 for them, yet, as the money would come in very slowly, he and his workmen would necessarily be kept a long time out of employ.

CAROLINE

To the farmer such delays would prove ruinous, if he could not sell his crops in time to proceed with the necessary cultivation of the farm for the ensuing season.

MRS. B.

In order to avoid such extremities, both the farmer and manufacturer would be obliged to divide their capital into two parts, and employ the one in raising or manufacturing commodities, and the other in disposing of them. To the occupations of agriculture or manufactures, they would find it necessary to add that of trade, a complication which would be equally injurious to each of the concerns. Commerce is one of the economical divisions of labour; if it sets apart a certain number of men, for the purpose of circulating and distributing the produce of the earth, it is in order that those who are engaged in raising and manufacturing that produce should be able to devote the whole of their capital, their time, and their talents, to their respective employments. It is worthy of observation, too, that none of these divisions are enforced by law, but exist under the choice' of the parties, and have been adopted from a view to their general interest. But although it is advantageous to separate commerce from other branches of industry, it is desirable that its operations should be facilitated as much as possible, both in order that agriculture and manufactures should not be deprived of too many labourers, and that commodities should be brought to market with the least possible expense. Good and numerous roads and navigable canals are extremely conducive to this end, as they enable the produce of the country to be conveyed with ease and expedition to the several markets; for ease and expedition economise time and labour, and economy of time and labour is productive of cheapness.

CAROLINE

Were there no roads, the farmer, being without means of sending his crops to market, would not produce more than could be consumed by his family, and perhaps some few customers in his neighbourhood, and he must be content to clothe himself with the fleeces of his flocks and the skins of his herds, for he would be unable to procure manufactured articles. Nor would the manufacturers be better off, as the market for the disposal of their goods would be equally limited.

MRS. B.

Neither towns nor manufactures could exist in such a state of things, because they could not be supplied with the produce of the country, which is still more necessary to their existence, than the workmanship of the towns is to the farmer. It is the surplus produce of the country which pays for the workmanship of the towns, and the surplus workmanship of the towns that pays for the produce of the country. The greater, therefore, the intercourse between town and country, the greater is the encouragement given to the industry of both; and it is scarcely possible to foretell the immense advantages that will be derived from the introduction of rail-roads.

History teaches us that in all old settled countries no material improvement has taken place in the cultivation of the lands without a considerable advance in the state of manufactures and commerce; and Adam Smith even goes so far as to say, that "through the greater part of Europe the commerce and manufactures of cities, instead of being the effect, have been the cause and occasion of the improvement and " cultivation of the country."

But as the forms of governments, and the manners and customs of our barbarous ancestors, have constantly interfered with and restricted the progress of wealth and civilisation of Europe, the natural order of things has frequently been reversed; and towns have arisen, not from the surplus wealth of the country, but as citadels and fortresses, in which the people found shelter from the oppression of their superiors and the incursions of their warlike neighbours. We must look to America for the natural effect of the progress of wealth end civilisation, and we shall there behold the habitations of farmers scattered over the face of the country, and towns built only after cultivation was far advanced.

CAROLINE

In expatiating on the advantages of facility of conveyance, it must not, however, be forgotten, that the land which is converted into roads is taken from tillage; and could we calculate the quantity of corn and hay which the roads, in a state of culture, might have produced, it would perhaps be found that some of them have occasioned more loss than gain.

To take land from cultivation for the purpose of roads appears to me very analogous to taking labourers from agriculture for the purpose of trade.

MRS. B.

The result is in both cases similar; for there can be no doubt but that the general effect of roads and canals is to increase the produce of the country. If we are indebted to merchants for the advantages of trade, roads and canals are the instruments with which they carry it on. Deprived of such means, their operations would be very circumscribed; there would be no trade but at sea-ports, and along the course of rivers.

The charge of conveyance from Liverpool to Manchester on the Duke of Bridgewater's canal is six shillings a ton, whilst the price of land-carriage is forty shillings.

CAROLINE

But since the railroad has been established between those towns, I suppose it supersedes all other conveyance.

MRS. B.

For passengers, no doubt, it does, and also for luggage that is not very heavy; but as I understand that the canal is in as great activity as ever, it must be preferred for weighty luggage, especially when time is of no great importance.

CAROLINE

If there had been a river from one of those towns to the other, the expense of carriage would have been still less than that of the canal.

MRS. B.

Probably not; a river is seldom uniformly navigable, and is always more or less circuitous in its course; and where the stream is powerful, it will admit of navigation only in one direction, as is the case in some of the American rivers. Before the Bridgewater canal was dug, the usual mode of conveyance of goods was along the Mersey and the Trevell, and the cost was twelve shillings a ton, just double that of conveyance on the canal. Macpherson observes, that "this spirited and patriotic enterprise of the Duke of Bridgewater is rewarded by a vast revenue, arising from his water-carriage and his formerly useless coal-mine; and the surrounding country is benefited a pound at least in every shilling paid to the Duke."

CAROLINE

This reminds me of a, circumstance that occurred

during a tour in Wales; we were admiring a neat fountain which supplied a village with water, and were informed by the landlord of the inn that he had constructed it, and had had the water conveyed from a distant spring, whence the people of the village had formerly been under the necessity of fetching it. A trifling sum was annually paid by each family for liberty to use this water, and the landlord thought it necessary to make many apologies for not allowing it them free of expense, and talked much of the money he had laid out in the enterprise. My father assured him that he was convinced the speculation was still more beneficial to the village than it was to himself; that as the inhabitants had the option of fetching water for themselves, the payment proved that it was because they could turn the time and labour they bestowed on the conveyance of water to better account; and upon inquiry we found the village had been in an improving state ever since the erection of this fountain. It had not only become more opulent, but had acquired habits of cleanliness, which had. proved very beneficial to the health of the people.

MRS. B.

There are three species of commerce in which merchants engage their capitals. The *home trade, foreign trade,* and the *carrying trade.*

The home trade comprehends all the internal and coasting trade of a country. The foreign trade is that in which we exchange our commodities for those of foreign countries; and the carrying trade consists in conveying the commodities of one foreign country to another. Let us at present confine our observations to the home trade.

CAROLINE

The home trade, I conclude, must be the most advantageous to the country, because it encourages the industry of our own people.

MRS. B.

What difference can it make whether our labourers are employed to work for us, or for foreigners? For if we export English goods, we receive an equal amount of foreign goods in exchange; so that foreign labourers work equally for us in return.

The only advantage of the home trade is that it usually affords a quicker return of capital, which is a further means of promoting industry. The nearer is the market at which the merchant disposes of his goods the sooner will his capital be returned to him, and the sooner will he be able to take other goods from the hands of the farmer or manufacturer. If a London merchant trades with Sheffield or Manchester, his capital may be returned to him in the course of a few weeks; if with America or the East Indies, it may be a year or two, or more, before he gets it back. The greater the vicinity of the market, therefore, the greater the number of sales and purchases he will be able to make in a given time. A capital of £1,000, for instance, might in the home trade be returned once a month, and enable the merchant, during the course of the year, to purchase £12,000 worth of goods; whilst, if he sent his merchandise to India, two years would probably elapse before he got his capital returned. In the first case, therefore, the £1,000 capital would afford twenty-four times more encouragement to industry than it would in the latter.

CAROLINE

You do not thence mean to infer, that in the first case the profits would be twenty-four times greater?

MRS. B.

Certainly not. Competition is, you know, perpetually tending to equalise the profits of capital, in whatever way it is employed. Profits will consequently be proportioned to the slow return of capital; and must, therefore, be reckoned annually, and not calculated upon every time the capital is returned.

CAROLINE

The period of the return of capital applies, then, not so much to the home or foreign trade, as to the distance of the market; for capital might be returned quicker in trading with Calais or Dunkirk than with Edinburgh and Cork?

MRS. B.

Very true; and how much is it to be regretted that jealousies and dissensions should so frequently impede and restrict the trade between neighbouring nations, which would otherwise be carried on with such great and reciprocal advantage! But we shall reserve till our next interview the observations we have to make on foreign trade.

CONVERSATION XIX

ON FOREIGN TRADE

ADVANTAGES OF FOREIGN TRADE.—IT EMPLOYS THE SURPLUS OF CAPITAL, AND DISPOSES OF A SURPLUS OF COMMODITIES.—OF BOUNTIES.—EFFECTS OF RESTRICTIONS ON FOREIGN TRADE.—EXTRACT FROM SAY'S POLITICAL ECONOMY.—EXTRACT FROM FRANKLIN'S WORKS.

CAROLINE

AT our last interview, Mrs. B., you were regretting that any restraint should be imposed on our trade with foreign countries; yet I cannot help thinking that every measure tending to discourage foreign commerce, and promote our own industry, would be extremely useful.

MRS. B.

You would find it difficult to accomplish both those objects; for in order to encourage our own industry we must facilitate the means of selling the produce of our manufactures, and extend their market as much as possible. On the other hand, if we prohibit exportation, we limit the production of our manufactures to the supply which can be consumed at home. If the woolen manufacturers of Leeds, after having supplied the whole demand of England for broad cloths, have any capital left, they will use it in the preparation of woolen goods for exportation.

CAROLINE

Why not rather employ it in the fabrication of other commodities which may be consumed at home?

MRS. B.

If there were a deficiency of capital in any other branch of industry at home, the redundancy would naturally be drawn to that branch; but if all the trade, that is all the exchanges, that could be made at home have been made, we send the residue of our commodities to foreign markets for sale.

CAROLINE

Yet it appears a great hardship on the poor to send goods abroad, which so many of them are in want of at home.

MRS. B.

The poor are supplied with whatever they can afford to purchase; and without the means of purchase you must recollect that there can be no effectual demand. It is not to be expected that farmers and manufacturers should labour for them merely from charitable motives, and were they so disposed, they would not long possess the means of continuing their benevolence. It would be very wrong, therefore, to consider this surplus produce as taken from the poor; for it would not have been produced had there been no demand for it in foreign countries.

CAROLINE

That is very true. In all employment of capital men labour with a view to profit; they work, therefore, only for those who will pay them the value of their produce; and it is easy to conceive that those who have no further want of English commodities may yet wish to procure foreign goods. The English merchant will therefore say, "Since there is no more demand for the goods I deal in, I will export the remainder, which will be purchased abroad, and I shall get foreign commodities in exchange;—though my countrymen do not require any more cotton goods, I know that they will purchase wines, coffee, sugar," &c.

MRS. B.

Very well. Let us examine now what would be the effect of confining the employment of commercial capital to the home trade. If the inhabitants of the West Indian islands,—Jamaica, for instance,—were to prohibit the exportation of coffee and sugar, and the planters were obliged to trade only within the island, the consequence would be, that the demand for coffee and sugar would be very small, and that an inconsiderable part only of the capital of the colony would find employment. The same effect would take place in Russia, if foreign merchants were not allowed to purchase the hemp and flax so abundantly produced in that country. If in Peru and Chile the exportation of indigo, bark, and other drugs were prohibited, the Europeans, who purchase them, would not be the only sufferers; the Americans would be impoverished for want of employment for their capital.

CAROLINE

All this is very clear, I admit. But what security have we that merchants will not employ their capital in foreign commerce, before the demand for it in the home trade is fully supplied?

MRS. B.

That security is derived from the natural distribution of capital according to the rate of profit. If foreign commerce employed more capital than the country could spare, the demand for it at home would raise the profits of the home trade, and the temptation of these increased profits would soon restore, that portion of capital which had been un-necessarily withdrawn from it

CAROLINE

The rate of profit, then, affords an excellent criterion of the employment of capital most advantageous to the community. When foreign commerce offers greater profits than the home trade, it proves that there is a greater demand for capital in that branch of industry?

MRS. B.

Yes; it proves that the country possesses a surplus quantity of produce either agricultural or manufactured, which cannot be disposed of in the home market; and if the owners of this surplus were prevented from exchanging it for foreign commodities, it would not in future be produced, and those who produced it would be thrown out of employment.

The first commodities a country usually exports are agricultural produce, which she exchanges for manufactured goods; this is still the case with America, on account of it being a newly-settled nation; it is also the case with Poland and Russia, those countries having made slower progress in wealth and population than the other communities of Europe. When nations are considerably advanced in wealth and population, all the food they raise is required at home, and manufactures are established in order to employ the increased numbers of people; in the course of time they find that they require more food than is produced at home, it then becomes expedient to export manufactured goods in exchange for corn, which they can obtain cheaper by importation than by raising it on inferior soils at home; and it is at this point that England is now arrived.

CAROLINE

I am surprised that foreign commerce with distant countries should ever offer sufficient profits to afford a compensation to the merchant for the disadvantages arising from the slow return of capital.

MRS. B.

If it did not, no merchant would engage in it. The greater the distance of the market to which he sends his goods, the greater must be the profits on their sale, to make up not only for the tardy return of his capital, but also for the charges of conveyance of the goods. Freight and insurance from sea risks are both to be deducted from the profits of the merchant in foreign trade.

CAROLINE

Then, since we are obliged to sell our goods at such high prices in distant markets, I wonder that we should find purchasers for them: would it not answer better for those countries to produce them at home?

MRS. B.

You may be assured that no nation will purchase from abroad what may be procured of the same quality and for less expense at home. But all countries are not equally capable of producing the same kind of commodities, either rude or manufactured. The gifts of nature are still more diversified in the different climates of the earth than the habits and dispositions of men. It would be impossible for us at any expense to produce the wines of Portugal, on account of the coldness of our climate; we can procure them only by an exchange of commodities: the Portuguese take our broad cloth in return: this, it is true, they might manufacture at home; but as our climate is peculiarly favourable to pasturage, and our workmen particularly skilful in manufactures, broad cloths could not be made in Portugal equally good at the same expense, including the charges of freight and insurance; and whilst the Portuguese can purchase them of us for less than they can fabricate them at home, it is certainly their interest to procure them in exchange for commodities the culture or fabrication of which is more suited to the nature of their climate and the habits of the people.

But the difference of price of our manufactured goods at home or abroad is not so great as you would imagine; in articles of small bulk it is very trifling. I recollect some years since purchasing an English pocket-book at Turin for nearly the same price that it would have cost in London.

CAROLINE

How, then, was the expense of conveyance defrayed; and what compensation was there for the slow return of capital?

MRS. B.

These expenses probably did not more than coun-terbalance the high rent and taxes paid by London shopkeepers, which I believe are comparatively insignificant at Turin. There ought, perhaps, also be some bounty on the exportation of such goods, which would enable the merchant to sell them at a lower price.

CAROLINE

Pray what is a bounty on goods?

MRS. B.

It is a pecuniary reward given by government for the exportation of certain goods. Governments, so far from partaking of your prejudices against foreign trade, often think it right to encourage the exportation of their manufactures by such artificial measures.

CAROLINE

A bounty, then, on any commodity has the effect of inducing merchants to export more of it than they would otherwise do, as it raises their profits?

MRS. B.

Yes; and in consequence of this, capital is drawn into that trade beyond its due proportion: a bounty therefore often tempts merchants to invest capital in a trade which otherwise would not answer; that is, to export goods which would not yield a profit, after paying the expenses of conveyance, without such encouragement; and this capital, were it not artificially drawn out of its natural course, would flow into channels which would yield profits without any expense to government.

CAROLINE

Here, then, my apprehension of foreign trade is well founded; for more capital is drawn into it than is required to preserve the equality of profits.

MRS. B.

That is sometimes the case; but it may also be unduly drawn, from one branch of foreign commerce to another. The effect of bounties, however, is generally counteracted by the nations with whom we trade. Alarmed at our thus in a manner forcing our goods upon them, and apprehensive of its interfering with the sale of their own manufactures, they immediately lay a duty on the commodity on which we grant a bounty, and oblige it to pay, on entering their territory, a sum at least equivalent to that which we bestow on it on quitting our own.

CAROLINE

What a pity that either party should interfere to check and restrain the natural course of commerce! The disease, however, seems to call for the remedy; as it is sometimes expedient to take one poison as an antidote to another.

MRS. B.

If we are so generous, or so absurd, as to enable foreigners to purchase our commodities at a cheaper rate, by paying a part of the price for them, under the form of bounty, are we not doing them a service, and ourselves an injury? and is it wise in them to endeavour to counteract such a measure?

CAROLINE

True; I did not consider it in that point of view. It is really laughable to see two nations, the one strenuously endeavouring to injure itself, whilst the other studiously avoids receiving a benefit; and thus, by the mutual counteraction of each other's artifice, they leave the trade to follow its natural course.

I am now perfectly satisfied of the advantage of obtaining, by means of foreign commerce, such articles as cannot be produced at home; but I confess I do not feel the same conviction with regard to commodities which might be produced at home, even though at some additional expense.

MRS. B.

Why should it not be the interest of a country as well as that of an individual to purchase commodities wherever they can be procured cheapest? It might be very possible, as it has been observed by an ingenious writer*, for England to produce at a great expense of labour the tobacco which we now import from Virginia; and the Virginians, with no less difficulty, might fabricate the broad cloths with which we furnish them; but if our climate is better adapted to pasturage, and that of Virginia to the culture of tobacco, it is evident that the exchange of these commodities is a mutual advantage.

CAROLINE

But are not the goods exchanged in trade of equal value? If we send the Virginians a thousand pounds worth of broad cloths, they will send us only a thousand pounds worth of tobacco in return. It may be a convenient measure, and the exchanging merchants will each make their profits; but I cannot perceive how the country can derive any accession of wealth from such traffic.

MRS. B.

The cost of production or natural value of both these commodities is lowest in the respective countries in which they are produced, and their exchangeable

* Sir Francis Divernois

value will be augmented by bringing them from places where they are plentiful to those where they are scarce. When we ship off £1,000 worth of broad cloths for Virginia, and the Virginians export £1,000 worth of tobacco for England, the commodities of each acquire an additional value on arriving at their new destination. The tobacco will be worth more when it arrives in England, because, not being cultivated here, it is more scarce and in greater demand with us; the broad cloth will be worth more when it reaches Virginia, because, not being fabricated in that country, it is more scarce and in greater demand there. The respective cargoes will perhaps each have acquired the additional value of £200 on being landed at their destined ports.

CAROLINE

Very true; but if we both cultivated tobacco and fabricated broad cloths, and if the Virginians did the same, each country would be supplied at home, and the expense of conveyance of the two cargoes exchanged would be saved.

MRS. B.

If we could raise tobacco at as little expense as it is done in Virginia, and the Virginians could manufacture broad cloths as cheap as they can purchase them of us, your argument would be just; but that is not the case. To make this clear to you, let us examine what quantity of labour is bestowed upon the production of these several commodities. If the broad cloth which we send to Virginia cost us the labour of one man, we will say, for 1,000 days, while the tobacco which we receive in exchange would have cost us 2,000 days' labour to produce at home, do we not save a thousand days' labour? and is not the advantage to the Virginians similar, if the tobacco, which cost them 1,000 days' labour to raise, will exchange for English broad cloth which they could not have manufactured under 2,000 days labour?

CAROLINE

By such an exchange, then, each country saves 1,000 days' labour?

MRS. B.

Yes; and to save is to gain; for the thousand days' labour thus economised is employed in the production of some other commodity, which is so much clear gain to each country.

CAROLINE

Then each country procures the commodity it wants at half the expense which would have been required to produce it at home.

MRS. B.

Just so. To put the question in other words, we may say, if by the employment of £50,000 in the Virginia trade we can obtain as much tobacco as would require £100,000 if cultivated at home, there is £50,000 economised, which will be employed in producing something else. The advantages of foreign commerce, it is true, are seldom carried so far as a saving of half the expenses of production; but they must always exist in a greater or less degree; for it is evident that no nation will purchase from abroad what can be produced equally cheap and good at home.

CAROLINE

When goods are equally good and cheap, I certainly

prefer buying them of shops in the neighbourhood rather than at a distance, because it is more convenient; but why merchants should feel the same preference I do not clearly see: provided the goods they receive in their warehouses are of the same quality and price, I should think it would be immaterial to them from whence they came?

MRS. B.

They, like you, find advantages in dealing with their neighbours; it enables them to ascertain better the character of the persons of whom they make their purchases; it affords them the means of protecting themselves against imposition, and of applying a legal remedy in case of necessity. As long as profits are equal, therefore, (independently of risk,) a merchant will always prefer employing his capital in the home trade; and it is only superior profits that can tempt him to enter on a trade in which he is exposed to greater risks. You may recollect, we formerly observed that the chances of gain must always be proportioned to the chances of loss.

CAROLINE

I confess that before this explanation I never could comprehend how foreign trade could be a mutual advantage to the countries engaged in it, for I imagined that what was gained by the one was lost by the other.

MRS. B.

All free trade, of whatever description, must be a mutual benefit to the parties engaged in it; the only difference that can exist with regard to profit is, that it may not always be equally divided between them.

An opposition of interests takes place, not between merchants or countries exchanging their commodities, but between rival dealers in the same commodity; and it is from that circumstance probably that yon have been led to form such an erroneous idea of commerce. Do you not recollect our observing, some time since, that competition amongst dealers to dispose of their commodities renders them cheap, whilst competition amongst purchasers renders them dear? When you make any purchase, are you not sensible that the greater the number of shops in the same neighbourhood dealing in the same commodity, the more likely you are to purchase it at a low price?

CAROLINE

Yes, because the shopkeepers endeavour to undersell each other.

MRS. B.

It is therefore the interest of the dealer to narrow competition, whilst it is that of the consumer to enlarge it. Now which do you suppose to be the interest of the country at large?

CAROLINE

That of the consumers; for every man is a consumer, even the dealers themselves, who, though they are desirous of preventing competition in their own individual trade, must wish for it in all other species of commerce.

MRS. B.

No doubt; it is by free and open competition alone that extravagant prices and exorbitant profits are prevented, and that the public are supplied with commodities as cheap as the dealer can afford to sell them.

CAROLINE

But in regard to luxuries, Mrs. B., may we not be allowed to encourage those of our own production in preference to those brought from foreign countries?

MRS. B.

The principle of free trade is applicable equally to commodities of every description. If the French can make silks, cambricks, and laces for us, better and cheaper than we can make them ourselves, is it not better to employ them in such fabrications, whilst we employ our own countrymen in weaving cottons and broad cloths, or polishing cutlery; in a word, in some kind of work in which we excel, and which will be exported to pay for the French luxuries?

CAROLINE

True. I am always forgetting that foreign commodities must be paid for; and it is much the same whether we manufacture the silk or the calicoes and hardware which are given in exchange for it.

MRS. B.

No, it is not the same; it is to the advantage of every country that their labouring classes should be employed on what they can do easiest and best Therefore, if we make calicoes better than the French, and that the French manufacture silks of a superior quality to ours, let us each continue our respective employments; for we shall sell our calicoes to the French for more than they would fetch at home, and they, in return, will sell their silks dearer to us than they could if sold in France.

CAROLINE

Then it is tit for tat, and neither countries are gainers or losers in exchanging calicoes for silks, for what we gain on the sale of calicoes we lose on the purchase of silks, and what the French gain on the sale of their silks is lost on the purchase of our calicoes.

MRS. B.

On the contrary both countries are gainers by employing themselves on what they can do best; for they each make a saving of labour, as I explained to you, in our trade with Virginia; and labour saved is so much labour gained to be employed on some other work; in other words, the cost of production of the articles exchanged is diminished in both cases.

The commercial state of France during Bonaparte's system of prohibition furnishes a very curious illustration of the evils resulting from restraints on free trade. The West-Indian produce, which the French were prohibited from purchasing, consists chiefly of sugar and coffee, luxuries of which they could not endure to be deprived; so that they were employed, at an immense expense of capital, in extracting a saccharine juice from various fruits and roots to answer in an inferior degree the purpose of sugar; they cultivated bitter endives, the root of which supplied them with a wretched substitute for coffee; their tea was composed of indigenous herbs of a very inferior flavour to that of China; in a word, labour was multiplied to produce commodities of inferior value, or they would have been altogether deprived of a variety of comforts to which they had been accustomed, and which, besides the pleasure derived from the enjoyment of them, we have observed to be one of the strongest incitements to industry.

But the privation of the consumers of luxuries is but a trifling evil compared with the consequences of such restrictions upon the labouring classes; for its effect is to increase the difficulty of raising produce, and, consequently, to diminish the quantity of capital, the fund upon which the poor subsist.

Mr. Say, who witnessed all the pernicious effects of this system, thus expresses himself: *"C'est un bien mauvais calcul que de vouloir obliger la zone temperée à fournir des produits à la zone torride. Nos terres produisent péniblement, en petite quantité, et en qualité médiocre, des matières sucrées et colorantes, qu'un autre climat donne avec profusion; mais elles produisent, au contraire, avec facilité, des fruits, des céréales que leur poids et leur volume ne permettent pas de tirer de bien loin. Lorsque nous condamnons nos terres à nous donner ce qu'elles produisent avec désavantage aux dépends de ce qu'elles produisent plus volontiers; lorsque nous achetons fort cher, ce que nous payerions à fort bon marché, si nous le tirions des lieux où il est produit avec avantage, nous devenons nous memes victimes de notre propre folie. Le comble de l'habilité est de tirer le parti le plus avantageux des forces de la nature; et le comble de la démence est de lutter contre elles; car c'est employer nos peines à detruire une partie des forces qu'elle voudroit nous prêter."*

CAROLINE

The prohibition of foreign commodities has, then, an effect precisely the reverse of that of machinery;

for it increases instead of diminishing the quantity of labour; and produces inferior) instead of more perfect commodities.

MRS. B.

And, consequently, the wealth, prosperity, and enjoyments of a country so situated, instead of augmenting, would decline. Let us hear what Dr. Franklin says on the subject of restrictions and prohibitions.

"Perhaps, in general, it would be better if government meddled no further with trade than to protect it, and let it take its course. Most of the statutes or acts, edicts, arrets, and placards, of parliaments, princes, and states, for regulating, directing, or restraining of trade, have, we think, been either political blunders, or jobs obtained by artful men, for private advantage, under pretence of public good. When Colbert assembled some wise old merchants of France, and desired their advice and opinion how he could serve and promote commerce: their answer, after consultation, was in three words only, '*Laissez nous faire.*' It is said by a very solid writer of the same nation, that *he* is well advanced in the science of politics who knows the full force of that maxim, *pas trap gouvemer,* which perhaps would be of more use when applied to trade than in any other public concern. It were, therefore, to be wished that commerce were as free between all the nations in the world as between the several counties of England. So would all, by mutual communication, obtain more enjoyment. Those counties do not ruin each other by trade, neither would the nations. No nation was ever ruined by trade, even seemingly the most disadvantageous. Whenever desirable superfluities are imported, industry is thereby excited and superfluity pro-duced."

CAROLINE

Well, I abandon the exclusive use of English luxuries; but the very argument you have used against them makes me think that it must be advisable to rely on home produce for the necessaries of life. Were we dependent on foreign countries for a supply of corn, what would become of us if those countries, in time of war, prohibited its exportation?

MRS. B.

Your question will lead us into a discussion on the corn trade, which it is too late for us to enter upon to-day; we will, therefore, reserve it for our next meeting.

CONVERSATION XX

Continuation of FOREIGN TRADE

ON THE CORN TRADE.—CONSEQUENCES OF DEFENDING UPON A
HOME SUPPLY OF CORN IN COUNTRIES OF GREAT CAPITAL
AND POPULATION.—IT PRODUCES HIGH PRICES IN ORDI-
NARY SEASONS, AND GREAT FLUCTUATION OF PRICES IN
TIMES OF SCARCITY AND OF ABUNDANCE.—WHY THIS IS
NOT THE CASE IN NEWLY-SETTLED COUNTRIES.—PRO-
PRIETY OF FREE TRADE IN GENERAL.—DANGER OF
INTRODUCING A NEW BRANCH OF INDUSTRY PREMA-
TURELY.—EXTRACT FROM MIRABEAU'S MONARCHIE
PRUSSIENNE ON THE ADVANTAGES OF FREE COMMERCIAL
INTERCOURSE.

MRS. B.

WHEN we last parted, you expressed a wish that we should
raise all our corn at home, in order to be completely independent of the casualties attending a foreign supply.

CAROLINE

Yes; for were we at war with those countries which usually furnished us with corn, they would withhold the supply;
or, should they experience a dearth, they would no longer
have it in their power to send us corn.

MRS. B.

We occasionally import corn from different parts of

America, from the shores of the Baltic, and those of the Mediterranean seas. Now, it is very improbable either that we should be in a state of warfare with those various countries at the same period of time, or that they should all be afflicted with a dearth of produce in the same season. There is much greater chance of a scarcity prevailing in any single country, than in every part of the world at once. Indeed, facts have fully demonstrated, that when the weather is unfavourable to the crops of one country, it is almost invariably found to be favourable to those of another. I believe no single instance can be produced of a simultaneous failure of the crops throughout the whole commercial world. In the year 1800, when England suffered so much distress from the deficiency of the harvest, the crops were very abundant in Spain; while the harvest of 1803, which was extremely plentiful in this country, was so deficient in Spain as to produce a famine. Now it is evident, that had a free corn trade existed between these countries, the distresses of both would have been alleviated.

CAROLINE

Under such circumstances it would certainly be right to import corn; I object only to doing so habitually, and not depending in ordinary times on the produce of our own country.

MRS. B.

If we apply to corn countries only in seasons of distress we shall find it very difficult to obtain relief. Those countries, after supplying themselves, raise corn only for nations which they usually supply with that article; but they will have but little to spare for a new customer, who from an accidental dearth at home is compelled to seek for food abroad; and we could obtain it only by out-bidding other competitors. The supply, therefore, would be both scanty and at a price which the lower ranks of people could ill afford to pay; so that there would be great distress, if not danger of a famine.

CAROLINE

To prevent such a calamity we have only to raise so large a quantity of corn at home as will afford a plentiful supply in years of average produce; then in seasons of abundance we have the resource of exportation, and in bad seasons we might still have a sufficiency.

MRS. B.

It is impossible to raise at all times a sufficiency without having often a superfluity. This is particularly the case with corn, as it is the most variable of almost all kinds of agricultural produce. If, there-fore, we wish to raise such a quantity as will always secure us against want, we must in common seasons have some to spare, and in abundant years a great superfluity.

Now the more corn-land we cultivate the higher will the price of corn be in average seasons. You start, Caroline; but, paradoxical as this may appear, if you reflect upon the causes which occasion the regular high price of corn, independently of the variations of supply and demand, you will understand it.

The more corn is grown in a country the greater will be the quantity of inferior land brought into cultivation, in order to produce it; and the price of corn, you know must pay the cost of its production on the worst soil on which it is raised*, otherwise it would cease to be produced. If, therefore, in order to ensure a home supply, we force an ungrateful soil, at a great expense of capital, to yield a scanty crop, we raise the price of all the corn of the country to that standard, and we thus enable the landed proprietors to increase their rents.

CAROLINE

That is very true; and then by enhancing the price of the first necessaries of life we must raise the rate of wages.

MRS. B.

Yes; but observe that this rise of wages does not at all better the condition of the labouring classes; it merely enables them to live at the advanced price of the necessaries of life.

Nor is this all; when the home supply of corn proves superabundant, what is to become of it? The unnatural high price at which it usually sells in our market, owing to the forced encouragement given to agriculture, renders it unsaleable in foreign markets until the price is fallen so low as to be ruinous to farmers.

CAROLINE

I cannot easily bring myself to look upon a superfluity of the necessaries of life as a calamity; — if it is injurious to the fanner, what an advantage it is to the lower classes of people!

MRS. B.

The advantage is of a very temporary nature. The farmer who cultivates poor land in hopes of a remune-

* See Conversation on Rent.

rating price, must be ruined if he continues to cultivate at the low price occasioned by superfluity: he will therefore throw up the inferior lands, and the consequence will be that less corn will be produced in succeeding years than is requisite for the supply; and the superfluity will be succeeded by dearth or famine. Thus the price of corn will be continually fluctuating between the low price of a glutted market and the high price of scarcity.

A redundance of the necessaries of life is in some respects attended with more pernicious consequences than the excess of any other species of commodity. If the market were overstocked with tea and coffee, those articles would fall in price, and would not only be more freely consumed by the people accustomed to enjoy them, but the reduction of price would bring them within reach of a lower and more extensive class of people. Now this cannot happen with bread, because it is already the daily and most common food of the lowest ranks of society, and though in seasons of great plenty they may consume somewhat more than usual, the difference will not be very considerable; they will rather avail themselves of the cheapness of bread to devote a larger share of their wages to other gratifications; they will eat more meat, drink more spirits, or wear better clothes. Great part of the superabundance of corn will therefore remain in the granary of the farmer, instead of supplying him with the means of carrying on the cultivation of his land; the labourers who raised that corn will probably be driven to the parish for want of work, and the consequences which will ensue to the community who would have bean fed by the fruits of their industry, may be easy to conceive.

CAROLINE

But do you then regard a low price of corn, under all circumstances, as an evil?

MRS. B.

On the contrary, I consider it as highly advantageous when it results from low cost of production; it is attended with injurious consequences only when it will not remunerate the former. But when corn can be raised at a small expense, it can afford to be sold at a low price. It is this which renders it desirable to bring only good land under tillage, and not to force poor soils to yield scanty and. expensive crops.

Countries that have plenty of good land and but little capital, find no branch of industry so advantageous as the productions of agriculture; and the exportation of corn, we have observed, is their first attempt at foreign commerce. Thus America, being a newly-settled country, and as yet but thinly inhabited, has great choice of fine soils, and can raise corn at a very small expense of production; accordingly we find, that she not only feeds her own population but regularly exports corn.

Poland and Prussia are still agricultural countries, exporting corn; but old established countries in general, such as England, which are far advanced in arts and manufactures, and have raised a population too great to be maintained by the produce of her good soils, will find it answer better to import some portion of the corn they consume, and to convert their inferior lands into pasture. This would not only lower the price of bread, but also that of meat, milk, butter, and cheese, the supply of which would be increased by the conversion of corn land into pasture. When the home crops proved abundant, they would import less; when scanty, they would import more. Thus without difficulty they would proportion the supply to the demand, and keep both bread and wages steadily at moderate prices.

CAROLINE

But with the additional expenses of freight and insurance, can we import corn from America cheaper than we can produce it at home?

MRS. B.

In ordinary seasons we certainly can.

CAROLINE

And do you suppose that the distressed state of agriculture is owing to our producing too much corn at home?

MRS. B.

I have no doubt but that it is one of the causes, but it is connected with many others, which render the question so complicated and intricate that we must leave it to wiser heads than our own to unravel.

The system of growing a home supply of corn, in countries where great capital affords the means of maintaining a very large population, is attended not only with the disadvantage of keeping the price of corn high in average seasons, but likewise occasions greater fluctuations of price in times of dearth or abundance than if those casualties were diminished by a free corn-trade with other countries.

Nothing is more injurious to the interests of the labouring classes than great and sudden fluctuations in the price of bread: they are either distressed by unexpected poverty, or intoxicated by sudden prosperity; but if that prosperity is the effect but of one fruitful season, it gives rise to expenses they are unable to maintain: it is but a gleam of sunshine on a wintry day, and the buds it untimely develops are nipped by the succeeding frost.

It would perhaps be difficult to say whether we have suffered most from a high or a low price of corn, within these last forty years; but we have acquired sufficient experience of the evils arising from both these extremes to think that the only course we can adopt to prevent great fluctuations of price is a free corn-trade.

CAROLINE

Well, Mrs. B., I see that you will not allow of any exception in favour of the corn-trade, and that I must consent to admit of the propriety of leaving all trade whatever perfectly free and open.

MRS. B.

That is certainly the wisest way. Instead of struggling against the dictates of reason and nature, and madly attempting to produce every thing at home, countries should study to direct their labours to those departments of industry for which their situation and circumstances are best adapted.

CAROLINE

Yet you must allow me to observe, that there are numerous instances of our having established flourishing manufactures of goods which we formerly procured entirely from foreign commerce: such, for instance, as china-ware, muslins, damask linen, and a variety of others. Now does not this imply that we may sometimes direct our labour to a new branch of industry with greater advantage than by importing the goods from foreign countries?

MRS. B.

It certainly does; and it shows also, that as soon as we are able to cultivate or fabricate the commodities we have been accustomed to procure from foreign parts as cheap as we can import them, we never fail to do so. But the period for the introduction of any new branch of industry should be left to the experience and discretion of the individuals concerned in it, and not attempted to be regulated or enforced by government. James I. attempted to compel his subjects to dye their woolen cloths in this country, instead of sending them to the Netherlands, as had been the usual practice; but the English-dyed woolen cloths proved both of worse quality and dearer than those of the Netherlands, and James was obliged to abandon his plan. Had the sovereign not interfered, dyers would have established themselves in this country as soon as the people had acquired sufficient skill to undertake the business; but the discouragement produced by an unsuccessful attempt probably retarded the natural period of adopting it.

If it were possible for a country both to cultivate and manufacture all kinds of produce with as little labour as it costs to purchase them from other countries, there would be no occasion for foreign commerce: but the remarkable manner in which Providence has varied the productions of nature in different climates, appears to indicate a design to promote an intercourse between nations, even to the most distant regions of the earth; an intercourse which would ever prove a source of reciprocal benefit and happiness, were it not often perverted by the bad passions and blind policy of man.

CAROLINE

And independently of the diversity of soils, climates, and natural productions, I do not suppose that it would be possible for any single country to succeed in all branches of industry, any more than for a single individual to acquire any considerable skill in a great variety of pursuits?

MRS. B.

Certainly not. The same kind of division of labour which exists among the individuals of a community, is also in some degree observable among different countries: "Nature," Mr. Senior observes, "seems to have intended that mutual dependence should unite all the inhabitants of the earth into one commercial family. For this purpose she has indefinitely diversified her own products in every climate and in almost every extensive district. For this purpose also she seems to have varied so extensively the wants and productive powers of the different races of men. The superiority of modern over ancient wealth depends, in a great measure, on the greater use we make of these varieties." And when particular branches of industry are not formed by local circumstances, it will generally be found the best policy to endeavour to excel a neighbouring nation in those manufactures in which we are nearly on a par, rather than to attempt com' petition in those in which by long habit and skill they have acquired a decided superiority. Thus will the common stock of productions be most improved, and all countries most benefited. Nothing can be more illiberal and short-sighted than a jealousy of the progressed of neighbouring countries, either in agriculture or manufactures. Their demand for our commodities, so far from diminishing, will always be found to increase with the means of purchasing them. It is the idleness and poverty, not the wealth and industry, of neighbouring nations that should excite alarm.

CAROLINE

A tradesman would consider it more for his interest to set up his shop in the neighbourhood of opulent customers than of poor people who could not afford to purchase his goods; and why should not countries consider trade in the same point of view?

MRS. B.

Mirabeau, in his *"Monarchie Prussienne,"* has carried this principle so far, that it has made him doubt whether the trade of France was injured by the revocation of the edict of Nantz, which drove so many skilful manufactures and artificers out of the country.

"Il est en général un principe sûr en commerce: plus vos acheteurs seront riches, plus vous leur vendrez: ainsi les causes qui enrichissent un peuple augmentent toujours l'industrie de ceux qui ont des affaires à négocier avec lui. Sans doute c'est une démence frénétique de chasser 200,000 individus de son pays pour enrichir celui des autres; mais la nature qui veut conserver son ouvrage ne cesse de réparer, par des compensations insensibles, les erreurs des homines; et les fautes les plus desastreuses ne sont pas sans remèdes. La grande vérité que nous offre cet exemple memorable, c'est

qu'il est insensé de détruire l'industrie et le commerce de ses voisins, puisqu'on anéantit en même tems chez soi-même ces trésors. Si de tels efforts pouvoient jamais produire leur effet, ils dépeupleroient le monde, et rendroient très-infortunée la nation qui auroit eu le malheur d'engloutir toute l'industrie, tout le commerce du globe, et de vendre toujours sans jamais acheter. Heureusement la Providence a tellement disposé les choses que les délires des souverains ne sauroient arrêter entièrement ses vues de bonheur notre espèce."

CAROLINE

The more I learn upon this subject, the more I feel convinced that the interests of nations, as well as those of individuals, so far from being opposed to each other, are in the most perfect unison.

MRS. B.

Liberal and enlarged views will always lead to similar conclusions, and teach us to cherish sentiments of universal benevolence towards each other; hence the superiority of science over mere practical knowledge.

CONVERSATION XXI

Subject of FOREIGN TRADE *continued.*

OF BILL OF EXCHANGE.—OF THE BALANCE OF TRADE.—CAUSE
OF THE REAL VARIATION OF THE EXCHANGE.—DISPROPOR-
TION OF EXPORTS AND IMPORTS.—CAUSE OF THE NOMI-
NAL VARIATION OF THE EXCHANGE.—DEPRECIATION OF
THE VALUE OF THE CURRENCY OF THE COUNTRY.

MRS. B.

I HOPE that you are now quite satisfied of the advantages
which result from foreign commerce?

CAROLINE

Perfectly so; but there is one thing which perplexes me.
In a general point of view I conceive that trade consists in
an exchange of commodities; but I do not understand how
this exchange takes place between merchants. The wine-
merchant, for instance, who imports wine from Portugal,
does not export goods in return for it; his trade is confined
to the article of wine.

MRS. B.

There are many general merchants who both export
and import various articles of trade. Thus the Spanish
merchant, the Turkey merchant, and the West-Indian

merchant, import all the different commodities which we receive from those countries, and generally export English goods in return. It is, however, the countries, rather than the individuals, who *exchange* their respective productions; for both the goods exported and imported are in all cases bought and sold, and never actually exchanged.

CAROLINE

But since the merchants of the respective countries do not literally exchange their goods, they must each of them send a sum of money in payment; and these sums of money will be nearly equivalent. If the London merchant has £1,000 to pay for wines at Lisbon, the Lisbon merchant will have nearly the same sum to pay for broad cloth in London. It is to be regretted, therefore, that the goods should not be actually exchanged, or that some mode should not be devised of reciprocally transferring the debts, in order to avoid so much useless expense and trouble.

MRS. B.

Such a mode has been devised, and these purchases and sales are usually made without the intervention of money, by means of written orders, called *bills of exchange.*

CAROLINE

Is not then a bill of exchange a species of paper-money like a bank-note?

MRS. B.

Not exactly; instead of being a promissory note, it is an order addressed to the person abroad to whom the merchant sends his goods, directing him to pay the amount of the bill, at a certain date, to some third person mentioned in the bill. Thus when a woolen merchant sends broad cloths to Portugal, he draws such a bill on the merchant to whom he consigns them; but instead of sending it with the goods to Portugal, he disposes of it in London; that is to say, he inquires whether any person wants such a bill for the purpose of discharging a debt in Portugal. He accordingly applies to some wine merchant who owes a sum of money to a mercantile house at Lisbon for wines imported from that country, and who finds it convenient to avail himself of this mode of payment, in order to avoid the expense of sending money to Portugal. He therefore gives the woolen-merchant the value of his bill, and having his own name or that of his correspondent in Portugal inserted in the bill as the third person to whom the amount of the bill is to be paid, transmits it to his correspondent in Portugal, who receives the money from the person on whom it is drawn.

CAROLINE

The same bill then is the means of paying for both commodities, the broad cloth and the wine; and it supersedes the necessity of transmitting two sums of money for that purpose. A bill of exchange is a most convenient and economical contrivance, and I feel very much inclined to avail myself of it. A friend of mine at York owes me a sum of money for purchases I have made for her in London; and my sister Emily is indebted about the same sum to a glover at York. I might, therefore, draw a bill of exchange on my friend, which Emily would buy of me, and forward it to the glover at York for the purpose of discharging her debt for the gloves; and he would receive the money from my friend on whom it was drawn. It is, if I understand you right, by such transfers of debts that commodities are really exchanged between merchants.

MRS. B.

I am glad to see that you understand the use of a bill of exchange so well. It will therefore be evident to you that if, when two countries are trading together, the value of the goods exported and imported be equal, the amount of the bills of exchange in payment of those goods will be so likewise; and the debts will be mutually settled without the necessity of transmitting money.

CAROLINE

That is quite clear: but it must, I suppose, frequently happen that the value of the goods exported and imported is not equal, and in that case the bills of exchange will not settle the whole of the respective debts, and some balance or sum of money will remain due from one country to the other.

MRS. B.

This is called the balance of trade. In order to explain to you in what manner such a debt is settled, let us take, for example, our trade with Russia:—If, in trading with that country, our exports and imports are exactly equal in value, the exchange between Russia and England is said to be at par, or equal; but if the value of our imports should have exceeded our exports, so that, for instance, we should have received more hemp and tallow *from* than we have sent broad cloths and hardware *to* Russia, there will be a greater amount of bills drawn by Russian merchants on

England than by English merchants on Russia: after their reciprocal debts are settled, therefore, as far as the bills will enable them to do so, there will remain a surplus of Russian bills drawn on England, which will require to be paid in money.

CAROLINE

Then some of our merchants will be under the necessity of sending money to Russia in payment of their debts.

MRS. B.

This every merchant endeavours to avoid, on account of the heavy expenses of freight and insurance of the money; as soon, therefore, as there appears to be a scarcity of English bills on Russia, every English merchant who is indebted to that country is eager to procure them. The competition of merchants for these bills raises their price, for they find it answer to give something more than the amount of the bill rather than send gold to Russia to pay for their hemp and tallow. The sum thus given for a bill above its amount is called a *premium,* and our exchange with Russia is, in this case, said to be *unfavourable, or below par.*

CAROLINE

That is to say, that a man who owes a sum of money to Russia must give something more than the amount of the debt in order to pay it?

MRS. B.

Yes; and the amount of the premium given depends, of course, on the degree of scarcity of the bills.

CAROLINE

And as the scarcity of the bills is owing to the value of our imports exceeding that of our exports, our exchange must be favourable or unfavourable with any country in proportion as the exports or imports prevail.

But our exchange with Russia, I suppose, can never fall below what it would cost to transport gold to Russia; for, as it is optional with our merchants to pay either in bills or money, if the premium on the bill were greater than the expense of sending money, they would prefer the latter mode of payment.

MRS. B.

Undoubtedly; and as the expense of sending gold to different countries varies according to the distance, and to the facility or difficulty of our intercourse with them, a favourable or unfavourable exchange with those countries will vary accordingly.

CAROLINE

But the premium given for bills of exchange, after all, does not supersede the necessity of our paying the balance of debt in gold; it merely removes the difficulty from one individual to another; for those merchants who finally cannot obtain bills must transmit money in payment.

MRS. B.

I beg your pardon; an unfavourable exchange in a great measure corrects itself: but this, it is true, requires some explanation. There are merchants who make it their business to trade in bills of exchange; that is to say, to buy them where they are abundant and cheap, and sell them where they are scarce and dear. Thus bills of exchange become an article of commerce like cloth, or any other commodity. Therefore when English bills on Russia are scarce, those merchants buy up the bills drawn by other countries on Russia, and supply the English market with them.

CAROLINE

But when English bills on Russia are scarce, there may perhaps be no surplus of bills on Russia in other countries to supply the English market.

MRS. B.

Generally speaking, when there is a deficiency of bills on Russia in one country, there will be a redundancy of them in some other; for though the exportations and importations of Russia with any particular country may be unequal, her general exportations and importations will, upon the whole, nearly balance each other; because if there was a constant excess of importation, Russia would be drained of money to pay for it; if, on the contrary, there was an excess of exportations, the money received in payment would accumulate, and depreciate the value of the currency of the country. The goods which Russia purchases, therefore, from foreign countries must, upon the long run, be to the same amount as the goods which she sells in exchange for them; so that if there is a balance of debt due *to* Russia from one country, there must be a balance of debt due *from* Russia to another country. The bills of exchange, therefore, drawn by Russia on foreign countries, and those drawn by foreign countries on Russia, will balance each other; and it is the business of the dealers in bills to discover where there is a superfluity, and where a deficiency of these bills, with a view to buy them in the one place, and sell them in the other.

CAROLINE

If, then, the bill-merchants, instead of supplying the English market with bills on Russia, bought up the surplus of Russian bills on England, it would equally answer the purpose of paying our debt to that country?

MRS. B.

Exactly. In our trade with Italy, for instance, we import large quantities of silk, olive oil, and various other articles, and our exportations are manufactured goods only to a trifling amount. The exchange would, in this case, be so unfavourable as to reduce us to the necessity of exporting gold in payment for the excess of imports, did not the bill-merchants come to our assistance. This useful class of men buy up the surplus of Italian bills on England, and send them for sale to Germany, France, Spain, or wherever there is a deficiency of bills on England, and where they will consequently sell with profit

CAROLINE

Thus Germany, France, or Spain, discharge our debt to Italy.

MRS. B.

Yes; provided any of those countries are in our debt; otherwise, you know they would not purchase our bills of exchange.

CAROLINE

One would imagine that these operations of the bill-merchants would invariably have the effect of counteracting the fluctuations of exchanges, and keep them constantly at par.

MRS. B.

If the business of the bill-merchant could be transacted with the same celerity and regularity as that of the bankers in London, who meet together every day, after the hours of business, to settle their respective accounts, it might influence the exchanges in the manner you suppose. But the speculations of the bill-merchant embrace so wide a sphere, and so many circumstances occur in the course of trade, or of political events, by which the exchanges are affected, that no individual prudence or foresight can prevent great fluctuations.

CAROLINE

Are then merchants often reduced to the necessity of sending abroad money in payment of foreign goods?

MRS. B.

Scarcely ever, I believe, excepting where there is a greater demand for money than for goods; for independently of the operations of the bill-merchants, there is yet another means of preventing that expense. When the English merchants who export goods to Russia find that the excess of imports over exports produces a scarcity of their bills on Russia, which enables them to sell them to the importing merchants at a premium, such an addition to their usual profits of trade induces them to increase their exportations, and has, in fact, the effect of a bounty, for they can now afford to export goods which, before, did not yield sufficient profits to enable them to do it; whilst, on the contrary, our importing merchants of Russian commodities, who are obliged to purchase these bills at a premium, (which has the effect of a duty, since it is a clear deduction from their profits,) will confine their importations to such commodities only as will leave them their usual profits, after deducting the premium upon the bills, with which they were to be paid.

CAROLINE

The premiums, then, which our importing merchants lose, our exporting merchants gain. This must undoubtedly have a considerable effect in encouraging exportation, and restraining importation, and tend rapidly to restore the equality of the exchange.

MRS. B.

The evil, then, of an unfavourable exchange immediately gives rise to the remedy which corrects it, and actually tends to equalise the exports and imports. But in order to have completely that effect, it would be necessary that the country with whom the exchange is unfavourable should require as much of our productions as we do of theirs, which is not always the case. The unfavourable exchange, however, enables the exporting merchant to afford to sell his goods abroad at a lower rate, because a part of his profit is derived from the premium on the exchange, and thus more persons abroad being able to purchase at the reduced price, the market for the goods is enlarged, and a greater quantity consumed.

CAROLINE

All these circumstances, then, together, must nearly supersede the necessity of sending money to balance the account?

MRS. B.

Very nearly so, I believe, except with such countries as, having mines of their own, may be said to produce money. If Spain and Portugal were to retain all the gold and silver which they derive from their mines, it would fall so much in value in those countries, that no laws could prevent its conveyance to others where its value was greater. It would be the most profitable article a Spanish or Portuguese merchant could export in payment for the goods imported; and, indeed, we find that they supply Europe with gold and silver, in the same manner as we supply it with the produce of our West Indian colonies, coffee and sugar. We have, in a former conversation, observed how the precious metals were diffused throughout all civilised nations, and the supply every where so proportioned to the demand, as to admit of no other variation of value than the small difference arising from the expense of bringing them from the mines to the different countries where they are wanted.

CAROLINE

But have I not heard of the exchange having been much below what it would cost to send money abroad?

MRS. B.

That is true; but I believe it is principally to be ascribed to another and a totally different cause, which nominally influences the exchanges to a very great extent. We formerly observed, that a depreciation of value of the currency of a country raises the price of commodities in that country. Whether the depreciation arises from an unnecessary increase of currency, from an adulteration of the coin, or from any other cause, it invariably produces this effect.

Let us suppose the currency of England to be depreciated 25 per cent; that is to say, that a sum worth £100 previous to the depreciation is now really worth only £75, though it retains its nominal value of £100. An English bill of exchange, which represents a certain portion of the currency, will partake of this depreciation, and will no longer be equal in value to a foreign bill of the same amount. It would require an English bill of £133, six shillings, and eight pence to exchange for a foreign one of £100; therefore, if before the depreciation the exchange were at par, this circumstance would make it immediately fall 25 per cent.

CAROLINE

Would not the evil, then, be remedied by increasing the exports, and diminishing the imports, as when the unfavourable state of the exchange arises from the unequal balance of trade?

MRS. B.

Certainly not. For though it is true that in both cases the exporting merchant can sell his bills at a premium, yet when this premium arises from a depreciation of the currency, it cannot be considered as any gain to him, because it is exactly balanced by the advanced price of the goods he exports, which operates as a loss.

CAROLINE

I think I understand it. The depreciation of currency which produces the premium on the bill of exchange produces also an increase in the price of the merchandise, and these effects, resulting from the same cause, must always correspond and be felt in the same proportion. Thus if a merchant exports cloth to Hamburgh which costs him £200, whatever profits he might expect under the ordinary state of the currency must be diminished 25 per cent, in consequence of his giving £50 more for his cloth than he would otherwise have done. Yet as he will sell the bill of exchange which he draws on Hamburgh for the payment of his cloth at a premium of £50 his profits will remain precisely the same, upon the whole transaction, as if every thing had gone on in its regular way.

MRS. B.

You have explained it perfectly well. Remember therefore that when the exchange is unfavourable in consequence of the depreciation of the currency) it is only *nominally,* not really unfavourable; for it may take place when the exports and imports are perfectly equal. And recollect, also, that the difference the exchange produces in the sale or purchase of bills is neither a loss nor a gain to the parties, and that it has no effect either on exportation or importation.

CAROLINE

But is it easy to distinguish between two causes which are so similar in their effects, and to ascertain at any time which of them it is that influences the exchange?

MRS. B.

Far from it: this has been a subject of much discussion, particularly during the late war. If it be true that the currency of the country has been increased beyond what was required, it must be considered as depreciated, and as having nominally affected the exchange.

On the other hand, as the system of warfare engaged us in very great expense on the Continent, whilst it was remarkably unfavourable to our exportations, the balance of foreign debt was very much against us, and the expense of transmitting gold considerably increased; so far the exchange may be said to have been *really* unfavourable. It is probable that both these causes contributed to the very low rate of our exchange during the late war.

Notwithstanding all the investigation which these subjects have undergone, there still prevails, even amongst our legislators, the old popular error respecting the balance of trade. Even at this day we find persons congratulating the country, that the exports exceed the imports, and that in consequence a balance of money remains due to us, which is considered as so much gain to the country.

CAROLINE

But do those who maintain such an opinion know, that this money would not be due to us, unless we had exported a surplus of merchandise to an equal amount?

MRS. B.

It is from that circumstance they conceive the advantage arises. They assert that since the poor are maintained by labour, the more work we perform for other countries, and the more money we receive for our work, the richer we must be.

CAROLINE

Not if we export the fruits of their labour and receive only gold in return: for the poor are maintained, not by the act of labour but by its produce; and if all that produce were exported, and nothing but gold received in exchange, we should be much in the situation of King Midas, who was starved because every thing he touched was converted into gold.

But do not the bill-merchants prevent this importation of gold, by transferring the bills of exchange from one country to another? for if our balance of trade is favourable with one country, it must be unfavourable with another.

MRS. B.

No doubt they do. If it were possible to have what is called a favourable balance of trade with every country, we should accumulate a quantity of the precious metals which would answer no other purpose than to depreciate our currency.

The most advantageous trade for both parties concerned is when the exports and imports are equal, so that the balance does not preponderate on either side; for it is as injurious to one country to part with money which is wanted at home for purposes of currency, as it is to the other to receive it when it is not wanted.

When a country receives bullion, it should not be in payment of a balance of debt, but as a commodity for which there is a demand. This demand will always take place in thriving countries, not only because gold and silver bullion are wanted by jewellers and silversmiths for the purposes of luxury: but also because, as the saleable produce of the country increases, an additional quantity of currency is required for its circulation.

CAROLINE

According to this theory of the balance of trade, it should always be against Spain and Portugal, and favourable to every other country; because it is through Spain and Portugal that all the treasures of the new world flow into Europe?

MRS. B.

True; but they are not sent immediately from those countries to the most distant parts of Europe, but are transferred through the intermediate countries. Thus France sends *Louis* to Geneva to pay for the watches she imports from that place; or to Italy, in payment of raw silks, olive oil, &c. So that the countries most distant from Spain and Portugal would consequently have what is absurdly called the balance of trade in their favour; whilst the intermediate countries would have it favourable with those which were nearer Spain than themselves, and unfavourable with those which were more distant.

This, however, is a general principle, which, though true in theory, requires modification if applied to practice; because there is a great variety of disturbing causes which prevent the free operation of the principle, and occasion fluctuations in the regular distribution of the wealth of America. However extraordinary it may appear, it is not very long since we sent considerable quantities of specie to Spain and Portugal, to maintain our troops in those countries: so much does war reverse the natural order of things. Instead of exporting our manufactures to bring back gold, we were obliged to drain our circulation, to send money in order to support our troops, whilst our manufacturers were either starving or became members of that very army which caused their ruin.

CAROLINE

But if Spain, from the abundance of her gold and silver, imports such large quantities of manufactured goods, is it not a check to her industry at home?

MRS. B.

It certainly is; though not so much as you would

imagine, because she does not obtain the gold and silver of America free of cost; she obtains it partly in the form of a tax imposed by the mother-country, or rent for the royal mines; and the rest by payment in produce or manufactured goods. But these goods are not necessarily manufactured in Spain or Portugal A Spanish merchant having imported goods from England and sent them to America, receives back gold and silver in payment, which are transmitted to England, if wanted there; Spain and Portugal being the entrepôt, in consequence of the strict regulations by which the gold and silver are compelled to be brought to *the* mother-country.

The want of industry in Spain, though it proceeds in a great measure from the nature of its religion and government, is also in part attributable to the effect which the influx of the precious metals has produced.

In Townsend's Travels in Spain, which abound with philosophical observations, it is stated, "that the gold and silver of America, instead of animating the country and promoting industry, instead of giving life and vigour to the whole community, by the increase of arts, of manufactures, and of commerce, had an opposite effect, and produced in the event weakness, poverty, and depopulation. The wealth which proceeds from industry resembles the copious yet tranquil stream, which passes silent, and almost invisible, and enriches the whole extent of country through which it flows; but the treasures of the new world, like a swelling torrent, were seen, were heard, were felt, were admired: yet their first operation was to desolate and lay waste the spot on which they fell." The shock was sudden; the contrast was too great. Spain overflowed with specie, whilst other nations were comparatively poor in the extreme. The price of labour, of provisions, and of manufactures, bore proportion to the quantity of circulating cash. The consequence is obvious; in the poor countries industry advanced; in the more wealthy it declined.

"Even in the present day (1806), specie, being about 6 per cent less valuable in Spain than it is in other countries, operates precisely in the same proportion against her manufactures and her population."

We may here, I think, conclude our observations on the principles of trade; and having now explained the different sources from which an income may be derived, we shall at our next meeting make a few inquiries into the nature and effects of expenditure and consumption.

CONVERSATION XXII

ON EXPENDITURE

OF THE DISPOSAL OF INCOME.—OF THE EXPENDITURE OF INDI-
VIDUALS.—EFFECTS ON CONSUMING CAPITAL.—INCREASE
OF INCOME OF A COUNTRY BENEFICIAL TO ALL CLASSES
OF PEOPLE.—EXCEPT IN CASES WHERE GOVERNMENT
INTERFERES WITH THE DISPOSAL OF CAPITAL.—OF SUMP-
TUARY LAWS.—OF LUXURY.—INDUSTRY PROMOTED BY
LUXURY.—PASSAGE FROM PALEY ON LUXURY.—SUDDEN
INCREASE OF WEALTH PREJUDICIAL TO THE LABOUR-
ING CLASSES.—PASSAGE FROM BENTHAM ON LEGISLA-
TION.—LUXURY OF THE ROMANS NOT THE RESULT OF
INDUSTRY.—OF THE DISADVANTAGES ARISING FROM THE
EXCESS OF LUXURY.

MRS. B.

I TRUST that you now understand both the manner in which capital is accumulated and the various modes of employing it to produce an income. It remains for us to examine how this income may be disposed of.

CAROLINE

I have already learnt that income may either be spent, or accumulated and converted into capital; and that the more a man economises for the latter purpose the richer he becomes.

MRS. B

This observation is equally applicable to the capital

of a country, which may be augmented by industry and frugality, or diminished by prodigality.

CAROLINE

The capital of a country, I think you said, consisted of the capital of its inhabitants taken collectively?

MRS. B.

It does; but you must be careful not to estimate the income of a country in the same manner, for it would lead to very erroneous calculations. Let us, for instance, suppose my income to be £10,000 a year, and that I pay £500 a year for the rent of my house; it is plain that this £500 constitutes a portion of the income of my landlord; and since therefore the same property, by being transferred from one to another, may successively form the income of several individuals, the income of the country cannot be estimated by the aggregate income of the people.

CAROLINE

And does not the same reasoning apply to the expenditure of a country; since the £500 a year which you spend in house-rent will be afterwards spent by your landlord in some other manner?

MRS. B.

True, because spending money is but exchanging one thing against another of equal value;—it is giving, for instance, one shilling in exchange for a loaf of bread, five guineas in exchange for a coat Instead of a shilling we are possessed of a loaf of bread; instead of five guineas, of a coat; we are therefore as rich before as after these purchases are made.

CAROLINE

If so, how is it that we are impoverished by spending money.

MRS. B.

It is not by purchasing, but by *consuming* the things we have purchased, that we are impoverished. When we have eaten the bread and worn out the coat, we are the poorer by five guineas and a shilling than we were before.

A baker is not poorer for purchasing a hundred sacks of flour, nor a clothier for buying a hundred pieces of cloth, because they do not consume these commodities.

When a man purchases commodities with a view of re-selling them he is a dealer in such commodities, and it is capital which he lays out; but when he purchases commodities for the purpose of using and consuming them, it is called expenditure. Expenditure, therefore, always implies consumption.

CAROLINE

I understand the difference perfectly: the one lays out capital with the view of re-selling his goods with profit; the other spends money with the view of consuming the goods he purchases with loss;—that is to say, the loss of the value of the goods he consumes.

MRS. B.

Just so. Thus, though the sum of money you spend will serve the purpose of transferring commodities successively from one person to another, yet the commodities themselves can be consumed but once.

Therefore the consumption of a country may, like its capital, be estimated by the aggregate consumption of its inhabitants; and the great question relative to the prosperity of the country, is, how far that consumption takes place productively, and how far unproductively.

CAROLINE

That certainty is a very important point; for in the former case it increases wealth, in the latter it destroys it.

Yet, Mrs. B., supposing a man were so prodigal as to spend not only the whole of his income, but even the capital itself, provided that it were spent in the maintenance of productive labourers, though it would ruin the individual, I do not conceive that it would injure the country; for whether a man lay out his capital in the maintenance of productive labourers with a view to profit, or whether he spend it in purchasing the fruits of their industry for the purpose of enjoyment, I can perceive no difference relative to the country; in both cases an equal number of people would be employed, and consequently an equal quantity of wealth produced. If his money went to the maintenance of unproductive labourers, and nothing substantial was had in exchange, that would alter the case; but if it is spent amongst tradesmen, who will furnish him with articles for his enjoyment, such as magnificent apparel, splendid equipages, sumptuous entertainments, he will then replace the capital which those tradesmen have been consuming, in order to produce these commodities, which capital will again be usefully employed in producing more.

MRS. B.

That is very true; and so far the prodigal has done no harm. In spending his capital amongst tradesmen, he has exchanged his various commodities for others of equal value, and the same quantity of capital exists as before the exchange took place; but what is the prodigal to do with the new stock that he has acquired?

CAROLINE

It will be applied to the gratification of his desires; he will regale with his friends at sumptuous feasts, he will use the equipages, and clothe himself and his servants in the rich apparel.

MRS. B.

Then he and his friends will consume amongst servants and dependants, in fetes and splendid entertainments, what the tradesmen furnished him with, instead of that which he gave in exchange for it; and as much capital will be lost to himself and to the community in the one case as in the other. The spending of capital is a sterile consumption of it, whilst its employment is a reproductive consumption.

CAROLINE

But if money were not thus spent, what would the tradesman do with the luxuries which he had prepared for the purpose of supplying the demand of persons who spend in order to enjoy?

MRS. B.

Such tradesmen would certainly find less employment; but you would not thence conclude that the community would be injured. You have already seen that capital cannot produce income unless it be consumed; if it be consumed by industrious persons, who work whilst they are consuming it, something of superior value will be produced, and that product, whatever it may be, will be exchanged against other productions; it will be distributed amongst another order of tradesmen, and will afford precisely the same amount of encouragement, though of a different kind. Whatever is saved from the extravagant consumption of the rich, is a stock to contribute to the comforts of the middling and lower ranks of society.

CAROLINE

Yet how often has it been said that a generous and liberal expenditure, however injurious to the individual, was a source from which the middling and lower classes drew their principal means of subsistence?

MRS. B.

There is not a more fatal delusion in political economy. By such wanton extravagance as we have been describing, the capital, which should annually furnish a subsistence to labourers, is wasted and destroyed, and the industrious are reduced to idleness and want They are covered with rags, because the prodigal has clothed himself in gorgeous apparel; they wander without a home, because the prodigal hat erected a palace; they must starve, because the wealth that should have fed them has been squandered in sumptuous feasts.

It is easy to comprehend that the prevalence of such conduct in a state must be followed by the gradual decay of its wealth and population.

CAROLINE

This is a most painful reflection; but on the other hand it would not, I suppose, be possible for a country to make any progress in wealth by which the poor were not more or less benefited?

MRS. B.

Certainly not, if no undue influence is exercised, and things are allowed to follow their natural course. Where property is secure, there is a general tendency to accumulation of capital. The great majority are governed by good sense and prudence, and their efforts to save and better their condition more than counterbalance the occasional loss that arises from the extravagance of spendthrifts. Besides, if expenditure were directed in too large a proportion towards the production of mere luxuries, and the number of persons employed in producing them were to be increased without at the same time augmenting the number of persons employed in producing articles of subsistence, the same quantity of provisions must be divided amongst a greater number of consumers; and as provisions, in consequence of being more scarce, would increase in price, the profits of agriculture would become so great, that the capital which had been applied to the production of luxuries would flow to the more advantageous employment of agriculture, and thus the natural distribution of capital would be restored.

CAROLINE

The more I hear on this subject, and the better I understand it, the greater is my admiration of that wise and beneficent arrangement which has so closely interwoven the interests of all classes of men.

MRS. B.

We are accustomed to trace the hand of Providence

chiefly in the natural world, but it is no less conspicuous in moral life, and cannot be more strongly exemplified than in that order of things which renders it essential to the interests of the rich not to turn the labour of the poor to the production of superfluities until they have provided an ample supply of the necessaries of life.

But these wise dispensations are often in a great measure subverted by the folly and ignorance of man. An injudicious interference of government, for instance, may give peculiar advantages to the employment of capital in one particular branch of industry, to the prejudice of others, and thus destroy that natural and useful distribution of it, which is so essential to the prosperity of the community.

CAROLINE

If ever the legislature could interfere with advantage, I should think it would be in some regulations respecting expenditure. I should be strongly tempted to restrain the use of luxuries, in order to induce the owners of capital to employ it in agriculture, and such homely manufactures as are suited to the consumption of the poor: such a measure could not fail to produce a more equal distribution of the comforts of life.

MRS. B.

Sumptuary laws have been instituted with that view in many countries. But after all we have said of the benefits resulting from the natural distribution of capital when unrestrained and uninfluenced by political regulations, I confess that I am surprised at your wishing to compel people to employ it in one way rather than in another.

CAROLINE

But if that one way should prove the right way?

MRS. B.

Then capital will follow that direction by its natural impulse, without requiring any foreign aid. Be assured that the only right way is to leave the use of capital to the care of those to whom it belongs; they will be the most likely to discover in what line it can be employed to the greatest advantage.

CAROLINE

Of their own advantage they are no doubt the best judges; but are you sure that they will be equally attentive to the advantage of the poor? Sumptuary laws appear to me to afford peculiar encouragement to the production of the necessaries of life. But the principal use of sumptuary laws would be to repress the expenditure of income. And since it is so desirable that capital should not be dissipated, surely the same principles will apply to income; would it not be advantageous to save great part of that also, in order to convert it into capital?

MRS. B.

Capital, you know, has arisen solely from savings from income; but you are aware that there must be a limit to such savings.

CAROLINE

Certainly there is a limit, because we could no live without consuming some part of it; but the less we consume, and the more we save, the better.

MRS. B.

That is pushing the principle too far: wealth is accumulated for the purpose of enjoyment; and if by a liberal though prudent expenditure, social affections are cultivated, and the happiness of mankind promoted and extended, I see no reason why we should be debarred from indulging in some of the best feelings of our nature.

Mr. Senior observes that "It seems at first sight that habits of unnecessary expenditure, as they have a tendency to diminish the wealth of an individual, must have the same effect on the wealth of a nation; and, separately considered, it appears clear that each act of unproductive consumption, whatever gratification it may afford to the consumer, must, *pro tanto,* impoverish the community. It is so much taken from the common stock and destroyed; and as the national capital is formed from the aggregate savings of individuals, it is certain that if each individual were to spend to the utmost extent of his means, the whole capital of the country would be gradually wasted away, and general misery would be the result But it appears equally certain that if each individual were to confine his expenditure to mere necessaries, the result would be misery quite as general and as intense."

The two extremes of parsimony and prodigality are perhaps equally pernicious; the one as destructive of the social and benevolent affections, the other as wasting the provision which nature has destined for the maintenance and employment of the poor.

But there is another point of view in which sumptuary laws have a dangerous tendency. By diminishing objects of desire you run great risk of giving a general check to industry.

Tell me why do the rich employ the poor?

CAROLINE

In order to derive an income from the profits of their labour.

MRS. B.

And what use do the rich make of this income?

CAROLINE

They either spend the whole, or they economise part in order to augment their capital.

MRS. B.

But why should they be desirous of increasing their capital?

CAROLINE

There are so many reasons for wishing to be rich, that I scarcely know how to enumerate them. The pride of wealth is a motive with some men, the love of independence with others; the apprehension of future reverses incites a third to accumulate; the wish to increase his means of doing good, stimulates the industry of another; the desire of providing for a family, and leaving them in affluence, is a powerful inducement with many; but the ambition of improving their situation in life, and of increasing their enjoyments by a more liberal expenditure, is, I think, the most general, and perhaps the strongest of all the motives for accumulating riches.

MRS. B.

If, then, laws be enacted which restrain a man from

spending any part of his income in luxuries, you take away one of his motives for wishing to augment his capital; and a growing capital is, you know, an increase of subsistence for the poor.

CAROLINE

I would wish to prohibit only that excess of luxury which you have censured as pernicious.

MRS. B.

It is extremely difficult to draw the line between necessaries and luxuries; united, they form a scale, the gradations of which are too numerous and minute to be distinct. We have considered as necessaries whatever the rate of wages of the lowest ranks of people have enabled them to command; they would consider as luxuries whatever they have not been accustomed to enjoy; though when they can afford it there is no excess. Excess depends not so much on the quantity or nature of the luxury, as upon its relative proportion to the means of the individual. A daily meal of meat is an excess of luxury to the family of a common labourer, because they are not used to it, and their wages will not, in general, enable them to command it; whilst a table abounding with expensive delicacies can scarcely be called excess of luxury to a man whose income is so large that such gratifications do not prevent his making considerable savings.

CAROLINE

Since, then, it is impossible to define what are and what are not luxuries, no general line of prohibition can be drawn. Yet it is surely much to be regretted that excessive expenditure, so mischievous in its effects, should neither be restrained nor punished.

MRS. B.

The ruin which extravagance entails on the prodigal is his natural punishment, and serves as a warning to deter others from similar imprudence. Any attempt to prevent such partial evil by sumptuary laws would, generally, tend to depress the efforts of industry. The desire of increasing our enjoyments, and of improving our situation in life, as it is one of the strongest sentiments implanted in our nature, so I conceive it to be essentially conducive to the general welfare. It is the active zeal of each individual exerted in his own cause, which, in the aggregate, gives an impulse to the progressive improvement of the world at large. The desire of bettering his condition is justly considered as a laudable disposition in a poor man, and it is a feeling dangerous to repress in any classes of society.

CAROLINE

_____ The man of wealth and pride
Takes up a space that many poor supply'd:
Space for his lake, his park's extensive bonds;
Space for his horses, equipage, and bounds.
The robe that wraps bis limbs in silken sloth,
Has robb'd the neighbouring fields of half their growth;
His seat, where solitary sports are seen,
Indignant spurns the cottage from the green.

What can you reply to these beautiful lines, Mrs. B.? I fear they are but too faithful a representation of the state of society.

MRS. B.

I must first inquire whether this man of wealth and

pride either spends or produces capital in order to procure these gratifications. If the former, he deserves all the censure we have bestowed upon the spendthrift. If the latter, his wealth may possibly be more increased by his industry than diminished by his luxury.

CAROLINE

In all probability he does neither; but being possessed of a considerable property, he lives upon his income; and such an expensive style of living must greatly diminish, if not wholly absorb, what he might otherwise economise.

MRS. B.

Still I cannot approve of compulsory measures to lessen his expenses. If it be desirable to stimulate and encourage the industry of man, and induce him to accumulate wealth, he must be at full liberty to dispose of it according to his inclinations. It is not only the possession of his property that must be secured to him, but the free use of it, in whatever manner he chooses. It is unquestionably true, that unless the rich impoverish themselves by spending their capital, they cannot impoverish their country.

CAROLINE

That is not enough; the question is, what are the best means of enriching the country?

MRS. B.

One man sits down contented with his little property; brings up his children with humble views and desires, and every year lays by something to provide for their future support in life.

Another of a more ambitious character rises early and labours hard, exerting every faculty of his mind to turn his capital to the best account; he likewise makes savings from his income, but they do not prevent his growing wealth from enabling him to spend more liberally, and enjoy more freely; and none of his enjoyments is more heartfelt than that of having raised his family in the world by the exertions of his industry.

CAROLINE

Every man who is striving to acquire wealth is certainly more or less actuated by the prospects of the various enjoyments which he hopes his increasing income will enable him to command. One wishes to become rich enough to marry; another to keep a carriage, or a country-house; a third to be able to settle his children respectably in the world.

MRS. B.

Such motives are strong incitements both to industry and frugality; and these useful habits often remain when the cause which gave rise to them no longer exists; it is far from uncommon to see men retain the taste for accumulating long after they have lost the inclination for spending.

Dr. Adam Smith observes, that before the introduction of refined luxuries, the English nobles had no other means of spending their wealth, than by maintaining in their houses a train of dependants, either in a state of absolute idleness, or whose only business was to indulge the follies or flatter the vanity of their patron; and this is in a great measure the case in

Russia, Poland, and several other parts of Europe, even at the present day. We find that the consumption of provisions by the household of an English noble man some centuries ago was perhaps a hundred times greater than it is at present. But you must not thence infer that the estate, which maintained such numerous retainers, produces less now than it did in those times; on the contrary, it is perhaps as much increased as the consumption of the household is diminished. The difference is, that the produce, instead of supporting a number of lazy dependants, maintains, probably a hundred times that number of industrious independent workmen, part of whom are employed in raising the produce of the estate, and part in supplying the nobleman with all the luxuries he requires: it was to obtain these luxuries that he dismissed his train of dependants, that he improved the culture of his land, and that, whilst studying only the gratification of his wishes, he contributed so essentially to the welfare of his country.

Here is a passage in Paley's Political Philosophy on the subject of luxury, extremely worthy your attention:—

"It appears that the business of one half of mankind is to set the other half at work; that is, to provide articles, which, by tempting the desires, may stimulate the industry, and call forth the activity of those upon the exertion of whose industry, and the application of whose faculties, the production of human provision depends. It signifies nothing to the main purpose of trade how superfluous the articles which it furnishes are, whether the want of them be real or imaginary; whether it be founded in nature or in opinion, in fashion, habit, or emulation; it is

enough that they be actually desired and sought after. Flourishing cities are raised and supported by trading in tobacco:
populous towns subsist by the manufactory of ribbons. A
watch may be a very unnecessary appendage to the dress
of a peasant, yet if the peasant will till the ground in order
to obtain a watch, the true design of trade is answered, and
the watchmaker, whilst he polishes the case, and files the
wheels of his machine, is contributing to the production of
corn, as effectually, though not so directly, as if he handled
the spade or the plough. If the fisherman will ply his nets,
or the mariner fetch rice from foreign countries, in order
to procure the indulgence of the use of tobacco, the market
is supplied with two important articles of provision by the
instrumentality of a merchandise which has no other apparent use than the gratification of a vitiated palate."

CAROLINE

This reminds me of an anecdote in Dr. Franklin's works.
He describes the admiration which was excited by a new
cap worn at church by one of the young girls of Cape May.
This piece of finery had come from Philadelphia; and with
a view of obtaining similar ornaments, the young girls had
all set to knitting worsted mittens, an article in request at
Philadelphia, the sale of which enabled them to gratify
their wishes.

MRS. B.

We often hear the poor reproached for aiming
at things above their situation; but I own that I de-
light in seeing them strive to ornament their cottages,
to raise a few flowers amongst the nutritious vegetables *in* their gardens, to deck their room, though it be

but with rows of damaged china cups and plates, or a few gaudy prints; it shows a desire of creditable appearance, and of aiming at something beyond the bare means of subsistence.

CAROLINE

The desire of improving their condition is not, however, in all cases a sufficient motive to rouse the industry of the lower classes. I once knew an easy indulgent landed proprietor, who having no ambition to increase his income could never be induced to raise his rents; his tenants, finding that they could pay their landlord and maintain their families as well as their neighbours, with much less labour, neglected their farms, and became so idle and disorderly, that the estate was the least productive of any in the country.

MRS. B.

The country thus suffered from the well-meant, but ill-judged indulgence of this landlord.

CAROLINE

But why was not the industry of these tenants stimulated by the desire of raising themselves in the world, which the forbearance of their landlord enabled them so easily to do?

MRS. B.

In the course of time it probably would have had that effect; but when uneducated men obtain an increase of wealth, the first use they generally make of it is to procure indulgences and exemption from labour; it is only after becoming sensible that idleness leads them back to poverty that they think of turning their wealth to better account. Well-educated people seldom require the experience of so severe a lesson, but amongst the lower classes it is not uncommon to find that a great, and especially a sudden accession of riches, terminates in ruin.

CAROLINE

There are frequently instances of poor people being ultimately ruined by a high prize in the lottery.

MRS. B.

And the lower the state of ignorance and degradation of mind of the poor man who gains the prize the more certain is his ruin. The different state of improvement of the lower classes in England, in Scotland, and in Ireland, are strongly exemplified in this respect. If you were to give a guinea to a Scotch peasant, he would deliberately consider how he could turn it to the best account; he would, perhaps, buy a pig, or something which would bring a future profit. An English peasant is not quite so long sighted, yet he would contrive to derive some substantial advantages from the gift of a guinea; he would probably lay it out in repairing his cottage, or in purchasing some new clothes for his children. But the Irishman, whose joy would be the greatest of the three at such an unexpected acquisition of wealth, would in all likelihood spend the whole of it in drinking whiskey with his friends, and thus disable himself for the labour of the following day.

CAROLINE

And do you suppose that a sudden and considerable increase of wages would be attended with mischievous affects to the labouring poor?

MRS. B.

In the first instance it probably would. In manufactures it is commonly found that an accidental increase of wages, arising from a sadden demand for workmen, is productive of intemperance and disorderly conduct; and this has been urged as a general objection to high wages; but this bad effect seldom takes place unless the augmentation be sudden and unlooked for, and it discontinues when the high wages become regularly established. You may almost consider it as certain, that uneducated men will derive no advantage from such an augmentation of income as raises them suddenly above their accustomed habits of life. The beneficial effects I have described to you in one of our preceding conversations as arising from increasing wealth and demand for labour must be gradual in order to prove useful to the lower classes.

CAROLINE

All that you have said reconciles me, in a great measure, to the inequality of the distribution of wealth; for it proves that, however great a man's possessions maybe, it is. decidedly advantageous to the country that he should still endeavour to augment them. Formerly I imagined, that whatever addition was made to the wealth of the rich was so much subtracted from the pittance of the poor, but now I see that it is, on the contrary, an addition to the general stock of wealth of the country, by which the poor benefit equally with the rich.

MRS. B.

Yes; every accession of wealth to a country must have not only employed labourers to produce it, but will in future employ other labourers, in order that the proprietor may derive an income from it. For every increase of capital is the result of a past and the cause of a future augmentation of produce; therefore whatever a man's property may be, he should be encouraged to improve it. I will read you an eloquent passage in Bentham's *Théorie de la Legislation* on the subject of luxury.

"*L'attrait du plaisir, la succession des besoins, le desir actif d'ajouter au bien être, produiront sans cesse, sous le régime de la sûreté, de nouveaux efforts vers de nouvelles acquisitions. Lea besoins, les jouissances, ces agens universels de la société, après avoir fait éclore les premières gerbes de blés, élèveront peu-à-peu les magazins de l'abondance toujours croissans et jamais remplis. Les desires s'etendent avec les moyens; l'horizon s'aggrandit, à mesure qu'on s'avance, et chaque besoin nouveau, également accompagné de sa peine et de son plaisir, devient un nouveau principe d'action; l'opulence qui n'est qu'un terme comparatif n'arrête pas même ce mouvement, une fois qu'il est imprimé; au contraire, plus on opère en grand, plus la recompense est grande, et par conséquent plus est grande aussi la force du motif qui anime l'homme au travail.*

"*On a vu que l'abondance se forme peu-à-peu par l'operation continue des mêmes causes qui ont produit la subsistance. Il n'y a donc point d'opposition entre ces deux buts. Au contraire, plus l'abondance augmente, plus on est sûr de la subsistance. Ceux qui blâment l'abondance sous le nom de luxe n'ont jamais saisi cette considération.*

"*Les intempéries, les guerres, les accidens de toute espèce attaquent souvent le fond de la subsistance; en sorte qu'une société, qui n'auroit pas de superflu et même beaucoup de superflu seroit sujette à manquer souvent du necéssaire: c'est ce qu'on voit chez les peuples sauvages. C'est ce qu'on a vu fréquement chez toutes les nations dans les tems de l'antique pauvreté. C'est ce qui arrive encore de nos jours dans les pays peu favorisés de la nature, tels que la Suéde, et dans ceux où le gouvernement contrarie les operations du commerce au lieu de se borner à le protéger. Mais les pays où le luxe abonde et où l'administration est éclairée, sont à l'abri de la famine. Telle est l'heureuse situation de l'Angleterre. Des manufactures de luxe deviennent des bureaux d'assurances contre la disette. Une fabrique de bierre ou d'amidon se convertira en moyen de subsistance. Que de fois n'a-t-on pas déclamé contre les chevaux et les chiens comme dévorant la subsistance des hommes! Ces profonds politiques ne s'élèvent que d'un degré au dessus de ces apôtres du désinteréssement, qui pour ramener l'abondance des bles courent incendier les magazins."*

CAROLINE

We had not yet considered luxury under this point of view; I confess that I was of the opinion of those who thought that dogs and horses devoured the subsistence of man, but I am much better pleased to think that the food which luxury raises for the nourishment of those animals may, in case of necessity, become nourishment for the human species; and, if a famine should take place, even the animals themselves would afford a resource.

MRS. B.

Hair powder, when in fashion, might be considered

as a kind of granary for the preservation of wheat, for though the powder would not, unless in cases of very great urgency, be converted into food, the quantity of corn annually grown for the purpose of making hair-powder would, during a moderate scarcity, find its way more readily to the baker's than to the perfumer's shop.

CAROLINE

And pray, Mrs. B., what do you think of the luxury of the Romans? We read in Pliny of a Roman lady who was dressed in jewels to the amount of £300,000 I recollect, also, an account of a dish of fish having cost £64.

MRS. B.

These are but trifling instances of profusion, in comparison of some others related of the Romans. Marc Antony expended £60,000 in an entertainment given to Cleopatra; and the supper of Heliogabalus cost £6,000 every night. But nothing can be said in apology for the luxuries of the Romans; they were peculiarly objectionable, because their wealth did not proceed from industry, but from plunder. Their extravagance and profusion, therefore, far from being a spur to industry, acted in a contrary direction; it encouraged the love of rapine in themselves, whilst it depressed the spirit of industry in the countries subject to their power, by destroying the strongest of all inducements to labour, the security of property. It has been well observed by Macpherson, that "the luxuries of the Romans cannot be considered as the summit of a general scale of prosperity; it was a scale graduated but by one division, which separated immense wealth and power from abject slavery, wretchedness, and want."

In considering the advantages to be derived from luxury, we must, however, carefully remember, that it acts in a two-fold manner; whilst on the one hand it encourages industry, on the other it increases expenditure; so far as its productive powers prevail over its prodigal effects, it is beneficial to mankind; but in the contrary case it becomes an evil, and when it encroaches on capital we have seen that it is an evil of the greatest magnitude.

The grand object to be kept in view in order to promote the general prosperity of the country, is the increase of capital. But it is not in the power of the legislature to promote this end in any other way than by providing for the security of property; any attempts to interfere either with the disposal of capital or with the nature and extent of expenditure, are equally discouraging to industry.

CAROLINE

Whoever, I conceive, augments his capital by savings from his income, increases the general stock of subsistence for the labouring classes; whilst he who spends part of his capital diminishes that stock of subsistence, and consequently the means of employing the labouring classes in its reproduction.

Every man ought, therefore, to consider it as a moral duty, independently of his private interest, to keep his expenditure so far within the limits of his income that he may be enabled every year to make some addition to his capital.

MRS. B.

And the question what that addition should be, must depend entirely upon the extent of his income, and his motives for expenditure. We can only point out illiberal parsimony and extravagant prodigality as extremes to be avoided; there are so many gradations in the scale between them, that every man must draw the line for himself, according to the dictates of his good sense and his conscience, and in so doing should consult the moral philosopher as well as the political economist. He who has a large family to maintain and establish in the world, though more strict economy be required of him, cannot be expected to make savings equal to those of a man of a similar income, who has not the same calls for expenditure.

But however large a man's income may be, he has no apology for neglect of economy. Economy is a virtue incumbent on all. A rich man may have sufficient motives to authorise a liberal expenditure, but he can have none for negligence and waste; and however immaterial to himself the loss which waste occasions, he should consider it as so much taken from that fund which provides maintenance and employment for the poor.

INDEX

A.

Accumulation of wealth, 72

Adulteration of the coin of the country, 302
    its effects on wages, 303
    has been adopted in almost all countries, 304

Agriculture, introduction of, 15, 35, 158
    whether preferable to other branches of industry, 185
    of the proportion it should bear to manufactures and commerce, 189
    most advantageous to newly-settled countries, 189
    yields two incomes, 230
    Métayer, system of, 245
    state of, in France, 246

Agricultural produce, high price of, 202
    not susceptible of unlimited increase, 203
    causes of its high price, 207
    causes which lower its price, 208
    high price of, necessary to proportion the consumption to the supply, 226
    the first commodity which a country exports, 337, 357

Alms-giving, effects of, 152,155

America, increase of population in, 126
    exports corn, 337
    agriculture of, 357
    effects of its discovery on the industry of Europe, 295